The Expositor's Bible
The Gospel Of St. Matthew

By

John Monro Gibson ~

Double 9
BOOKS

The Expositor's Bible
The Gospel Of St. Matthew
by John Monro Gibson

ISBN: 978-93-61150-27-2

Published by

DOUBLE 9 BOOKS

2/13-B, Ansari Road
Daryaganj, New Delhi – 110002
info@double9books.com
www.double9books.com
Tel. 011-40042856

ABOUT THE AUTHOR

John Monro Gibson's "Expositor's Bible" stands as one of his masterpieces, showcasing his brilliance as an author who skillfully bridges the nation-states of ancient, non-secular, and literary narratives. With a profound commitment to connecting human beings through his writing, Gibson weaves a tapestry that intertwines the threads of history and spirituality. His creativity and ardour shine via each page, inviting readers into a journey that explores numerous nation-states of human revel in. Gibson's eloquent prose resultseasily navigates the intricacies of his subject matter, presenting a harmonious combo of beauty and accessibility. Through his superb storytelling, readers are brought to a spectrum of emotions and sundry landscapes, enriching their information of the human condition. In the fingers of John Monro Gibson, literature will become a conduit for shared studies, as his works captivate with each sophistication and ease, ensuring that readers from all walks of life can have fun with and admire his first rate narratives.

CONTENTS

I
THE COMING OF THE CHRIST

Matt. i.

THE New Testament opens appropriately with the four Gospels; for, though in their present form they are all later in date than some of the Epistles, their substance was the basis of all apostolic preaching and writing. As the Pentateuch to the Old Testament, so is the fourfold Evangel to the New.

That there should be a manifold presentation of the great facts which lie at the foundation of our faith and hope, was both to be expected and desired. The Gospel of Jesus Christ, as proclaimed by the first preachers of it, while in substance always the same, would be varied in form, and in number and variety of details, according to the individuality of the speaker, the kind of audience before him, and the special object he might have in view at the time. Before any form of presentation had been crystallized, there would therefore be an indefinite number of Gospels, each "according to" the individual preacher of "Christ and Him crucified." It is, therefore, a marvellous proof of the guidance and control of the Divine Spirit that out of these numerous oral Gospels there should emerge four, each perfect in itself, and together affording, as with the all-round completeness of sculpture, a life-like representation of the Lord Jesus Christ. It is manifestly of great advantage to have these several portraits of our Lord, permitting us to see Him from different points of view, and with varying arrangements of light and shade; all the more that, while three of them set forth in abundant variety of detail that which is more external, — the face, the features, the form, all the expression of that wondrous Life, — the fourth, appropriately called on this account "the Gospel of the heart of Jesus," unveils more especially the hidden riches of His inner Life. But, besides this, a manifold Gospel was needed, in order to meet the wants of man in the many-sidedness of his development. As the heavenly "city lieth four square," with gates on the east, and the west, and the north, and the south, to admit strangers coming from all points of the compass; so must there be in the presentation of the Gospel an open door for all mankind. How this great purpose is attained by the fourfold Gospel with which the New Testament opens can be readily shewn; and even a brief statement of it may serve a useful purpose as introductory to our study of that which is known as the First Gospel.

The inscription over the cross was in three languages: Hebrew, Latin, and Greek. These languages represented the three great civilizations which were the final outcome of ancient history—the Jewish, the Roman, the Greek. These three were not like so many nations selected at random, but stood for three leading types of humanity. The Jew was the man of the past. He could claim Moses and the prophets; he had Abraham for his father; his records went back to the Genesis of all things. He represented ancient prerogative and privilege, the conservatism of the East. The Roman was the man of the present. He was master of the world. He represented power, prowess, and victory; and while serving himself heir to the culture which came from the shores of the Egean Sea, he had combined with it the rude strength and restless activity of the barbarian and Scythian of the North. The Greek was the man of the future. He had lost his political empire, but still retained an empire in the world of thought. He represented humanity, and the ideal, and all the promise which was afterwards to be realized in the culture of the nations of the West. The Jew was the man of tradition, the Roman the man of energy, the Greek the man of thought. Turning now to the Gospels, we find the wants of each of these three types provided for in a wondrous way. St. Matthew addresses himself especially to the Jew with his Gospel of fulfilment, St. Mark to the Roman with "his brief and terse narrative of a three years' campaign," St. Luke to the Greek with that all-pervading spirit of humanity and catholicity which is so characteristic of his Evangel; while for those who have been gathered from among the Jews and Romans and Greeks—a people who are now no longer Jews or Greeks, but are "all one in Christ Jesus," prepared to receive and appreciate the deeper things of Christ—there is a fourth Gospel, issued at a later date, with characteristics specially adapted to them: the mature work of the then venerable John, the apostle of the Christian.

It is manifest that for every reason the Gospel of St. Matthew should occupy the foremost place. "To the Jew first" is the natural order, whether we consider the claims of "the fathers," or the necessity of making it clear that the new covenant was closely linked to the old. "Salvation is of the Jews;" the Christ of God, though the Saviour of the world, had been in a very special sense "the Hope of Israel," and therefore it is appropriate that He should be represented first from the standpoint of that nation. We have, accordingly, in this Gospel, a faithful setting forth of Christ as He presented Himself to the mind and heart of a devout Jew, "an Israelite indeed, in whom was no guile," rejoicing to find in Him One who fulfilled ancient prophecy and promise, realized the true ideal of the kingdom of God, and substantiated His claim to be Himself the divine Saviour-King for whom the nation and the world had waited long.

The opening words of this Gospel suggest that we are at the Genesis of the New Testament, the genesis not of the heavens and the earth, but of Him who was to make for us "new heavens and a new earth, wherein dwelleth righteousness." The Old Testament opens with the thought, "Behold I make all things;" the New Testament with that which amounts to the promise, "Behold I make all things new." It begins with the advent of "the Second Man, the Lord from Heaven." That He was indeed a "Second Man," and not merely one of the many that have sprung from the first man, will presently appear; but first it must be made clear that He is man indeed, "bone of our bone, flesh of our flesh;" and therefore the inspired historian begins with His historic genealogy. True to his object, however, he does not trace back our Lord's descent, as does St. Luke, to the first man, but contents himself with that which is especially interesting to the Jew, setting Him forth as "the son of David, the son of Abraham." There is another difference between the genealogies, of a more serious kind, which has been the occasion of much difficulty; but which also seems to find readiest explanation in the different object each Evangelist had in view. St. Luke, writing for the Gentile, is careful to give the natural descent, while St. Matthew, writing for the Jew, sets forth that line of descent—diverging from the other after the time of David—which made it clear to the Jew that He was the rightful heir to the kingdom. The object of the one is to set Him forth as the Son of Man; of the other to proclaim Him King of Israel.

St. Matthew gives the genealogy in three great epochs or stages, which, veiled in the Authorized Version by the verse division, are clearly exhibited to the eye in the paragraphs of the Revised Version, and which are summed up and made emphatic at the close of the genealogical tree (ver. 17). The first is from Abraham to David; the second from David to the captivity in Babylon; the third from the captivity to Christ. If we glance at these, we shall find that they represent three great stages in the development of the Old Testament promises which find their fulfilment in the Messiah.

"To Abraham and to his seed were the promises made." As given to Abraham himself, the promise ran thus: "In thy seed shall all the nations of the earth be blessed." As made to David, it indicated that the blessing to the nations should come through a king of his line. These were the two great promises to Israel. There were many others; but these stand out from the rest as constituting the mission and the hope of Israel. Now, after long waiting, both are to be fulfilled in Christ. He is the chosen Seed in Whom all nations shall be blessed. He is the Son of David, who is to sit upon His throne for ever, and reign, not over Israel alone, but over men, as "Prince of Peace" and "King of Glory." But what has the captivity in Babylon to do with it? Very much; as a little reflection will show.

The captivity in Babylon, as is well known, was followed by two great results: (1) it cured the people of idolatry for ever, so that, while politically the kingdom had passed away, in reality, and according to the spirit, it was then for the first time constituted as a kingdom of God. Till then, though politically separate from the Gentile nations, spiritually Israel had become as one of them; for what else than a heathen nation was the northern kingdom in the days of Ahab or the southern kingdom in the time of Ahaz? But after the captivity, though as a nation shattered into fragments, spiritually Israel became and continued to be one. (2) The other great result of the captivity was the Dispersion. Only a small remnant of the people came back to Palestine. Ten of the tribes passed out of sight, and but a fraction of the other two returned. The rest remained in Babylon, or were scattered abroad among the nations of the earth. Thus the Jews in their dispersion formed, as it were, a Church throughout the ancient world, — their eyes ever turned in love and longing to the Temple at Jerusalem, while their homes and their business were among the Gentiles — in the world, but not of it; the prototype of the future Church of Christ, and the soil out of which it should afterwards spring. Thus out of the captivity in Babylon sprang, first, the spiritual as distinguished from the political kingdom, and, next, the world-wide as distinguished from the merely national Church. Clearly then the Babylonish captivity was not only a most important historical event, but also a stage in the grand preparation for the Advent of the Messiah. The original promise made to Abraham, that in his seed should all the nations of the earth be blessed, was shown in the time of David to be a promise which should find its fulfilment in the coming of a king; and as the king after God's heart was foreshadowed in David, so the kingdom after the Divine purpose was foreshadowed in the condition of the people of God after the captivity in Babylon, purified from idolatry, scattered abroad among the nations, with their innumerable synagogues (prototypes of our churches) and their peculiarities of faith and life and worship. Abraham was called out of Babylon to be a witness for God and the coming Christ; and, after the long training of centuries, his descendants were taken back to Babylon, to scatter from that world-centre the seed of the coming kingdom of God. Thus it comes to pass that in Christ and His kingdom we see the culmination of that wonderful history which has for its great stages of progress Abraham, David,[1] the Captivity, Christ.

So much for the earthly origin of the Man Christ Jesus; but His heavenly descent must also be told; and with what exquisite simplicity and delicacy is this done. There is no attempt to make the words correspond with the greatness of the facts. As simple and transparent as clear glass, they allow the facts to speak for themselves. So it is all the way through this Evangel. What a contrast here to the spurious Gospels afterwards produced, when men had nothing to tell, and so must put in their own poor fictions, piously intending sometimes to add lustre to the too simple story of the Infancy, but only with the effect of degrading it in the eyes of all men of taste and judgment. But here there is no need of fiction, no need even of rhetoric or sentiment. The fact itself is so great, that the more simply it is told the better. The Holy One of Israel came into the world with no tinsel of earthly pomp; and in strict harmony with His mode of entrance, the story of His birth is told with like simplicity. The Sun of Righteousness rises like the natural sun, in silence; and in this Gospel, as in all the others, passes on to its setting through the heaven of the Evangelist's thought, which stands, like that other heaven, "majestic in its own simplicity."

The story of the Incarnation is often represented as incredible; but if those who so regard it would only reflect on that doctrine of heredity which the science of recent years has brought into such prominence, if they would only consider what is involved in the obvious truth that, "that which is born of the flesh is flesh," they would see that it was not only natural but necessary that the birth of Jesus Christ should be "on this wise." Inasmuch as "the first man is of the earth, earthy," "the Second Man" must be "of heaven," or He will be no Second Man at all; He will be sinful and earthy like all the others. But all that is needful is met in the manner so chastely and beautifully set forth by our Evangelist, in words which, angelic in their tone and like the blue of heaven in their purity, so well become the angel of the Lord.

Some wonder that nothing is said here of Nazareth and what took place there, and of the journey to Bethlehem; and there are those who are fain even to find some inconsistency with the third Gospel in this omission, as if there were any need to wonder at omissions in a story which tells of the first year on one page and the thirtieth on the next! These Gospels are not biographies. They are memorials, put together for a special purpose, to set forth this Jesus as the Son of God and Saviour of the world. And the special object, as we have seen, of St. Matthew is to set Him forth as the Messiah of Israel. In accordance with this object we have His birth told in such a way as to bring into prominence those facts only in which the Evangelist specially recognised a fulfilment of Old Testament prophecy. Here again the names give us the main thoughts. Just as Abraham, David, Babylon, suggest the main object of the genealogy, so the names Emmanuel, Jesus, suggest the main object of the record of His birth. "All this was done that it might be fulfilled which was spoken by the prophet."

The first name mentioned is "Jesus." To understand it as St. Matthew did, we must bear in mind that it is the old historic name Joshua, and that the first thought of the Hebrew mind would be, Here is One who shall fulfil all that was typified in the life and work of the two Old Testament heroes who bore that name, so full of hopeful significance.[2] The first Joshua was Israel's captain on the occasion of their first settlement in the land of promise after the bondage in Egypt; the second Joshua was Israel's high priest at their second settlement in the land after the bondage in Babylon. Both were thus associated with great deliverances; but neither the one nor the other had given the rest of full salvation to the people of God (see Heb. iv. 8); what they had done had only been to procure for them political freedom and a land they could call their own,—a picture in the earthly sphere of what the Coming One was to accomplish in the spiritual sphere. The salvation from Egypt and from Babylon were both but types of the great salvation from sin which was to come through the Christ of God. These or such as these must have been the thoughts in the mind of Joseph when he heard the angel's words: "Thou shalt call His name Joshua; for it is He that shall save His people from their sins."

Joseph, though a poor carpenter of Nazareth, was a true son of David, one of those who waited for the salvation of Israel, who had welcomed the truth set forth by Daniel, that the coming kingdom was to be a kingdom of the saints of the Most High,—not of political adventurers, as was the idea of the corrupt Judaism of the time; so he was prepared to welcome the truth that the coming Saviour was One who should deliver, not from the rule of *Rome*, but from the guilt and power and death of *Sin*.

As the name Joshua, or Jesus, came from the earliest times of Israel's national history, the name Emmanuel came from its latest, even out of the dark days of King Ahaz, when the hope of the people was directed to the birth of a Child who should bear this name. Some have thought it enough to show that there was a fulfilment of this hope in the time of Ahaz, to make it evident that St. Matthew was mistaken in finding its fulfilment in Christ; but this idea, like so many others of the same kind, is founded on ignorance of the relation of the Old Testament history to the New Testament times. We have seen that though Joshua of the early times and his successor of the same name did each a work of his own, yet both of them were in relation to the future but prototypes of the Great Joshua who was to come. In the same way exactly, if there was, as we believe, a deliverance in the time of Ahaz, to which the prophet primarily referred, it was, as in so many other cases, but a picture of the greater one in which the gracious purpose of God, manifested in all these partial deliverances, was to be "fulfilled," *i.e.*, filled to the full. The idea in the name "Emmanuel" was not a new one even in the time of King Ahaz. "I will be with you;" "Certainly I will be with you;" "Fear not, for I am with you,"—such words of gracious promise had been echoed and re-echoed all down the course of the history of the people of God, before they were enshrined in the name prophetically used by Isaiah in the days of King Ahaz; and they were finally embodied, incarnated, in the Child born at Bethlehem in the fulness of the time, to Whom especially belongs that name of highest hope, "Emmanuel," "God with us."

If, now, we look at these two names, we shall see that they not only point to a fulfilment, in the largest sense, of Old Testament prophecy, but to the fulfilment of that which we all need most—the satisfaction of our deepest wants and longings. "God is light;" sin is darkness. With God is the fountain of life; "sin when it is finished bringeth forth death." Here shines the star of hope; there lies the abyss of despair. Now, without Christ we are tied to sin, separated from God. Sin is near; God is far. That is our curse. Therefore what we need is God brought near and sin taken away—the very blessings guaranteed in these two precious names of our Lord. As Emmanuel, He brings God near to us, near in His own incarnate person, near in His loving life, near in His perfect sympathy, near in His perpetual presence according to the promise, "Lo, I am with you alway, even unto the end of the world." As Jesus, He saves us from our sins. How he does it is set forth in the sequel of the Gospel, culminating in the sacrifice of the cross, "to finish the transgression, and to make an end of sins, and to make reconciliation for iniquity, and to bring in everlasting righteousness." For He has not only to bring God down to us, but also to lift us up to God; and while the incarnation effects the one, the atonement, followed by the work of the Holy Spirit, is necessary to secure the other. He touches man, the creature, at his cradle; He reaches down to man, the sinner, at His cross—the end of His descent to us, the beginning of our ascent with Him to God. There we meet Him; and saved from sin, we know Him as our Jesus; and reconciled to God, we have Him with us as Emmanuel, God with us, always with us, with us throughout all life's changes, with us in death's agony, with us in the life to come, to guide us into all its wisdom and honour and riches and glory and blessing.

FOOTNOTES

[1] To some minds it may present itself as a difficulty that the great name of Moses should not find a place in the series; was not he as much of an epoch-maker as David? The answer is that, from the point of view of prophecy and promise, he was not. This, which lies implicitly in St. Matthew's summary, is set forth explicitly by St. Paul in his epistle to the Galatians, where he shows that the Law, as a stage in the dealings of God with the nation, did not belong to the main course of development, but came in as an episode, was "added because of transgressions" (Gal. iii. 16-19).

[2] The Hebrew name Joshua, of which Jesus is simply the Greek transliteration, combines the two words Jehovah and Salvation (cf. Num. xiii. 16).

II
HIS RECEPTION

Matt. ii.

THIS one chapter contains all that St. Matthew records of the Infancy. St. Mark and St. John tell us nothing, and St. Luke very little. This singular reticence has often been remarked upon, and it certainly is most noteworthy, and a manifest sign of genuineness and truthfulness: a token that what these men wrote was in the deepest sense not their own. For if they had been left to themselves in the performance of the task assigned them, they could not have restrained themselves as they have done. The Jews of the time attached the greatest importance to child-life, as is evident from the single fact that they had no less than eight different words to mark the successive stages of development from the new-born babe up to the young man; and to omit all reference to these stages, except the slight notice of the Infancy in this chapter, was certainly not "according to Matthew" the Jew, — not what would have been expected of him had he been left to himself. It can only be explained by the fact that he spoke or was silent according as he was moved or restrained by the Holy Ghost. This view is strikingly confirmed by comparison with the spurious Gospels afterwards published, by men who thought they could improve on the original records with their childish stories as to what the boy Jesus said and did. These awkward fictions reflect the spirit of the age; the simple records of the four Evangelists mirror for us the Spirit of Truth. To the vulgar mind, they may seem bare and defective, but all men of culture and mature judgment recognise in their simplicity and naturalness a note of manifest superiority.

Much space might be occupied in setting forth the advantages of this reticence, but a single illustration may suggest the main thought. Recall for a moment the well-known picture entitled, "The Shadow of the Cross," designed and executed by a master, one who might surely be considered qualified to illustrate in detail the life at Nazareth. We have nothing to say as to the merit of the picture as a work of art; let those specially qualified to judge speak of this; but is it not generally felt that the realism of the carpenter's shop is most painful? The eye is instinctively averted from the too obtrusive details; while the mind gladly returns from the startling vividness of the picture to the vague impressions made on us by the mere hints in the sacred Scriptures. Was it not well that our blessed Saviour should grow in retirement and seclusion; and if so, why should that seclusion be invaded? If His family life was withdrawn from the eyes of the men of that time, there remains the same reason why it should be withdrawn from the eyes of the men of all time; and the more we think of it, the more we realize that it is better in every way that the veil should have been dropped just where it has been, and that all should remain just as it was, when with unconscious skill the sacred artists finished their perfect sketches of the child Jesus.

Perhaps, however, the question may be asked: If St. Matthew would tell us so little, why say anything at all? What was his object in relating just what he has set down in this chapter? We believe it must have been to show how Christ was received. It seems, in fact, to correspond to that single sentence in the fourth Gospel, "He came unto His own, and His own received Him not;" only St. Matthew gives us a wider and brighter view; he shows us not only how Jerusalem rejected Him, but how the East welcomed Him and Egypt sheltered Him. Throughout the entire Old Testament our attention is called, not merely to Jerusalem, which occupied the centre of the ancient world, but to the kingdoms round about, especially to the great empires of the East and South—the empire of the East represented in succession by Ancient Chaldea, Assyria, Babylonia, Media, and Persia; and that of the South—the mighty monarchy of Egypt, which under its thirty dynasties held on its steady course alongside these. How natural, then, for the Evangelist whose special mission it was to connect the old with the new, to take the opportunity of showing that, while His own Jerusalem rejected her Messiah, her old rivals of the East and of the South gave Him a welcome. In the first chapter the Child Jesus was set forth as the Heir of the promise made to Abraham and his seed, and the fulfilment of the prophecy given to the chosen people; now He is further set forth as the One who satisfies the longings of those whom they had been taught to regard as their natural enemies, but who now must be looked upon as "fellow-heirs" with them of God's heritage, and "partakers of His promise in Christ by the Gospel." It will be seen, then, how the second chapter was needed to complete the first, and how the two together give us just such a view of the Advent as was most needed by the Jews of the period, while it is most instructive and suggestive to men of all countries and of all time. As, then, the last paragraph began with, "Now the birth of Jesus Christ was on this wise," we may regard this as beginning with, "Now the reception of Jesus Christ was on this wise."

According to the plan of these expositions, we must disregard details, and many interesting questions, for the consideration of which it is surely enough to refer to the many well-known and widely-read books on the Life of Christ; and confine ourselves to those general thoughts and suggestions which seem best fitted to bring out the spirit of the passage as a whole.

Let us, then, look first at the manner of His reception by Jerusalem, the city which as Son of David He could claim as peculiarly His own. It was the very centre of the circle of Old Testament illumination. It had all possible advantages, over every other place in the world, for knowing when and how the Christ should come. Yet, when He did come, the people of Jerusalem knew nothing about it, but had their first intimation of the fact from strangers who had come from the far East to seek Him. And not only did they know nothing about it till they were told, but, when told, they were troubled (ver. 3). Indifference where we should have expected eagerness, trouble where we should have looked for joy.

We have only to examine the contemporary accounts of the state of society in Jerusalem to understand it thoroughly, and to see how exceedingly natural it was. Those unacquainted with these records can have no idea of the gaiety and frivolity of the Jewish capital at the time. Every one, of course, knows something of the style and magnificence in which Herod the Great lived; but one is not apt to suppose that luxurious living was the rule among the people of the town. Yet so it seems to have been. Dr. Edersheim, who has made a special study of this subject, and who quotes his authorities for each separate statement, thus describes[3] the state of things: "These Jerusalemites—townspeople as they called themselves—were so polished, so witty, so pleasant.... And how much there was to be seen and heard in those luxuriously furnished houses, and at these sumptuous entertainments! In the women's apartments friends from the country would see every novelty in dress, adornments, and jewellery, and have the benefit of examining themselves in looking-glasses.... And then the lady-visitors might get anything in Jerusalem, from a false tooth to an Arabian veil, a Persian shawl, or an Indian dress!" Then, after furnishing what he calls "too painful evidence of the luxuriousness at Jerusalem at that time, and of the moral corruption to which it led," he concludes by giving an account of what one of the sacred books of the time describes as "the dignity of the Jerusalemites," mentioning particulars like these: "the wealth which they lavished on their marriages; the ceremony which insisted on repeated invitations to the guests to a banquet, and that men inferior should not be bidden to it; the dress in which they appeared; the manner in which the dishes were served, the wine in white crystal vases; the punishment of the cook who failed in his duty," and so on.

If things of that kind represented the dignity of the people of Jerusalem, we need not ask why they were troubled when they heard that to them had been born in Bethlehem a Saviour who was Christ the Lord. A Saviour who would save them from their sins was the very last thing people of that kind wanted. A Herod suited them better, for it was he and his court that set the example of the luxury and profligacy which characterised the capital. Do not all these revelations as to the state of things in the capital of Israel set off more vividly than ever the pure lustre of the quiet, simple, humble, peaceful surroundings of the Babe of Bethlehem and Boy of Nazareth? Put the "dignity" and trouble of Jerusalem over against the humility and peace of Bethlehem, and say which is the more truly dignified and desirable. When we look at the contrast we cease to wonder that, with the exception of a very few devout Simeons and Annas, waiting for the consolation of Israel, Jerusalem, as a whole, was troubled to hear the rumour of the advent of her Saviour-King.

Herod's trouble we can so readily understand that we need not spend time over it, or over what he did to get rid of it, so thoroughly in keeping as it was with all that history tells us of his character and conduct. No wonder that the one thought in *his* mind was "Away with Him!"

But who are these truly dignified men, who are now turning their backs on rich and gay Jerusalem, and setting their faces to the obscurity and poverty of the village of Bethlehem? They are men of rank and wealth and learning from the far East—representatives of all that is best in the old civilizations of the world. They had only the scantiest opportunities of learning what was the Hope of Israel, and how it should be realised; but they were earnest men; *their* minds were not taken up with gaiety and frivolity; they had studied the works of nature till their souls were full of the thought of God in His glory and majesty; but their hearts still yearned to know if He, Whose glory was in the heavens, could stoop to cure the ills that flesh is heir to. They had heard of Israel's hope, the hope of a child to be born of David's race, who should bring divine mercy near to human need; they had a vague idea that the time for the fulfilment of that hope was drawing near; and, as they mused, behold a marvellous appearance in the heavens, which seemed to call them away to seek Him whom their souls desired! Hence their long journey to Jerusalem and their eager entrance into Bethlehem. Had their dignity been the kind of dignity which was boasted of in Jerusalem, they would no doubt have been offended by the poverty of the surroundings, the poor house with its scanty furniture and its humble inmates. But theirs was the dignity of mind and soul, so they were not offended by the poor surroundings; they recognised in the humble Child the object of their search; they bowed before Him, doing Him homage, and presented to Him gifts as a tribute from the East to the coming King of righteousness and love.

What a beautiful picture; how striking the contrast to the magnificence of Herod the Great in Jerusalem, surrounded by his wealthy and luxurious court. Verily, these were wise men from the East, wise with a wisdom not of this world—wise to recognise the hope of the future, not in a monarch *called* "the Great," surrounded by the world's pomp and luxury, but in the fresh young life of the holy heaven-born Child. Learned as they were, they had simple hearts—they had had some glimpse of the great truth that it is not learning the world needs so much as life, new life. Would that all the wise men of the present day were equally wise in heart! We rejoice that so many of them are; and if only all of them had true wisdom, they would consider that even those who stand as high in the learning of the new West as these men did in the learning of the old East, would do themselves honour in bowing low in presence of the Holy Child, and acknowledge that by no effort of the greatest intellect is it possible to reach that truth which can alone meet the deepest wants of men—that there is no other hope for man than the new birth, the fresh, pure, holy life which came into the world when the Christ was born, and which comes into every heart that in simple trustfulness gives Him a welcome as did these wise men of old. There, at the threshold of the Gospel, we see the true relation of science and religion.

"Let knowledge grow from more to more,
But more of reverence in us dwell;
That mind and soul, according well,
May make one music as before."

All honour to these wise men for bending low in presence of the Holy Child; and thanks be to God for allowing His servant Matthew to give us a glimpse of a scene so beautiful, so touching, so suggestive of pure and high and holy thought and feeling.

The gifts of the East no doubt provided the means of securing a refuge in the South and West. That Egypt gave the fugitives a friendly welcome, and a safe retreat so long as the danger remained, is obvious; but here again we are left without detail. The one thing which the Evangelist wishes to impress upon us is the parallel between the experience of Israel and Israel's Holy One. Israel of the Old Testament, born in Palestine, had to flee into Egypt. When the time was ripe for return, the way was opened for it; and thus the prophet speaks of it in the name of the Lord: "When Israel was a child, then I loved him, and called My son out of Egypt." Now that the Holy One of Israel has come to fulfil old Israel's destiny, the prophetic word, which had been only partially realised in the history of the nation, is fulfilled in the history of the Anointed One. Hence, just as it happened with the nation, so did it happen with the nation's representative and King: born in His own land, He had to flee into Egypt, and remain there till God brought Him out, and set Him in His land again.

Other points of agreement with the prophetic word are mentioned. It is worthy of note that they are all connected with the dark side of prophecy concerning the Messiah. The reason for this will readily appear on reflection. The Scribes and Pharisees were insistent enough on the bright side, the side that favoured their ideas of a great king, who should rescue the people from the Roman yoke, and found a great world-kingdom, after the manner of Herod the Great or of Cæsar the mighty. So there was no need to bring strongly out that side of prophecy which foretold of the glories of the coming King. But the sad side had been entirely neglected. It is this, accordingly, which the Evangelist is prompted to illustrate.

It was, indeed, in itself an occasion of stumbling that the King of Israel should have to flee to Egypt. But why should one stumble at it, who looked at the course of Israel's history as a nation, in the light the prophets threw upon it? It was an occasion of stumbling that His birth in Bethlehem should bring with it such sorrow and anguish; but why wonder at it when so great a prophet as Jeremiah so touchingly speaks of the voice heard in Ramah, "Rachel weeping for her children and would not be comforted," — a thought of exquisite beauty and pathos as Jeremiah used it in reference to the banished ones of his day, but of still deeper pathos as now fulfilled in the sorrow at Ramah, over the massacre of her innocents, when not Israel but Israel's Holy One is banished from the land of His birth. Again, it was an occasion of stumbling that the King of Israel, instead of growing up in majesty in the midst of the Court and the capital, should retire into obscurity in the little village of Nazareth, and for many years be unheard of by the great ones of the land; but why wonder at it when the prophets again and again represent Him as growing up in this very way, as "a root out of a dry ground," as a twig or "shoot out of the stem of Jesse," growing up "out of His place," and attracting no attention while He grew. Such is the meaning of the words translated, "He shall be called a Nazarene." This does not appear in our language; hence the difficulty which many have found in this reference, there being no passage in any of the prophets where the Christ is spoken of as a Nazarene; but the word to Hebrew ears at once suggests the Hebrew for "Branch," continually applied to Him in the prophets, and especially connected with the idea of His quiet and silent growth, aloof from the throng and unnoticed by the great.

This completes, appropriately, the sketch of His reception. Unthought of by His own, till strangers sought Him; a source of trouble to them when they heard of Him; His life threatened by the occupant, for the time, of David's throne, He is saved only by exile, and on returning to His people passes out of notice: and the great world moves on, all unconscious and unconcerned, whilst its Saviour-King is preparing, in the obscurity of His village home, for the great work of winning a lost world back to God.

FOOTNOTE

[3] *Life and Times of Jesus the Messiah,* vol. i., p. 130.

III
HIS HERALD

Matt. iii. 1-12.

THIRTY years have gone since all Jerusalem was in trouble at the rumour of Messiah's birth. But as nothing has been heard of Him since, the excitement has passed away. Those who *were* troubled about it are ageing or old or dead; so no one thinks or speaks of it now. There have been several political changes since, mostly for the worse. Judæa is now a province of Rome, governed by procurators, of whom the sixth, called Pontius Pilate, has just entered on his office. Society is much the same as before—the same worldliness and luxurious living after the manner of the Greek, the same formalism and bigotry after the manner of the Scribe. There is no sign, in Jerusalem at least, of any change for the better.

The only new thing stirring is a rumour in the street. People are telling one another that a new prophet has arisen. "In the Palace?"—"No." "In the Temple?"—"No." "Surely somewhere in the city?"—"No." He is in the wilderness, clad in roughest garb, subsisting on poorest fare—a living protest against the luxury of the time. He makes no pretence to learning, draws no fine distinctions, gives no curious interpretations, and yet, with only a simple message,—which, however, he delivers as coming straight from God Himself,—is drawing crowds to hear him from all the country side. So the rumour spreads throughout the town, and great numbers go out to see what it is all about; some perhaps from curiosity, some in hope that it may be the dawn of a brighter day for Israel, all of them no doubt more or less stirred with the excitement of the thought that, after so many silent centuries, a veritable prophet has come, like those of old. For it must be remembered that even in gay Jerusalem the deep-rooted feelings of national pride and patriotism had been only overlaid, not superseded, by the veneer of Greek and Roman civilisation, which only seemed for the moment to satisfy the people.

So they go out in multitudes to the wilderness; and what do they see? "A man clothed in fine raiment," like the Roman officials in the palace, which in those degenerate days were Jerusalem's pride? "A reed shaken by the wind," like the time-serving politicians of the hour? Nay, verily; but a true prophet of the Lord, one reminding them of what they have read in the Scriptures of the great Elijah, who suddenly appeared in the wild mountain region of Gilead, at a time when Phœnician manners were making the same havoc in Israel that Greek manners are now making in Jerusalem. Who can he be? He seems to be more than a prophet. Can he be the Christ? But this he entirely disclaims. Is he Elijah then? John probably knew that he was sent "in the spirit and power of Elijah," for so his father had learned from the angel on the occasion of the announcement of his birth; but that was not the point of their question. When they asked, "Art thou Elijah?" they meant "Art thou Elijah risen from the dead?" To this he must, of course, answer, "No." In the same way he must disclaim identity with any of the prophets. He will not trade upon the name of any of these holy men of old. Enough that he comes, a nameless one, before them, with a message from the Lord. So, keeping himself in the background, he puts his message before them, content that they should recognise in it the fulfilment of the well-known word of prophecy: "A voice crying in the wilderness, Prepare ye the way of the Lord, make His paths straight."

John wishes it to be distinctly understood that he is not that Light which the prophets of old have told them should arise, but is sent to bear witness to that Light. He has come as a herald to announce the approach of the King, and to call upon the people to prepare for His coming. Think not of me, he cries, ask not who I am; think of the coming King, and make ready for Him, —"Prepare ye the way of the Lord, make *His* paths straight."

How is the way of the Lord to be prepared? Is it by summoning the people to arms all over the land, that they may repel the Roman invader and restore the ancient kingdom? Such a proclamation would no doubt have struck a chord that would have vibrated through all the land. That would have been after the manner of men; it was not the way of the Lord. The summons must be, not to arms, but to *repentance*: "Wash you, make you clean: put away the evil of your doings." So, instead of marching up, a host of warriors, to the Roman citadel, the people troop down, band after band of penitents, to the Jordan, confessing their sins. After all it is the old, old prophetic message over again, —the same which had been sent generation after generation to a backsliding people, its burden always this: "Turn ye unto Me, saith the Lord of Hosts, and I will turn unto you, saith the Lord of Hosts."

Like many of the old prophets, John taught by symbol as well as by word. The preparation needed was an inward cleansing, and what more fitting symbol of it than the water baptism to which he called the nation? "In that day," it was written in the prophets, "there shall be a fountain opened to the house of David and to the inhabitants of Jerusalem, for sin and for uncleanness." The prophecy was about to be fulfilled, and the baptism of John was the appropriate sign of it. Again, in another of the prophets the promise ran, "Then will I sprinkle clean water upon you, and ye shall be clean; from all your filthiness and from all your idols will I cleanse you ... and I will put my spirit within you." John knew well that it was not given to him to *fulfil* this promise. He could not grant the real baptism, the baptism of the Holy Ghost; but he could baptise with water; he could give the sign and assurance to the truly penitent heart that there was forgiveness and cleansing in the coming One; and thus, by his baptism with water, as well as by the message he delivered, he was preparing the way of the Lord. All this, we cannot but observe, was in perfect accord with the wonderful prophetic utterance of his father Zacharias, as recorded by St. Luke: "Thou, child, shalt be called the prophet of the Highest: for thou shalt go before the face of the Lord to prepare His ways; to give knowledge of salvation unto His people by the remission of their sins," —not to give salvation, which only Christ can give, but the knowledge of it. This he did not only by telling of the coming Saviour, and, when He came, pointing to Him as "the Lamb of God that taketh away the sin of the world;" but also by the appropriate sign of baptism, which gave the same knowledge in the language of symbol addressed to the eye.

The summons of the prophet of the wilderness is not in vain. The people come. The throngs increase. The nation is moved. Even the great ones of the nation condescend to follow the multitude. Pharisees and Sadducees, the leaders of the two great parties in Church and State, are coming; many of them are coming. What a comfort this must be to the prophet's soul. How gladly he will welcome them, and let it be known that he has among his converts many of the great ones of the land! But the stern Baptist is a man of no such mould. What cares he for rank or position or worldly influence? What he wants is reality, simplicity, godly sincerity; and he knows that, scarce as these virtues are in the community at large, they are scarcest of all among these dignitaries. He will not allow the smallest admixture of insincerity or hypocrisy in what is, so far, a manifest work of God. He must test these new-comers to the uttermost, for the sin of which they need most to repent is the very sin which they are in danger of committing afresh in its most aggravated form in offering themselves for baptism. He must therefore test their motives; he must at all risks ensure that, unless their repentance is genuine, they shall not be baptised. For their own sakes, as well as for the work's sake this is necessary. Hence the strong, even harsh language he uses in putting the question *why* they had come. Yet he would not repel or discourage them. He does not send them away as if past redemption, but only demands that they bring forth fruit worthy of the repentance they profess. And lest they should think that there was an easier way of entrance for them than for others, lest they should think that they had claims sufficient because of their descent, he reminds them that God can have his kingdom upon earth, even though every son of Abraham in the world should reject Him: "Think not to say within yourselves, We have Abraham to our father: for I say unto you, that God is able of these stones to raise up children unto Abraham."

It is as if he said, The coming kingdom of righteousness and truth will not fail, even if Pharisees and Sadducees and all the natural children of Abraham refuse to enter its only gate of repentance; if there is no response to the Divine summons where it is most to be expected, then it can be secured where it is least to be expected; if flesh become stone, then stone can be made flesh, according to the word of promise. So there will be no gathering in of mere formalists to make up numbers, no including of those who are only "Jews outwardly." And there will be no half measures, no compromise with evil, no parleying with those who are unwilling or only half willing to repent. A time of crisis has come,—"now also the axe is laid unto the root of the trees." It is not lifted yet. But it is there lying ready, ready for the Lord of the vineyard, when He shall come (and He is close at hand); then, "*every tree which bringeth not forth good fruit is hewn down and cast into the fire.*"

Yet not for judgment is He coming,—John goes on to say,—but to fulfil the promise of the Father. He is coming to baptise you with the Holy Ghost and with fire—to purify you through and through and to animate you with a new life, glowing, upward-striving, heaven-aspiring; and it is to prepare you for this unspeakable blessing that I ask you to come and put away those sins which must be a barrier in the way of His coming, those sins which dim your eyes so that you cannot see Him, which stop your ears so that you cannot recognise your Shepherd's voice, that clog your hearts so that the Holy Spirit cannot reach them,—repent, *repent*, and be baptised all of you; for there cometh One after me, mightier than I, whose meanest servant I am not worthy to be,—He shall baptise you with the Holy Ghost and with fire, if you are ready to receive Him; but if you are not, still you cannot escape Him, "Whose fan is in His hand, and He will thoroughly cleanse His threshing floor; and He will gather His wheat into the garner, but the chaff He will burn up with unquenchable fire" (R.V.).

The work of John must still be done. It specially devolves upon the ministers of Christ; would they were all as anxious as he was to keep in the background, as little concerned about position, title, official rank, or personal consideration.

IV
HIS BAPTISM

Matt. iii. 13-17.

"THE baptism of John, was it from Heaven or of men?" This question must have been asked throughout the length and breadth of the land in the days of his mission. We know how it was answered; for even after the excitement had died away, we are told that "all men counted John for a prophet." This conviction would of course prevail in Nazareth as well as everywhere else. When, therefore, the Baptist removed from the wilderness of Judæa and the lower reaches of the Jordan to the ford of Bethany, or Bethabara,—now identified with a point much farther north, within a single day's journey of Nazareth,—the people of Galilee would flock to him, as before the people of Judæa and Jerusalem had done. Among the rest, as might naturally be expected, Jesus came. It was enough for Him to know that the baptism of John was of Divine appointment. He was in all things guided by His Father's will, to whom He would day by day commit His way. Accordingly, just as day by day He had been subject to His parents, and just as He had seen it to be right to go up to the Temple in accordance with the Law, so He recognised it to be His duty to present Himself, as His countrymen in such large numbers were doing, to receive baptism from John. The manner of the narrative implies that He came, not as if He were some great person demanding special recognition, but as simply and naturally as any of the rest: "Then cometh Jesus from Galilee to the Jordan unto John, to be baptised of him."

John looks at Him. Does he know Him at all? Perhaps not; for though they are cousins, their lives have been lived quite apart. Before their birth their mothers met; but it is doubtful if they themselves have seen each other before, and even if they have, in earlier years, they may both be so changed that recognition is uncertain. The one has had his home in the South; the other, in the North. Besides, the elder of the two has spent his life mostly in the desert, so that probably he is a stranger now even to his own townspeople, and his father and mother, both very old when he was born, must be dead and gone long ago. Perhaps, then, John did not know Jesus at all; certainly he did not yet know Him as the Messiah. But he sees something in Him that draws forth the homage of his soul. Or possibly he gathers his impressions rather from what Jesus says. All the rest have confessed sin; He has no sin of His own to confess. But words would no doubt be spoken that would convey to the Baptist how this disciple looked on sin, how the very thought of it filled Him with horror, how His whole soul longed for the righteousness of God, how it was a sacred passion with Him that sin should perish from the hearts of men, and righteousness reign in its place. Whether then, it was by His appearance, the clear eye, the calm face,—an open window for the prophet to look through into His soul,—or whether it was by the words He spoke as He claimed a share in the baptism, or both combined, John was taken aback—surprised a second time, though in just the opposite way to that in which he had been surprised before. The same eagle eye that saw through the mask of Pharisee and Sadducee could penetrate the veil of humility and obscurity; so he said: "I have need to be baptised of Thee, and comest Thou to me?"

Think of the majesty of this John. Remember how he bore himself in presence of the Pharisees and Sadducees; and how he faced Herod, telling him plainly, at the risk of his life, as it afterwards proved, "It is not lawful for thee to have thy brother's wife." Remember that all Judæa, and Jerusalem, and Galilee had been bowing down in his presence; and now, when an obscure nameless One of Nazareth comes to him, only as yet distinguished from others by the holiness of His life and the purity of His soul, John would not have Him bow in his presence, but would himself bend low before Him: "I have need to be baptised of Thee, and comest Thou to me?" Oh for more of that grand combination of lofty courage and lowly reverence! Verily, "among them that are born of women there hath not risen a greater than John the Baptist."

But Jesus answering said unto him, "Suffer it now; for thus it becometh us to fulfil all righteousness" (R.V.). Though about to enter on His Messianic work, He has not yet taken its burden on Him; accordingly He comes, not as Messiah, but in the simplest and most unassuming way; content still, as He has been all along till now, to be reckoned simply as of Israel. This is what we take to be the force of the plural pronoun "us."

On the other hand, it should be remembered that Jesus must have recognised in the summons to the Jordan a call to commence His work as Messiah. He would certainly have heard from His mother of the prophetic words which had been spoken concerning His cousin and Himself; and would, therefore, as soon as He heard of the mission of John, know well what it meant—He could not but know that John was preparing the way before Him, and therefore that His time was close at hand. Of this, too, we have an indication in His answer to the expostulation of John. "Suffer it now," He says; as if to say, I am as yet only one of Israel; My time is at hand, when I must take the position to which I am called, but meantime I come as the rest come: "Suffer it *now*; for thus it becometh us to fulfil all righteousness."

While then Jesus came simply in obedience to the will of God, He must have come with a very heavy burden. His study of the Scriptures must have made Him painfully familiar with the dark prospects before Him. Well did He know that the path of the Messiah must be one of suffering, that He must be despised and rejected, that He must be wounded for the people's transgressions and bruised for their iniquity; that, in a word, He must be the suffering Priest before He can be the reigning King. This thought of His priesthood must have been especially borne in upon Him now that He had just reached the priestly age. In His thirteenth year—the Temple age—He had gone to the Temple, and now at the age when the priest is consecrated to his office, He is summoned to the Jordan, to be baptised by one whom He knows to be sent of God to prepare the way before Him. Those Scriptures, then, which speak of the priestly office the Messiah must fill, must have been very much in His mind as He came to John and offered Himself to be baptised. And of all these Scriptures none would seem more appropriate at the moment than those words of the fortieth Psalm: "Lo, I come: in the volume of the book it is written of Me, I delight to do Thy will, O My God."

At this point we can readily see the appropriateness of His baptism, and also an element in common between it and that of the people. They had come professing to be willing to do the will of God by turning from sin to righteousness. He had no need to turn from sin to do the will of God; but He had to turn from the quiet and peaceful home life at Nazareth, that He might take up the burden laid upon Him as Messiah. So He as well as they had to leave the old life and begin a new one; and in this we can see how fitting it was that He as well as they should be baptised. Then, just as by baptism—the symbol, in their case, of separation from sin and consecration to God—John made "ready a people prepared for the Lord;" so by baptism—the symbol, in His case, of separation from private life and consecration to God in the office of Messiah,—the Lord was made ready for the people. By baptism John opened the door of the new Kingdom. From the wilderness of sin the people entered it as subjects; from the seclusion of private life Jesus entered it as King and Priest. They came under a vow of obedience unto Him; He came under a vow of obedience unto death, even the death of the Cross.

This, then, is the moment of His taking up the Cross. It is indeed the assumption of His royalty as Messiah-King; but then He knew that He must suffer and die before He could enter on His glory; therefore, as the first great duty before Him, He takes up the Cross. In this we can see a still further appropriateness in the words already quoted, as is suggested in the well-known passage in the Epistle to the Hebrews: "Sacrifice and offering thou wouldest not, but a body hast thou prepared me: in burnt offerings and sacrifices for sin thou hast had no pleasure. Then said I, Lo, I come (in the volume of the book it is written of me) to do thy will, O God." Ah, who can understand the love in the heart of Jesus, who can measure the sacrifice He makes as He bends before John, and is baptised into the name of "the Christ," the Saviour of mankind!

The act of solemn consecration is over. He comes up out of the water. And lo, the heavens are opened, and the Spirit of God descends upon Him, and a voice from heaven calls, "This is My beloved Son, in Whom I am well pleased."

"The heavens were opened." What was the precise natural phenomenon witnessed we can only conjecture, but whatever it was, it was but a symbol of the spiritual opening of the heavens. The heaven of God's love and of all holy Angels, shut from man by sin, was opened again by the Christ of God. Nothing could be more appropriate, therefore, than that just at the moment when the Holy One of Israel had bowed Himself to take up His heavy burden, when for the first time it was possible to say, "Behold the Lamb of God, that taketh away the sin of the world!" the heavens should open to welcome Him, and in welcoming Him, the Sin-bearer, to welcome all whose sins He came to take away.

"And He saw the Spirit of God descending like a dove, and lighting upon Him." This was His anointing for the work He had come to do. The priests of the line of Aaron had been anointed with oil; He was anointed with that of which the oil was but a symbol, — the Holy Spirit descending from the open heaven. From His birth, indeed, He had been guided by the Spirit of God. But up to this time He had, as we have seen, nothing more than was needed to minister to that growth in wisdom which had been going on in private life these thirty years, nothing more than was necessary to guide Him day by day in His quiet, unexacting duties at home. Now He needs far more. Now He must receive the Spirit without measure, in the fulness of His grace and power; hence the organic form of the symbol. The emblem used when the apostles were baptised with the Holy Ghost was tongues of fire, indicating the partial nature of the endowment; here it is the dove, suggesting the idea of completeness and, at the same time, as every one sees, of beauty, gentleness, peace, and love. Again let it be remembered that it is on Him as our representative that the Spirit descends, that His baptism with the Holy Ghost is in order that He may be ready to fulfil the word of John, "He shall baptise you with the Holy Ghost and with fire." Heaven opened above Him means all heavenly blessings prepared for those who follow Him into the new Kingdom. The descent of the Spirit means the bestowment on Him and His of heaven's best gift as an earnest of all the rest.

Last of all there is the voice, "This is My beloved Son, in whom I am well pleased," spoken not merely to Himself individually,—all along, in the personal sense, He was God's beloved Son, in whom He was well pleased,—but to the Messiah, as the Representative and Head of a new redeemed humanity, as the First-born among many brethren, as One who at the very moment was undertaking suretyship on behalf of all who had already received Him or should in the ages to come receive Him as their Priest and King—"*This* is My beloved Son, in whom I am well pleased."

Blessed be the God and Father of our Lord Jesus Christ, who hath blessed us with all spiritual and heavenly blessings in Him: with an open heaven, a present Spirit, a reconciled Father's voice. Blessed be our loving Lord and Saviour, that He came so humbly to the Jordan, stooped so bravely to the yoke, took up our heavy Cross, and carried it through these sorrowful years to the bitter, bitter end. And blessed be the Holy Spirit of all grace, that He abode on Him, and abides with us. May the grace of the Lord Jesus Christ, and the love of God, and the communion of the Holy Ghost, be with us all!

V
HIS TEMPTATION

Matt. iv. 1-11.

MUCH has been written on the possibility of temptation in the experience of a sinless Being. The difficulties which have been raised in this region are chiefly of a metaphysical kind, such as it is possible—for some minds, we might say inevitable—to raise at every point in that mysterious complexity which we call life. Without attempting to enter profoundly into the question, may not an appeal be made to our own experience? Do we not all know what it is to be "tempted without sin,"—without sin, that is, in reference to the particular thing to which we are tempted? Are there not desires in our nature, not only thoroughly innocent, but a necessary part of our humanity, which, nevertheless, give occasion to temptation? But on its being recognised that to follow the impulse, however natural, would lead to wrongdoing, the temptation is instantly repelled and integrity perfectly preserved. In such a case there is temptation, conflict, victory—all without sin. Surely then what is possible to us on occasion was also possible to our Lord on all occasions, all through His pure and spotless life. His taking our nature indeed involved not only the possibility, but the necessity, of temptation.

The passage before us records what is known as *the* Temptation, by which it is not, of course, meant that it was the only one. Our Lord was all His life exposed to the assaults of the Tempter, which seem indeed to have increased in violence as He approached the end of His life. Why, then, is this attack singled out for special record? The reason seems obvious. It marks the beginning of the life-work of the Messiah. In His quiet home at Nazareth Jesus must have had the ordinary temptations to which childhood and youth are subject. That was the time of quiet preparation for the great campaign. Now the war must begin. He must address Himself to the mighty undertaking of destroying the works of the devil. The great adversary, therefore, wisely endeavours to mar it at the outset, by a deliberately planned series of assaults, directed against all the vulnerable points of that human nature his great antagonist must wear. From this time onward our Lord's whole life was to be a warfare, not against the rage of wicked men only, but against the wiles of the unseen adversary, whose opposition must have been as bitter and relentless as that of his representatives in flesh and blood. From the nature of the case, the conflict waged in the spiritual sphere could not appear in the history. It belonged to that hidden life, of which even the closest disciples could see but very little. We get a hint of it occasionally in certain looks and words betokening inward conflict, and in those frequent retirings to solitary places to pray; but of the actual soul experience we have no record, except in the case of this first pitched battle, so to call it, of the lifelong conflict. It is evident that our Lord Himself must have given His disciples the information on this deeply interesting subject which enabled them to put it on record, for the encouragement and comfort of His people in all time to come. Blessed be His Holy Name, for this unveiling of His hidden life.

The greater portion, indeed, is still veiled. A dark cloud of mystery hangs over the forty days. Nothing else is told of them in this Gospel than that Jesus fasted for that time—an indication of sustained intensity in the life of His spirit. From St. Mark and St. Luke we learn that the temptation lasted throughout the entire period—a fact not at all inconsistent with sustained spiritual elevation, for it is just at such periods that man is most exposed to the assaults of the enemy. We may not penetrate the darkness of these forty days. Like the darkness in Gethsemane, and again, from the sixth to the ninth hour on Calvary, it forbids entrance. These were times when even "the disciple whom Jesus loved" could not be with Him. These are solitudes that can never be disturbed. Only this we know: that it was necessary that our Saviour should pass through these dark "cloud-gates" as He entered on and as He finished His priestly work on earth.

But though we cannot comprehend what our Lord did for us during these forty days, when He "recovered Paradise to all mankind," we may, remembering that He was tempted, not only as our Representative but as our Exemplar, endeavour with all humility and reverence to enter into this soul-experience of our Lord, so far as the vivid representation of its main features in the inspired record warrants.

It is always difficult to tell the story of soul-experience in such a way as to come home to the common mind and heart of humanity. It will not do to tell it in the language of philosophy or psychology, which none but those familiar with such discussions could understand. It must be addressed to the imagination as well as to the pure reason. If this had been sufficiently kept in view, it might have saved many a difficulty on the part of those who have set themselves to discover exactly what were the outward circumstances of the temptation, forgetting that here especially it is the inward and spiritual with which we have to do, not the outward and physical. It is not what happened to the body of Jesus,—whether it was actually carried to a pinnacle of the

Temple or not,—with which we have any concern in connection with the subject of temptation; but what happened to His soul: for it is the soul of man, not his body, which is tempted.

It is above all things necessary to hold firmly to the reality of the temptation. It was no mere sham fight; it was just as real as any we have ever had when most fiercely assailed by the tempter. This will, of course, dispose of the vulgar idea that the devil appeared in recognisable shape, like one of Doré's fiends. Some people cannot rise above the folly of imagining that there is nothing real that is not material, and therefore that our Saviour could have had no conflict with Satan, if Satan had not assumed some material shape. The power of temptation consists in its appearance of being suggested without sinister intent. Our Lord was tempted "like as we are," and therefore had not the advantage of seeing the tempter in his proper person. He may have appeared "as an angel of light," or it may have been only as an invisible spirit that he came. However that may be, it was unquestionably a spiritual experience; and in that consists its reality and value.

In order firmly to grasp the reality of the conflict, we must not only bear in mind that our Lord had to contend with the same invisible adversary whom we must encounter, but that He had to meet him just as we have to meet him—not as God, but as man. The man Christ Jesus was tempted, and in His human nature He triumphed. He had "emptied Himself" of His divine attributes; and to have had recourse to them when the battle raged too fiercely for His resources as a man, would have been to have acknowledged defeat. What need was there to show that God could triumph over Satan? There needed no Incarnation and no wilderness contest for that. Had it not been as a man that He triumphed there had been no victory at all. It is true that He went into the wilderness in the power of the Spirit; but so may we go into any wilderness or anywhere. It was through Divine strength He triumphed, but only in that strength made perfect in human weakness according to the promise which is valid for us all. Here too "He was tempted like as we are," with the same ways and means of resisting the temptation and overcoming it as are available to us. It follows from all this that we should not look at this temptation scene as something quite foreign to ourselves, but should endeavour to enter into it, and, as far as possible, to realise it.

Observe first the close connection with the baptism. This is made prominent and emphatic in all the three accounts. Evidently, then, it supplies the key to it. The baptism of Christ was His consecration to the work of His Messiahship. And let us not imagine that He had any ready-made plan for the accomplishment of it. His was no stereotyped life-work, such as that which most of us take up, in which we can learn from those who have gone before how they set about it, and proceed accordingly. Even with all that advantage most of us have to do not a little hard thinking, before we can lay our plans. Could it be, then, that He who had such a work before Him had no need to think over it, and plan it, and weigh different methods of procedure, and face the difficulties which every one who enters on a new enterprise has to meet? Do not let us forget for a moment that He was a real man, and that in planning the course He would pursue, as in all other points, He was tried like as we are.

Accordingly, no sooner is He baptised, than He withdraws by Himself alone, as Moses and others had done when about to enter on their work, to commune with God and to take counsel with His own thoughts. Was He free from all misgiving? Let us not imagine that it was impossible for Him to doubt. Tempted in all points like as we are, He must have known this sore temptation. One may well suppose, then, that He was visited again and again with misgivings during these forty days, so that it was not at all unnatural that temptation should take the form: "If Thou be the Son of God — —"

Look now at the first temptation, and mark the double human weakness to which it was addressed. On the one hand *doubt* — "*If* Thou art the Son of God;" on the other, *hunger* — for He had fasted long and had as strong a craving for bread as any of us would have had in the circumstances. See now the force of the temptation. He is suffering from hunger; He is tempted to doubt. How can He have relief? "If Thou be the Son of God, *command that these stones be made bread.*" Special powers are entrusted to Him for His work as Messiah. Should He not use them now? Why not? So in his subtlety suggests the tempter. In vain. He had taken His place among His brother-men, and would not separate Himself from them. They could not command stones to be made bread; and would He cease to be their Brother? What saith the Law? A well-known passage leaps into His memory: "Man shall not live by bread alone, but by every word that proceedeth out of the mouth of God." Man must trust in God, and when he is hungry in the wilderness, as Israel was of old, must look upwards for his help. So must I; so will I. And He bears the hunger, repels the doubt, and conquers His subtle foe.

The thought of the doubt that must exist in other minds if not in His own, gives occasion for a second assault. To have proved His power by commanding the stones to be made bread would only have gratified a personal craving. But would it not advance His work to make some signal display of the powers by which He shall be accredited — do something that would attract universal attention; not in the desert, but in Jerusalem; — why not show to all the people that God is with Him by casting Himself from the pinnacle of the Temple? "If Thou be the Son of God, cast Thyself down; for it is written, He shall give His angels charge concerning Thee; and in their hands they shall bear Thee up, lest at any time Thou dash Thy foot against a stone." One sees at once the added force of this temptation. The hunger remains, together with the weakness of body and faintness of spirit which always accompany it. And the very weapon He used to repel the first assault is turned against Him now, for His adversary has found a passage of Scripture, which he uses with great effect. Moreover, the appeal seems to be to that very spirit of trustfulness which stood Him in such stead in His first encounter. Is He not hard beset? What then? Does He in this emergency summon to His aid any ally denied to us in similar stress of trial? No: He does exactly what we have to do in the same case: meets Scripture quoted with a bias by other Scripture thought of without prejudice. He recognises that the Scripture first presented to His mind is only a part of the truth which bears on the case. Something more must be had in view, before the path of duty is clear. To meet the distracting thought, this word occurs, "Thou shalt not tempt the Lord thy God." It is one thing to trust, another to tempt. I was trusting when I refused to command the stones to be made bread. But I should be tempting God were I to cast myself down from a pinnacle of the Temple. I should be experimenting upon Him, as did the children of Israel at Meribah and at Massah (for that is the connection of the words He quotes) when they said, "Is the Lord among us or not?" I must not experiment, I must not tempt, I must simply trust. Thus victory is gained a second time.

If it is not right to begin His work by any such display as that which the tempter has just suggested, how shall it be begun? A question surely of unexampled difficulty. The air was full of expectancy in regard to the coming of King Messiah. The whole nation was ready to hail him. Not only so, but even the heathen nations were more or less prepared for His coming. Why not take advantage of this favourable state of things at home and abroad? Why not proclaim a kingdom that will satisfy these widespread expectations, and gather round itself all those enthusiasms; and, after having thus won the people, then proceed to lead them on to higher and better things? Why not? It would be bowing down to the prince of this world. It is clearly a temptation of the Evil One. To yield to it would be to fall down before him and worship him in exchange for the kingdoms of this world and the glory of them. It would be gaining the allegiance of men by methods which are not of God, but of the great adversary. He recognises the device of Satan to lure Him from the path of self-denial which He sees to be the path of duty; accordingly, with energy He says, "Get thee hence,

Satan; for it is written, Thou shalt worship the Lord thy God, and Him only shalt thou serve." In establishing My kingdom I must show Myself to be a servant and worshipper of God and of Him only; accordingly, no worldly methods must be used, however promising they may seem to be; the battle must be fought with spiritual weapons, the kingdom must be established by spiritual forces alone, and on truth and love alone must I depend: I choose the path of the Cross. "Get thee hence, Satan."

The crisis is passed. The path of duty and of sorrow lies plain and clear before Him. He has refused to turn aside to the right hand or to the left. The tempter has been foiled at every point, and so must withdraw, for the time, at least. "Then the devil leaveth Him; and, behold, angels came and ministered unto Him."

VI
BEGINNING OF HIS GALILEAN MINISTRY

Matt. iv. 12-25.

DID our Lord's ministry begin in Galilee? If so, why did He not Himself set the example of "beginning at Jerusalem"? As a matter of fact we learn from the fourth Gospel that He did begin at Jerusalem; and that it was only after He was rejected there that He changed the scene of His labours to the North. Why then do the three Evangelists not mention this earlier ministry in the South? The answer to this question seems suggested by the stress laid by each of the three on the fact of John's imprisonment, as giving the date after which Christ commenced His work in the North. Here, for example (ver. 12), it is put thus: "Now when He heard that John was delivered up, He withdrew into Galilee." Their idea, then, seems to be that the Judæan ministry of Christ belonged rather to the closing months of John's career; and that only after John's mission, the sphere of which had been mainly in the South, had closed, could the special work of Christ be regarded as having begun.

If we review the facts we shall see how natural and accurate was this view of the case. John was sent to prepare the way of the Lord, to open the door of Jerusalem and Judæa for His coming. At first the herald meets with great success. Jerusalem and Judæa flock out to him for his baptism. The way seems ready. The door is opened. The Messiah has come; and John has pointed Him out as "the Lamb of God that taketh away the sin of the world." Now the Passover is at hand. People will be gathered together from all parts of the land. What better time for the Lord to come to His temple? And, as we are told in the fourth Gospel, Jesus takes the opportunity, goes up to Jerusalem, enters into the Temple, and at once begins to cleanse it. How is He received? As one whose way has been prepared, whose claims have been duly authenticated by a prophet of the Lord, as all acknowledge John to be? Not at all. Forth step the Temple officials and ask Him by what authority He does these things. He has come unto His own; His own receive Him not. He does not, however, too hastily accept their suicidal refusal to receive Him. He gives them time to think of it. He tarries in the neighbourhood, He and John baptising in the same region; patiently waiting, as it would seem, for signs of relenting on the part of the rulers and Pharisees,—one of whom, indeed, has come by night and made inquiries; and who can tell what the result will be—whether this Nicodemus may not be able to win the others over, so that after all there will be waiting for the King the welcome He ought to have, and which He is well entitled to expect after the reception given to His herald? But no: the impression of John's preaching and baptism is wearing off; the hardness of heart returns, and passes into positive bitterness, which reaches such a height that at last Herod finds the tide so turned that he can hazard what a few months before would have been the foolhardy policy of seizing John and shutting him in prison. So ends the mission of John—beginning with largest hope, ending in cruellest disappointment.

The early Judæan ministry of Christ, then, as related by St. John may be regarded as the opportunity which Christ gave to the nation, as represented by the capital and the Temple, to follow out the mission of John to its intended issue—an opportunity which the leaders of the nation wasted and threw away, and which therefore came to nothing. Hence it is that the three Evangelists, without giving any of the details which were afterwards supplied by St. John, sum up the closing months of the forerunner's ministry in the one fact which suggests all, that John was silenced, and shut up in prison. We see, then, that though Jesus did in a sense commence His work in Galilee, He did not do so until He had first given the authorities of the city and the Temple the opportunity of having it begin, as it would seem most natural that it should have begun, in the centre of the old kingdom.

But though it was His treatment in the South which was the immediate cause of this withdrawal to the North and the beginning of the establishment of the new kingdom there, yet this was no unforeseen contingency—this too was anticipated in the prophetic page, for herein was fulfilled the word of Isaiah the prophet, spoken long ago of this same northern land: "The land of Zabulon and the land of Nepthalim, by the way of the sea, beyond Jordan, Galilee of the Gentiles; the people which sat in darkness saw great light; and to them which sat in the region and shadow of death light is sprung up."

It is the old story over again. No room in the inn, so He must be born in a manger; no safety in Judæa, so He must be carried to Egypt; no room for Him in His own capital and His Father's house, so He must away to the country, the uttermost part of the land, which men despised, the very speech of which was reckoned barbarous in the polite ears of the metropolitans, a region which was scarce counted of the land at all, being known as "Galilee of the Gentiles," a portion of the country which had been overrun more than any other by the foreign invader, and therefore known as "the region and shadow of death;" here it is that the new light will arise, the new power be first acknowledged, and the new blessing first enjoyed—one of the many illustrations of the Lord's own saying, "Many of the last shall be first, and the first last."

Here, then, our Lord begins the work of setting up His kingdom. He takes up the same message which had seemed to return void to its preacher in the South. John had come saying, "Repent ye; for the kingdom of heaven is at hand." The people of the South had seemed to repent; and the kingdom seemed about to come in the ancient capital. But the repentance was only superficial; and though it still remained true that the kingdom was at hand, it was not to begin in Jerusalem.

So, in the new; and, to human appearance, far less promising field in the North, the work must be begun afresh; and now the same stirring words are ringing in Galilee, as rang a few months before in Judæa: "Repent; for the kingdom of heaven is at hand."

It is now in fact close at hand. It is interesting to note its first beginnings. "And Jesus walking by the Sea of Galilee,[4] saw two brethren, Simon called Peter, and Andrew his brother, casting a net into the sea; for they were fishers. And He saith unto them, Follow Me, and I will make you fishers of men. And they straightway left their nets, and followed Him. And going on from thence He saw other two brethren, James the son of Zebedee, and John his brother, in a ship with Zebedee their father, mending their nets; and he called them and they immediately left the ship and their father, and followed Him."

Observe in the first place that, though John is in prison, and to all human appearance failure has been written on the work of his life, the failure is only seeming. The multitudes that had been stirred by his preaching have relapsed into their old indifference, but there are a few whose souls have been permanently touched to finer issues. They are not of the lordly Pharisees or of the brilliant Sadducees; they cannot even claim to be metropolitans; they are poor Galilean fishermen: but they gave heed when the prophet pointed them to the Lamb of God, the Messiah that was to come; and though they had only spent a short time in His company, yet golden links had been forged between them; they had heard the Shepherd's voice; had fully recognised His Kingly claims; and so were ready, waiting for the word of command. Now it comes. The same Holy One of Nazareth is walking by the shores of their lake. He has been proclaiming His Kingdom, as now at last beginning; and, though the manner of its establishment is so entirely different from anything to which their thoughts have been accustomed in the past, their confidence in Him is such that they raise no doubt or question. Accordingly, when they see Him coming alone and unattended, without any of the trappings or the suits of royalty, without any badge or sign of office, with a simple word of command,—a word of command, moreover, which demanded of them the sacrifice of all for His sake, the absolute trusting of themselves and all their future to His guidance and care,—they do not hesitate for a single moment; but first Andrew and Simon his brother, and a little further on James and John his brother, straightway leave nets, father, friends, home, everything, and follow Him.

Such was the first exercise of the royal authority of the new King. Such was the constitution of His—Cabinet shall we call it?—or of His Kingdom itself, shall we not rather say? for so far as we can see, His cabinet at this moment was all the kingdom that He had. Let us here pause a moment and try to realise the picture painted for us in that grey morning time of what we now call the Christian Era. Suppose some of our artists could reproduce the scene for us: in the background the lake with the deserted boats upon the shore, old Zebedee with a half sad, half bewildered look upon his face, wondering what was happening, trying to imagine what he would do without his sons, and what his sons would do without him and the boat and the nets; and, in the foreground, the five men walking along, four of them without the least idea of where they were going or of what they had to do. Or suppose that, instead of having a picture of it now, with all the light that eighteen centuries have shed upon it, we could transport ourselves back to the very time and stand there on the very spot and see the scene with our own eyes; and suppose that we were told by some bystander, That man of the five that looks like the leader of the rest thinks himself a king: he imagines he has been sent to set up a kingdom of Heaven upon the earth; and he has just asked these other four to join him, and there they are setting out upon their task. What should we have thought? If we had had only flesh and blood to consult with, we should have thought the whole thing supremely ridiculous; we should have expected to see the four men back to their boats and nets again in a few days, sadder but wiser men. How far Zebedee had a spiritually enlightened mind we dare not say; perhaps he was as willing that his sons should go, as they were to go; but if he was, it could not have been flesh and blood that revealed it to him; he as well as his sons must have felt the power of the Spirit that was in Christ. But if he did not at all understand it or believe in it, we can fancy him saying to the two young men when they left: "Go off now, if you like; you will be back again in a few days, and foolish as you have been, your old father will be glad to take you into his boat again."

It is worth while for us to try to realise what happened in its veriest simplicity; for we have read the story so often, and are so thoroughly familiar with it, that we are apt to miss its marvel, to fail to recognise that it is perhaps the most striking illustration in all history of the apostle's statement, "God hath chosen the foolish things of the world to confound the wise, and God hath chosen the weak things of the world to confound the things which are mighty, ... that no flesh should glory in His presence."

Where was ever a weaker thing in this world than the beginning of this kingdom? It would be difficult to imagine any commencement that would have seemed weaker in worldly eyes. Stand by once again and look at it with only human eyes; say, is it not all weakness together?—weakness in the leader to imagine He can set up a kingdom after such a fashion, weakness in the followers to leave a paying business on such a fool's errand. But "the foolishness of God is wiser than men; and the weakness of God is stronger than men." And now that we look back upon that scene, we recognise it as one of the grandest this earth has ever witnessed. If it were painted now, what light must there be in the Leader's eye, what majesty in His step, what glory of dawning faith and love and hope in the faces of the rest—it must needs be a picture of Sunrise, or it would be utterly unworthy of the theme!

Now follow them: where will they go, and what will they do? Will they take arms and call to arms the country-side? Then march on Jerusalem and take the throne of David, and thence to Rome and snatch from Cæsar the sceptre of the world? "And Jesus went about all Galilee, teaching in their synagogues, and preaching the Gospel of the Kingdom, and healing all manner of sickness and all manner of disease among the people." Teaching—preaching—healing: these were the methods for setting up the kingdom. *"Teaching"*—this was the new light; *"preaching* the Gospel of the Kingdom"—this was the new power, power not of the sword but of the Word, the power of persuasion, so that the people will yield themselves willingly or not at all, for there is to be not a shadow of constraint, not the smallest use of force or compulsion, not the slightest interference with human freedom in this new kingdom; and *"healing"*—this is to be the great thing; this is what a sick world wants, this is what souls and bodies of men alike are crying out for—"healing all manner of sickness and all manner of disease among the people." Heavenly light, heavenly power, heavenly healing—these are the weapons of the new warfare; these the regalia of the new kingdom. "And the report of Him went forth into all Syria; and they brought unto Him all that were sick, holden with divers diseases and torments, possessed with devils, and epileptic, and palsied; and He healed them" (R.V.). Call to mind, for a moment, how in the extremity of hunger He would not use one fraction of the entrusted power for His own behoof. "Himself He cannot save." But see how He saves others. No stinting now of the heavenly power; it flows in streams of blessing: "They brought unto Him all that were sick, ... and He healed them."

It is Daybreak on the shores of Galilee. The Sun of Righteousness has risen with healing in His wings.

FOOTNOTE

[4] It is worthy of notice that He has had the same experience even in Galilee as before, for He is cast out of His own place Nazareth, so that He cannot really begin there. He gave them the first opportunity in Galilee as He had given Jerusalem first of all, but they too had rejected it, had driven Him out, and hence it is that the beginning was not in the village up in the hills, but down by the lakeside in the midst of the busy life that thronged its shores.

VII
THE GOSPEL OF THE KINGDOM

("SERMON ON THE MOUNT")

Matt. v., vi., vii.

IT may seem almost heresy to object to the time-honoured title "Sermon on the Mount;" yet, so small has the word "sermon" become, on account of its application to those productions of which there is material for a dozen in single sentences of this great discourse, that there is danger of belittling it by the use of a title which suggests even the remotest relationship to these ephemeral efforts. No mere sermon is this, only distinguished from others of its class by its reach and sweep and power: it stands alone as the grand charter of the commonwealth of heaven; or, to keep the simple title the evangelist himself suggests (iv. 23), it is "The Gospel (or good news) of the Kingdom." To understand it aright we must keep this in mind, avoiding the easy method of treating it as a mere series of lessons on different subjects, and endeavouring to grasp the unity of thought and purpose which binds its different parts into one grand whole.

It may help us to do this if we first ask ourselves what questions would naturally arise in the minds of the more thoughtful of the people, when they heard the announcement, "The kingdom of heaven is at hand." It was evidently to such persons the Lord addressed Himself. "Seeing the multitudes," we read "He went up into the mountain," perhaps for the purpose of selecting His audience. The idle and indifferent would stay down on the plain; only those who were in some measure stirred in spirit would follow Him as He climbed the steep ascent from the shore of the lake to the plateau above; and in their minds they would in all probability be revolving such questions as these: (1) "What is this kingdom, what advantages does it offer, and who are the people that belong to it?" (2) "What is required of those that belong to it? what are its laws and obligations?" And if these two questions were answered satisfactorily, a third would naturally follow— (3) "How may those who desire to share its privileges and assume its obligations become citizens of it?" These, accordingly, are the three great questions dealt with in succession.

I. The Nature and Constitution of the Kingdom (vv. 2-16): first in itself, and then in relation to the world

1. In itself ("The Beatitudes"), vv. 2-12.

The answer to the questions in the people's hearts is given in no cold didactic way. The truth about the heavenly kingdom comes warm from a loving heart yearning over the woes of a weary and heavy-laden humanity. Its first word is "Blessed"; its first paragraph, Beatitudes. Plainly the King of heaven has come to bless. There is no thunder nor lightning nor tempest on this mount; all is calm and peaceful as a summer's day.

How high the key-note struck in this first word of the King! The advantages usually associated with the best earthly government are very moderate indeed. We speak of the commonwealth, a word which is supposed to mean the common welfare; but the common welfare is quite beyond the power of any earthly government, which at most can only give protection against those enemies that would hinder the people from doing what they can to secure their own welfare. But here is a kingdom which is to secure the well-being of all who belong to it; and not well-being only, but something far beyond and above it: for "eye hath not seen, nor ear heard, neither have entered into the heart of man, the things which God hath prepared for them that love Him," and which His ambassador wrapped up in that great word "Blessed," the key-note of the Gospel of the Kingdom.

As He proceeds to show wherein this blessedness is to be found, we are struck by the originality of the conception, and its opposition to vulgar ideas. What the ordinary way of thinking on the subject is to this day can be readily seen in that very word "wealth," which in its original significance means welfare, but from the mistaken idea that a man's life consists in the abundance of the things which he possesses has come to mean what it means now. Who can tell the woes that result from the prevalence of this grand mistake—how men are led off in pursuit of happiness in a wrong direction altogether, away from its true source, and set to contending and competing with one another, so that there is constant danger—a danger averted only by the degree in which the truth enshrined in the Beatitudes prevails—that "the common wealth" will become the common woe? What a different world this would be if only the teaching of Christ on this one subject were heartily accepted—not by a few here and there, but by society at large! Then should we see indeed a kingdom of heaven upon earth.

For observe wherein our new King finds the universal weal. We cannot follow the beatitudes one by one; but glancing over them we see, running through them all, this great truth—that blessedness is essentially spiritual, that it depends not so much on a man's condition as on his character, not so much on what he has as on what he is. It needs no great effort of imagination to see that if men in general were to make it their main object and endeavour in life to be what they ought to be, rather than to scramble for what they can get, this earth would speedily become a moral paradise.

In expounding the blessedness of the kingdom the Master has unfolded the character of its members, thus not only explaining the nature of the kingdom and the advantages to be enjoyed under it, but also showing who those are that belong to it. That this was intended seems evident from the first and the last of the beatitudes both ending with the emphatic words "theirs is the kingdom of heaven." It is as if on the two gates at the hither and farther end of this beautiful garden were inscribed the words, "The truly blessed ones, the citizens of the commonwealth of heaven, are those who are at home here." Originality of conception is again apparent. A kingdom so constituted was an entirely new thing in the world. Previously it had been a matter of race or of place or of forced subjection. The forefathers of these people had belonged to the kingdom of Israel, because they belonged to Israel's race; themselves belonged to the empire of Rome, because their country had been conquered and they were obliged to acknowledge Rome's sway; moreover, they were subjects of Herod Antipas, simply because they lived in Galilee. Here was a kingdom in which race distinctions had no place, which took no account of territorial limits, which made no appeal to force of arms or rights of conquest—a kingdom founded on character.

Yet it is no mere aristocracy of natural virtue. It is not a Royal Academy of the spiritually noble and great. Its line seems rather to stretch down to the lowest, for who else are the poor in spirit? And the mourners and the meek are no elect classes of nature's nobility. On the other hand, however, it runs up to heights even quite out of sight of the easy-going virtue of the day; for those who belong to this kingdom are men full of eager aspirations, bent on heart purity, given to efforts for the good of others, ready even to suffer the loss of all things for truth and righteousness' sake. The line is stretched so far down that even the lowest may enter; yet it runs up so high that those have no place in it who are satisfied with mere average morality, who count it enough to be free from vices that degrade the man, and innocent of crimes that offend the state. Most respectable citizens of an earthly commonwealth such honest men may be; but no kingdom of heaven is open to such as they. The foundations of common morality are of course assumed, as is made specially evident in the next division of the great discourse; but it would have been quite misleading had the Herald of heaven's kingdom said "Blessed are the honest," or "Blessed is the man who tells no lies." The common virtues are quite indispensable; but there must be something beyond these—first a sense of need of something far higher and better, then a hungering and thirsting after it, and as a necessary consequence some attainment of it, in order to citizenship in the kingdom of heaven and enjoyment of its blessedness.

The last beatitude breaks forth into a song of joy. No light-hearted joy, as of those who shut their eyes to the dark things in life, but joy in facing the very worst the world can do: "Blessed are ye when men shall revile you, and persecute you, and shall say all manner of evil against you falsely, for My sake. Rejoice, and be exceeding glad." O wonderful alchemy of heaven, which can change earth's dust and ashes into purest gold! Think, too, what riches and royalty of spirit in place of the poverty with which the series began.

These eight beatitudes are the diatonic scale of heaven's music. Its key-note is blessing; its upper octave, joy. Those who heard it first with quickened souls could no longer doubt that the kingdom of heaven was at hand; indeed, was there on the mountain that day!

2. *In relation to the world* (vv. 13-16).

The original promise to Abraham was twofold: "I will bless thee," "Thou shalt be a blessing" (Gen. xii. 2). The beatitudes correspond to the former, the passage before us to the latter. The beatitudes are, so to speak, the home affairs of the kingdom of heaven; the passage which follows is occupied with foreign relations. Those spoke of blessedness within, this speaks of usefulness without; for the disciples of Christ are known not only by their personal character and disposition, but also by their influence on others.

The relations of the members of the kingdom to "those that are without" is a complex and difficult subject; but the essence of it is set forth with surpassing clearness, comprehensiveness and simplicity by the use of two unpretentious but most expressive figures, almost infinite in their suggestiveness—salt and light. This is our first experience of a well-known characteristic of the teaching of Christ—viz., His use of the simplest and most familiar objects of nature and circumstances of daily life, to convey highest and most important truth; and at once we recognise the touch of the Master. We cannot fail to see that out of all nature's infinity He has selected the two illustrations,—the only two, which exactly fit and fill the purpose for which He employs them. To the thoughtful mind there is something here which prepares for such tokens of mastery over nature as are found later on in the hushing of the storm and the stilling of the sea.

"Salt" suggests the conservative, "light" the liberal, side of the politics of the kingdom; but the two are not in opposition, they are in fullest harmony, the one being the complement of the other. Christian people, if they are what they profess to be, are all conservatives and all liberals: conservators of all that is good, and diffusers of all that is of the nature of light. Each of these sides of Christian influence is presented in succession.

"*Ye are the salt of the earth.*" The metaphor suggests the sad fact that, whatever tendency to upward development there may be in the world of nature, there is a contrary tendency in the world of men, so far as character is concerned. The world has often made great advances in civilisation; but these, unless counter-acted by forces from above, have always been accompanied by a degeneracy in morals, which in course of time has brought about the ruin of mighty states. All that is best and most hopeful in mere worldly civilisation has in it the canker of moral evil,

"That rotting inward slowly moulders all."

The only possible counteractive is the introduction of an element into society which will hold in check the forces that make for unrighteousness, and be itself an elevating and purifying influence. Such an element Christians were to be in the world.

Such, to a large extent, they have been. That they were the salt of the Roman empire during the evil days of its decline, no student of history can fail to see. Again, in the "dark ages" that followed, we can still trace the sweetening influence of those holy lives which were scattered like shining grains of salt through the ferment and seething of the times. So it has been throughout, and is still. It is true that there is no longer the sharp distinction between Christians and the world which there was in days when it cost something to confess Christ. There are now so many Christians in name who are not so in reality, and, on the other hand, so many in reality who are not so in name, and moreover so many who are Christians neither in name nor in reality, but who are nevertheless unconsciously guided by Christian principles as the result of the wide diffusion of Christian thought and sentiment—that the conservative influence of distinctive Christianity is very difficult to estimate and is far less appreciated than it should be. But it is as real and efficient as ever. If Christianity, as a conservative force in society, were to be suddenly eliminated, the social fabric would fall in ruins; but if only the salt were all genuine, if Christian people everywhere had the savour of the eight beatitudes about them, their conservative power as to all that is good, and restraining influence as to all that is evil, would be so manifest and mighty that none could question it.

If the salt would only keep its savour—there is the weak point. We know and feel it after the experience of all these centuries. And did not our omniscient Lord lay His finger on it at the very outset? He needed not that any one should tell Him what was in man. He knew that there was that in His truth which would be genuinely and efficiently conservative; but He knew equally well that there was that in man which would to a large extent neutralise that conservative power, that the salt would be in constant danger of losing its savour. Hence, after the encouraging words "Ye are the salt of the earth," He gives an earnest warning which necessarily moderates the too sanguine anticipations that would otherwise have been excited.

Alas! with what sad certainty has history proved the need of this warning! The salt lost its savour in the churches of the East, or it would never have been cast out and trodden underfoot of the Mohammedan invaders. It lost its savour in the West, or there would have been no papal corruption, growing worse and worse till it seemed as if Western Christendom must in turn be dissolved—a fate which was only averted by the fresh salt of the Reformation revival. In modern times there is ever the same danger, sometimes affecting all the churches, as in the dark days preceding the revival under Whitefield and Wesley, always affecting some of them or some portions of them, as is too apparent on every hand in these days in which we live. There is as much need as ever to lay to heart the solemn warning of the King. It is as pungent as salt itself. "Of what use," He asks, "is tasteless salt? It is fit only to be cast out and trodden under foot of men." Equally useless is the so-called Christian, who has nothing in character or life to distinguish him from the world; who, though he may be honest and truthful and sober, a very respectable citizen of an earthly kingdom, has none of the characteristic marks of the kingdom of heaven, none of the savour of the beatitudes about him. It is only because there are still so many savourless Christians that the value of the Church as a conservative influence on society is so little recognised; and that there are so many critics, not all unintelligent or wilfully unfair, who begin to think it is time that it were cast out and trodden under foot of men.

"Ye are the light of the world." We need not stay to show the liberality of light. Its peculiar characteristic is giving, spending; for this purpose wholly it exists, losing its own life in order to find it again in brightness diffused on all around.

Observe, it is not "Ye carry the light," but "Ye *are* the light." We are apt to think of light in the abstract—as truth, as doctrine, as something to be believed and held and expounded. We quote the familiar words, "Great is the Truth, and it shall prevail," and we imagine they are true. They are true indeed, in the long run, but not as often understood, certainly not in the region of the moral and spiritual. Of course truth in the abstract, especially moral and spiritual truth, ought to prevail; but it never does when men's interests lie, or seem to lie, in the contrary direction. Such truth, to be mighty, must be vitalised; it must glow in human hearts, burn on human tongues, shine in human lives. The King of truth knew this well; and hence He placed the hope of the future, the hope of dispelling the world's darkness, not in abstract truth, but in truth incarnate in the true disciple: "*Ye* are the light of the world."

In the strictest and highest sense, of course, Christ Himself is the Light of the world. This is beautifully set forth in discourses reported by another Evangelist (John viii. 12, ix. 5); and, indeed, it has been already taught by implication in the Evangel before us, where, as we have seen, the opening of Christ's ministry is likened to sunrise in the land of Zebulon and Naphtali (chap. iv. 16). But the personal Christ cannot remain upon the earth. Only for a few years can He be in this way the Light of the world, as He expressly says in one of the passages above referred to (John ix. 5); and He is speaking now not for the next few years but for the coming centuries, during which He must be represented by His faithful disciples, appointed to be His witnesses (Acts i. 8) to the ends of the earth; so at once He puts the responsibility on them, and says, "Ye are the light of the world."

This responsibility it was impossible to avoid. As a matter of course, the kingdom of heaven must be a prominent object in the sight of men. The mountain of the Lord's house must be established on the top of the mountains (Isa. ii. 2), and therefore may not be inconspicuous: "A city set on a hill cannot be hid." It has been often said, but it will bear repeating, that Christians are the world's Bible. People who never read a word of either Old or New Testament will read the lives of those who profess to draw their inspiration thence, and will judge accordingly. They will form their opinions of Christ and of His kingdom by those who call themselves or are called by others Christians. "A city set on a hill *cannot* be hid." Here we have a truth complementary to that other conveyed in the symbol of salt. It taught that true Christians exert a great deal of silent, unobserved influence, as of salt hidden in a mass; but, besides this, there is their position as connected with the kingdom of heaven which forbids their being wholly hid.

Indeed, it is their duty to see to it that they are not artificially hid: "Neither do men light a lamp, and put it under the bushel, but on the stand; and it shineth unto all that are in the house" (R.V.). How beautifully does the illustration lend itself to the needed caution against timidity, without giving the least encouragement to the opposite vice of ostentation! Why does light shine? Simply because it cannot help it; it is its nature; without effort or even consciousness, and making no noise, it quietly does its duty; and in the doing of it does not encourage but even forbids any looking at itself—and the brighter it is, the more severely does it forbid it. But while there is no ostentatious obtrusiveness on the one hand, there is no ignoble shirking on the other. Who would ever think of kindling a light and then putting it under a bed? Yet how many Christians do that very thing when they are called to work for Christ, to let the light He has given them shine in some of the dark places where it is most needed!

Here, again, our Lord lays His finger on a weak spot. The Church suffers sorely, not only from quantities of savourless salt,—people calling themselves Christians who have little or nothing distinctively Christian about them,—but also from bushel-covered lights, those who are genuinely Christian, but who do all they can to hide it, refusing to speak on the subject, afraid to show earnestness even when they feel it most, carefully repressing every impulse to let their light shine before men, doing everything, in fact, which is possible to render their testimony to Christ as feeble, and their influence as Christians as small, as it can be. How many in all our Christian communities are constantly haunted by a nervous fear lest people should think them forward! For one person who makes a parade of his Christianity there are a hundred or a thousand who want always to shrink into a corner. This is not modesty; it is the sign of an unnatural self-consciousness. The disciples of Christ should act simply, naturally, unconsciously, neither making a display on the one hand nor hiding their light on the other. So the Master puts it most beautifully and suggestively: "Let your light so shine before men, that they may see your good works" (not the worker—that is of no consequence—but the works), "and glorify your Father which is in heaven."

So closes the first great division of the Manifesto of the King. It had begun with "goodwill to men"; it has shown the way of "peace on earth"; it closes with "glory to God in the highest." It is a prolonged echo of the angels' song. The Gospel of the Kingdom, not only as set forth here in these beautiful paragraphs, but in all its length and breadth and depth and height, in all its range and scope and application, is but an expansion of its very first proclamation: "Glory to God in the highest, on earth peace, goodwill to men."

II. The Law of the Kingdom (v. 17-vii. 12)

1. *General principles* (vv. 17-20).

After blessing comes obligation—after beatitude, law. It is the same order as of old. The old covenant was in its origin and essence a covenant of promise, of blessing. Mercy, not duty, was its key-note. When God called Abraham to the land of promise, His first word was: "I will bless thee, and make thy name great; and thou shalt be a blessing" (Gen. xii. 2). Later on came the obligation resulting, as in Genesis xvii. 1: "Walk before me, and be thou perfect." So in the history of the Nation, the promise came first and the law followed it after an interval of four hundred years—a fact of which special use is made by the Apostle Paul (Gal. iii. 17, 18). The Mosaic dispensation itself began by an acknowledgment of the ancient promise ("I am the God of your fathers"—Ex. iii. 6), and a fresh declaration of Divine mercy ("I know their sorrows, and am come to deliver them"—Ex. iii. 7, 8). When Mount Sinai was reached, the entire covenant was summarised in two sentences, the first reciting the blessing, the second setting forth the resulting obligation: "Thus shalt thou say to the house of Jacob, and tell the children of Israel; Ye have seen what I did unto the Egyptians, and how I bare you on eagles' wings, and brought you unto Myself. Now, therefore, if ye will obey My voice indeed, and keep My covenant, then ye shall be a peculiar treasure unto Me above all people" (Ex. xix. 3-5). The very Decalogue itself is constructed on the same principle; for before a single commandment is given, attention is called to the great salvation which has been wrought on their behalf: "I am the Lord thy God, which brought thee out of the land of Egypt, out of the house of bondage." Thus closely does the proclamation of the new kingdom follow the lines of the old; far above and beyond it in respect of development, in essence it is the same.

It was therefore most appropriate that, in entering on the subject of the law of His kingdom Christ should begin with the caution, "Think not that I am come to destroy the law or the prophets." On this point there would necessarily be the greatest sensitiveness on the part of the people. The law was their glory—all their history had gathered round it, the prophets had enforced and applied it; their sacred Scriptures, known broadly as "The Law and the Prophets," had enshrined it. Was it, then, to be set aside for new legislation? The feeling was quite natural and proper. It was necessary, therefore, that the new King should set Himself right on a matter so important. He has not come to overturn everything. He accepts the old covenant more cordially and thoroughly than they do, as will presently appear; He will build on it as a sure foundation; and whatever in His legislation may be new grows naturally out of the old. It is, moreover, worthy of notice that while the Mosaic economy is specially in His mind, He does not entirely leave out of consideration the elements of truth in other religious systems; and therefore defines the attitude He assumes as a Legislator and Prophet, in terms of the widest generality: "I am not come to destroy, but to fulfil."

While in the widest sense He came not to destroy but to fulfil, so that He could with fullest liberality acknowledge what was good and true in the work of all former teachers, whoever and wherever they had been, thus accepting and incorporating their "broken lights" as part of His "Light of the world" (compare John i. 9), He can speak of the old covenant in a way in which it would have been impossible to speak of the work of earth's greatest and best. He can accept it as a whole without any reservation or deduction: "For verily I say unto you, Till heaven and earth pass, one jot or one tittle shall in no wise pass from the law, till all be fulfilled." Observe, however, that this statement is not at all inconsistent with what He teaches concerning the temporary character of much of the Mosaic legislation; it simply makes it clear that whatever passes away, does not pass by destruction, but by fulfilment—*i.e.*, the evolution of its hidden life—as the bud passes into the rose. The bud is there no longer; but it is not destroyed, it is fulfilled in the rose. So with the law as infolded in the Old Testament, unfolded in the New. How well fitted to inspire all thoughtful minds with confidence must have been the discovery that the policy of the new kingdom was to be on the lines, not of brand-new experimental legislation, but of Divine evolution!

Not only does He Himself do homage to the law, but takes order that His followers shall do the same. It is no parting compliment that He pays the old covenant. It is to be kept up both in the doing and in the teaching, from generation to generation, even in its least commandments. Not that there is to be such insistence on very small matters as to exclude altogether from the kingdom of heaven those who do not press every jot and tittle; but that these will be reckoned of such importance, that those who are lax in doctrine and practice in regard to them must be counted among the least in the kingdom; while those who destroy nothing, but seek to fulfil everything, will be the great ones. What a foundation is laid here for reverence of all that is contained in the law and the prophets! And has it not been found that even in the very smallest features of the old covenant, even in the details of the tabernacle worship, for example, there is for the devout and intelligent Christian a treasury of valuable suggestion? Only we must beware of putting jots and tittles in the place that belongs to the weightier matters of the law, of which we have warnings sufficient in the conduct of the scribes and Pharisees. Their righteousness had the appearance of extending to the minutest matters; but, large as it seemed in popular eyes, it was not nearly large enough; and accordingly, in closing this general definition of His relation to the old covenant, our Lord had to interpose this solemn warning: "I say unto you, that except your righteousness shall exceed the righteousness of the scribes and Pharisees, ye shall in no case enter the kingdom of heaven." Theirs was a righteousness as it were of the tips of the fingers, whereas He must have "the whole body full of light"; theirs was a righteousness that tithed mint and anise and cummin, and neglected judgment, mercy and faith; theirs was in the narrow sphere of the letter, that which He demanded must be in the large and lofty region of the Spirit.

2. *Illustrations from the Moral Law* (vv. 21-48).

The selection of illustrative instances is made with consummate skill. Our Lord, avoiding that which is specially Jewish in its interest, treats of matters that are of world-wide importance. He deals with the broadest principles of righteousness as adapted to the universal conscience of mankind, starting at the lowest point of mere earthly morality and rising to the very highest development of Christian character, thus leading up to the magnificent conclusion: "Be ye therefore perfect, even as your Father which is in heaven is perfect."

He begins with the crime which the natural conscience most strongly and instinctively condemns, the crime of murder; and shows that the scribes and Pharisees, and those who had been like them in bygone days, really destroyed the sixth commandment by limiting its range to the muscles, so that, if there were no actual killing, the commandment was not broken; whereas its true sphere was the heart, the essence of the forbidden crime being found in unjustifiable anger, even though no word is uttered or muscle moved,—a view of the case which ought to have been suggested to the intelligent student of the law by such words as these: "Thou shalt not hate thy brother in thine heart" (Lev. xix. 17); or again: "Whoso killeth his neighbour ignorantly, whom he hated not in time past, ... is not worthy of death, inasmuch as he hated him not in time past" (Deut. xix. 4). Hatred in the heart, then, is murder. How searching! And how terribly severe the sentence! Even in its least aggravated form it is the same as that decreed against the actual shedding of blood. All the three sentences are death-penalties, only there are aggravations in the penalty where there are aggravations in the offence. Such is the Saviour's teaching on the great subject of sin. Yet there are those who imagine that the Sermon on the Mount is all the gospel they need!

The two practical applications which follow press the searching subject home. The one has reference to the Throne of Grace, and teaches that all offences against a brother must be put away before approaching it. The other has reference to the Throne of Judgment, and teaches by a familiar illustration drawn from common experience in the courts of Palestine that it is an awful thing to think of standing there with the memory of a single angry feeling that had not been forgiven and utterly removed (v. 26).

The crime of adultery furnishes the next illustration; and He deals with it on the same lofty principles and with the same terrible severity. He shows that this crime, too, is of the heart—that even a wanton look is a commission of it; and again follows up His searching exposition by a twofold practical application, first showing that personal purity must be maintained at any cost (vv. 29, 30), and then guarding the sacredness of home, by that exaltation of the marriage bond which has secured the emancipation of woman and her elevation to her proper sphere, and kept in check those frightful evils which are ever threatening to defile the pure and sacred spring from which society derives its life and sustenance (vv. 31, 32).

Next comes the crime of perjury—a compound sin, which breaks at the same time two commandments of the Decalogue, the third and the ninth. Here, again, our Lord shows that, if only due homage is paid in the heart to reverence and to truth, all swearing is superseded. Let a man habitually live in the fear of the Lord all the day long, and "his word is as good as his oath"—he will always speak the truth, and will be incapable of taking the name of the Lord in vain. It is of course to be remembered that these are the laws of the kingdom of Christ; not laws meant for the kingdoms of this world, which have to do with men of all sorts, but for a kingdom made up of those who hunger and thirst after righteousness, who seek and find purity of heart. This passage accordingly has no bearing on the procedure of secular courts of justice. But, though the use of oaths may still be a necessity in the world, in the kingdom of heaven they have no place. The simple "Yea, yea," "Nay, nay," is quite enough where there is truth in the inward parts and the fear of God before the eyes; and the feeling of reverence, not only for God Himself but for all the works of His hands, will effectually prevent the most distant approach to profanity.

The sin of revenge furnishes the next illustration. The Pharisaic perversion of the old law actually sanctioned private revenge, on the ground of a statute intended for the guidance of the courts of justice, and given for the sake of curbing the revengeful spirit which without it would lead a prosecutor to demand that his enemy should suffer more than he had inflicted. In this way they really destroyed that part of the Mosaic legislation, whereas He fulfilled it by developing still further,—bringing, in fact, to perfection,—that spirit of humanity which had dictated the law at the first. The true spirit of the Mosaic legislation was to discourage private revenge by assigning such cases to the courts, and curbing it still further by the limitation of the penalty imposed. Was not this spirit most nobly fulfilled, carried to its highest development, when the Saviour laid it down as the law of His kingdom that our revenge is to be the returning of good for evil?

The four practical illustrations (vv. 39-42) have been a source of difficulty, but only to those who forget that our Saviour is all the while warning against "the letter that killeth," and showing the need of catching "the spirit" of a commandment which "giveth life" to it. To deal with these illustrations according to the letter, as telling us exactly what to do in particular cases, is not to fulfil but to destroy the Saviour's words. The great thing, therefore, is to catch their spirit; then they will be found of use, not for so many specified cases, but for all cases whatever. As an illustration of the difficulties to which we refer, mention may be made of the prejudice against the passage which suggests the turning of the other cheek, on the ground that it encourages a craven spirit. Take it as a definite command, and this would be in many cases the result. It would be the result wherever fear or pusillanimity was the motive. But where is there in all this passage the least trace of fear or pusillanimity? It is all love and magnanimity. It is the very antipodes of the craven spirit. It is the heroism of self-denying love!

The last illustration cuts at the root of all sin and crime, the tap-root of selfishness. The scribes and Pharisees had made use of those regulations, most needful at the time, which separated Israel from other nations, as an excuse for restricting the range of love to those prepared to render an equivalent. Thus that wonderful statute of the old legislation, "Thou shalt love thy neighbour as thyself," was actually made a minister to selfishness; so that, instead of leading them to a life above the world, it left them not a whit better than the lowest and most selfish of the people. "If ye love them which love you, what reward have ye? Do not even the publicans the same?" Thus was the noble "royal law according to the Scripture" destroyed by the petty quibbling use of the word "neighbour." Our Lord fulfilled it by giving to the word neighbour its proper meaning, its widest extent, including even those who have wronged us in thought or word or deed, "I say unto you, Love your *enemies*, bless them that curse you, do good to them that hate you, and pray for them which despitefully use you, and persecute you."

How lofty, how far beyond the reach of the natural man!—but not impossible, or it would not have been demanded. It is one of the things of the kingdom concerning which the assurance is given later on: "Ask, and ye shall receive; seek, and ye shall find." Still, the Master knows full well that it is no small demand He is making of poor human nature. So at this point He leads our thoughts upward to our Father in heaven, suggesting in that relationship the possibility of its attainment (for why should not a child be like its father?) and the only example possible, for this was a range of righteousness beyond the reach of all that had gone before—He Himself as the Son of the Father would later set it forth before the eyes of men in all its lustre. But that time is yet to come, and meantime He can only point upward to the Highest, and urge them to this loftiest height of righteousness by the tender plea, "That ye may be the children of your Father which is in heaven: for He maketh His sun to rise on the evil and on the good, and sendeth rain on the just and on the unjust."

How beautiful and expressive are these symbols from nature, and how encouraging the interpretation of nature His use of them suggests! And what shall we say of their suggestiveness in the higher sphere of the spirit?

Already the Sun of Righteousness is rising with healing in His wings; and in due time the rain of the Spirit will fall in fulness of blessing; so shall His disciples receive all that is needful to raise them to the very highest in character and conduct, in beatitude and righteousness; and accordingly their Master may well finish His whole exposition of the morals of the kingdom with the stirring, stimulating call, "Be ye therefore perfect, even as your Father which is in heaven is perfect."

3. *Illustrations from Religious Duty* (vi. 1-18).

The righteousness of the kingdom is still the great subject; for the reading of the Revised Version in the first verse of the chapter is evidently the correct one. The illustrations of the preceding passage have all come under the head of what we call morality as distinguished from religion, but it is important to observe that our Lord gives no sanction to the separation of the two.

Morality divorced from religion is a flower without root, which may bloom for a while, but in the end must wither away; religion without morality is—nothing at all; worse than nothing, for it is a sham. It is evident, of course, that this great word "righteousness," as used by our Lord, has a far wider scope than is given to it by those who take it merely as the equivalent of truth and honesty, as if a man could in any proper sense of the word be righteous, who was ungenerous to his neighbours, unfilial to God, or not master of himself.

Again, we have a principle laid down: "Take heed that ye do not your righteousness before men, to be seen of them" (R.V.). It is the same great principle as before, though the caution in which it is embodied is different. For if we compare ver. 20 of the preceding chapter, and remember its subsequent development in the verses which follow, we find that it agrees with the warning before us in insisting on righteousness of the heart as distinguished from that which is merely outward. The difference lies in this, that whereas, in the cases already dealt with, external conformity with the law is good so far as it goes, but does not go nearly far enough ("except your righteousness shall exceed," exceed, *i.e.*, by reaching back and down to the deepest recesses of the heart), in the cases now to be taken up external conformity is not good in itself, but really evil, inasmuch as it is mere pretence. Accordingly the caution now must needs be much stronger: "*Be ye not* as the hypocrites."

It is not, however, the being seen which is condemned, otherwise the caution would be at variance with the earnest counsel in chap. v. 16, and would, in fact, amount to a total prohibition of public worship. As before, it is a matter of the heart. It is the hidden motive which is condemned: "Take heed that ye do not your righteousness before men, *to be seen of them*."

The principle is applied in succession to Almsgiving, to Prayer, to Fasting.

Almsgiving is no longer regarded as distinctively a religious duty. Nor can it be put under the head of morality according to the common idea attached to that word. It rather occupies a kind of borderland between them, coming under the head of philanthropy. But whence came the spirit of philanthropy? Its foundation is in the holy mountains. Modern philanthropy is like a great fresh-water lake, on the shores of which one may wander with admiration and delight for great distances without discovering any connection with the heaven-piercing mountains. But such connection it has. The explorer is sure to find somewhere an inlet showing whence its waters come, a bright sparkling stream which has filled it and keeps it full; or springs below it, which, though they may flow far underground, bring the precious supplies from the higher regions, perhaps quite out of sight. If these connections with the upper springs were to be cut off, the beautiful lake would speedily dry up and disappear. Almsgiving, therefore, is in its right place here: its source is in the higher regions of the righteousness of the kingdom. And in these early days the lakes had not been formed, for the springs were only beginning to flow from the great Fountain-head.

The general object our Lord has in view, moreover, leads Him to treat the subject, not in relation to those who receive, but to those who give. There may be good done through the gifts of men who have no higher object in view than the sounding of their own trumpet; but, so far as they themselves are concerned, their giving has no value in the sight of God. Everything depends on the motive: hence the injunction of secrecy. There may indeed be circumstances which suggest or even require a certain measure of publicity, for the sake of the object or cause to which gifts are devoted; but so far as the giver is concerned, the more absolute the secrecy the better. For though it is possible to give in the most open and public way without at all indulging the petty motive of ostentation, yet so weak is human nature on that side of it, that our Lord puts His caution in the very strongest terms, counselling us not only to avoid courting the attention of others, but to refrain from even thinking of what we have done; for that seems to be the point of the striking and memorable words "Let not thy left hand know what thy right hand doeth."

The trumpet-blowing may be a great success. What the Master thinks of that success is seen in the caustic irony of the words "Verily I say unto you, they have their reward." There it is—and you can see just how paltry and pitiful it is; for there is nothing a man is more ashamed of than to be caught in even the slightest attempt to parade himself. But if the praise of men is never thought of, it cannot be said "they have their reward." Their reward is to come; and though it doth not yet appear, it will certainly be worthy of our Father Who seeth in secret.

Under the head of *Prayer* two cautions are given. The one may be dismissed in a few words, not only because it exactly corresponds with the preceding case, but because among us there is scarcely any temptation to that against which it is directed. The danger now is all the other way. The temptation for true children of the kingdom is not to parade their devotion for show, but to conceal it for shame. Still there are some directions in which even yet the caution against ostentation in prayer is needed—as, for instance, by those who in public or social prayer assume affected tones, or try in any way to give an impression of earnestness beyond what is really felt. Of the sanctimonious tone we may say that it has its reward in the almost universal contempt it provokes.

The other caution is directed, not against pretence, but against superstition. It will be seen, however, that the two belong to the same category, and therefore are most appropriately dealt with together. What is the sin of the formalist? It is that his heart is not in his worship. What is the folly of the vain repetitionist? It is the same—that his heart is not in his words. For there is no discouragement of repetition, if it be prompted by genuine earnestness. Our Lord again and again encouraged even importunate prayer, and Himself in the Garden offered the same petition three times in close succession. It is not, then, repetition, but "*vain* repetition,"—empty of heart, of desire, of hope—that is here rebuked; not much prayer, but "much speaking," the folly of supposing that the mere "saying" of prayers is of any use apart from the emotions of the heart in which true prayer essentially consists.

To guide us in a matter so important, our Lord not only cautions against what prayer ought not to be, but shows what it ought to be. Thus, incidentally as it were, He hands to us this pearl of great price, this purest crystal of devotion, to be a possession of His people for ever, never to lose its lustre through millenniums of daily use, its beauty and preciousness becoming rather more and more manifest to each successive generation.

It is given especially as a model of *form*, to show that, instead of the vain repetitions condemned, there should be simplicity, directness, brevity, order—above all, the plain, unadorned expression of the heart's desire. This main object is accomplished perfectly; a whole volume on the form of prayer could not have done it better, or so well. But, besides this, there is instruction as to the *substance* of prayer. We are taught to rise high above all selfish considerations in our desires, seeking the things of God first; and when we come to our own wants, asking nothing more than our Father in heaven judges to be sufficient for the day, while all the stress of earnestness is laid on deliverance from the guilt and power of sin. Then as to the *spirit* of prayer, mark the filial reverence implied in the invocation,—the fraternal spirit called for by the very first word of it, and the spirit of forgiveness we are taught to cherish by the very terms in which we ask it for ourselves. All this and more is superadded to the lesson for the sake of which the model prayer has been given.

The third application is to *Fasting*. In another place (ix. 14) will be found the principle to be followed in regard to times of fasting. Here it is taken for granted that there will be such times, and the principle announced at the beginning of the chapter is applied to the exercise. Let it be done in secret, before no other eye than His Who seeth in secret; thus only can we have the blessed recompense which comes to the heart that is truly humbled in the sight of God.

This principle plainly condemns that kind of fasting which is done only before men, as when in the name of religion people will abstain from certain kinds of food and recreation on particular days or at appointed times, without any corresponding humbling of the heart. The fasting must be before God, or it is a piece of acting, "as the hypocrites," who play a part before men, and when they go home put off the mask and resume their proper life. "Be ye not as the hypocrites;" therefore see that your fasting is before God; and then, if the inward feeling naturally leads to restriction of the pleasures of the table or of society, or to any other temporary self-denial, let it by all means be followed out, but so as to attract just as little attention as possible; and not only so, but if any traces of the secret exercise still remain when the penitential hour with God alone is over, these are to be carefully removed before returning to the ordinary intercourse of life. Our "penitence and prayer" are for ourselves only, and for God. Before men our *light* should shine.

The three illustrations cover by suggestion the whole ground; for prayer may well be understood in that large scriptural sense in which praise is included, and fasting is suggestive of all mortification of the flesh and humbling of the spirit. The first shows true religion in its outgoing, the second in its upgoing, while the third abases self; and all three are mutually helpful, for the higher we soar God-ward in praise and prayer, the lower shall we bend in reverent humility, and the further will our hearts go out in world-wide charity.

All depends on truth in the inward parts, on the secret life of the soul with God. How impressively is this stated throughout the whole passage! Observe the almost rhythmical repetitions: "Be ye not as the hypocrites," three times repeated; "Verily I say unto you, they have their reward," the very words three times repeated; "Let thine alms be *in secret*," "Pray to thy Father which is *in secret*," "That thou appear not unto men to fast, but unto thy Father which is *in secret*"; and once more, three times repeated, "Thy Father which seeth in secret Himself shall reward thee." No vain repetitions these. They press the great lesson home with a threefold force.

4. *Duty in relation to the World and the things of it* (vi. 19-vii. 12).

From this point onwards the plan of the discourse is not so apparent, and some have given up the idea of finding orderly sequence in it; yet there seems to be no insuperable difficulty, when the right point of view is taken. The perplexity seems to have arisen from supposing that at this point an entirely new subject begins, whereas all that follows on to chapter vii. 12, arranges itself easily under the same general head—the Righteousness of the Kingdom. According to this arrangement of the discourse there is an introduction of fourteen verses (v. 3-16), and a concluding passage of almost exactly the same length (vii. 13-27); while the main discussion occupies nearly three chapters, the subject throughout being the Righteousness of the Kingdom, dealt with, first as morality (v. 17-48), second as religion (vi. 1-18), and finally as spirituality (vi. 19-vii. 12), beginning and ending with a general reference to the law and the prophets (v. 17, vii. 12). The first of these divisions had to do with righteousness as between man and man;[5] the second with righteousness before God alone; while the third, on the consideration of which we now enter, deals with righteousness as between the children of the kingdom and the world in the midst of which it is set up. And just as in the paragraphs already considered we have been shown that our Lord came not to destroy but to fulfil the code of ethics, and the rules for Divine service in the law and the prophets, so in this it will be made equally apparent that He came not to destroy but to fulfil the principles involved in the political code by which Israel was separated from the nations of the world to be the Lord's peculiar people.

The subject before us now, therefore, is the relations of the children of the kingdom to the world; and it is dealt with—

(1) *As regards the good things of the world.* From the Beatitudes we have already learned that the blessedness of the children of the kingdom is to consist not in the abundance of the things they possess, but in qualities of soul, possessions in the realm of the unseen. Yet the children of the kingdom cannot do without the good things of this world; what, then, has the law of

the kingdom to say in regard to their acquisition and use? The subject is large and difficult; but with amazing clearness and force, comprehensiveness and simple practical utility, it is set forth in a single paragraph, which is also characterised by a surpassing beauty of language. As before, the straight and narrow path is marked off by cautions on the right and on the left. On the one side must be shunned the Scylla of *greed*, on the other the Charybdis of *care*. The one is the real danger of seeking too much, the other the supposed danger of having too little, of "the good things of life."

It is not, however, a question of quantity. As before, it is a question of the heart. On the one hand, it is not the danger of having too much, but of seeking too much; on the other, it is not the danger of having too little, but of fearing that there will not be enough. It is a mistake, therefore, to say that the one caution is for the rich and the other for the poor. True, indeed, the rich are in greater danger of Scylla than of Charybdis, and the poor in more peril from the pool than from the rock; still a rich man may be, often is, a victim of care, while a poor man may readily have his heart far too much set on the yearly or weekly increase of his little store. It seems better, then, to make no distinction of classes, but to look at each caution as needed by all.

(*a*) Against seeking the good things of the world too earnestly (vv. 19-24). It is important to notice the strong emphasis on the word "treasure." This is evident not only from the reduplication of it—for the literal translation would be, "Treasure not for yourselves treasures upon the earth"—but also from the reason against it assigned in ver. 21: "Where thy treasure is, there will thy heart be also." It is clear, then, that there is no prohibition of wealth, but only of making it "thy treasure." But against this the law of the kingdom is in the highest degree decided and uncompromising. The language is exceedingly forcible, and the reasons marshalled are terribly strong. With all faithfulness, and with growing earnestness, the Master shows that to disobey this law is foolish, pernicious, fatal. It is *foolish*; for all earthly treasures are perishable, eaten by moth, consumed by rust, stolen by thieves, while the heavenly treasures of the spiritually-minded are incorruptible and safe for evermore. It is not only foolish, but most *pernicious*,—injurious to that which is most sensitive and most precious in the life, that which is to the soul what the eye is to the body, the darkening of which means the darkening of the whole body, not the mere clouding of the vision, but the condition suggested by the awful words "full of darkness"; while the corresponding deterioration in the lower ranges of the life is indicated by what follows: "If therefore the light that is in thee be darkness, how great is that darkness!" It is not only foolish and most pernicious, but *fatal*, for "No man *can* serve two masters"; so that to set the heart on the world means to give up the kingdom. It is vain to try to satisfy two claimants of the heart. One or other must be chosen: "Ye *cannot* serve God and mammon."

(*b*) Against anxiety about the things of the world. The Revised Version has, by its correct translation, now removed the difficulty which seemed to lie in the words "Take no thought." To modern ears these words seemed to encourage thoughtlessness and to bless improvidence. Our translators of the seventeenth century, however, had no such idea. It is the result of a change of meaning in a current phrase. At the time the translation was made, "to take thought" meant to be anxious, as will appear from such a passage as that in the first book of Samuel (ix. 5), where Saul says to his servant, "Come and let us return; lest my father leave caring for the asses, and *take thought* for us," evidently in the sense of "be anxious about us."[6] It is then, manifestly, not against thoughtfulness and providence, but against anxious care that the caution is directed.

Although this evil seems to lie in the opposite direction from that of avarice, it is really the same both in its root and its fruit, for it is due to the estrangement of the heart from our Father in heaven, and amounts, in so far as it prevails, to enslavement to the world. The covetous man is enslaved in one way, the anxious man in another; for does not our common language betray it every time we think or speak of "*freedom* from care"? We need not wonder, then, that our Lord should connect what He is about to say on this evil so closely with what He has said on the other, as He does by use of the word *therefore*: "Therefore I say unto you, Be not anxious for your life."

But though, like the other, it is slavery, the sin of it is not nearly so great, and hence the difference of tone, which cannot but be observed as this new caution is given. It is no longer strong condemnation, but gentle expostulation; not dark threatening now, but tender pleading. As before, reason after reason is given against yielding to the all too natural weakness of the human heart. We are encouraged to remember what God has given already: the life, with such amazing powers and capabilities; the body, with all its marvellous intricacy and adaptation: and can it be supposed that He is likely to withhold the food to maintain the life, the raiment to clothe the body?—to remember how the little birds of the air and the modest lilies of the field are not forgotten: how then can we think that our Father would forget us, who are of so much more value than they?—to remember that the very fact that we know Him as our Father should be guarantee enough, preventing us from an anxious solicitude pardonable in the heathen, who have no such knowledge of a Father in heaven Who knoweth what His children need;—to remember also how vain and fruitless is our care, seeing we cannot in the very smallest lengthen the life for which we fret, while our times are wholly in the hand of Him Who gave it at first and daily satisfies its wants. Such is a bare outline of the thought in this passage, to attempt to expound or illustrate which would be to spoil it. The best way to deal with such a passage is first to study it carefully to see that its meaning and the point of all its parts is clearly apprehended, and then quietly, slowly, lovingly to read it over and let its heavenly music enter into the soul. Then, when the reading is finished and the great lesson has filled the heart with trustful love, we may look back upon it and observe that not only is a great spiritual lesson taught, but incidentally we are encouraged and directed to interrogate nature and learn what she has to teach, to gaze on her beauty and lovingly look at what she has to show. Thus we find, as it were by the way, in the simple words of our King, the germ principles of science and of art.

But these are wayside pearls; no special attention is called to them. These glimpses of nature come so naturally from the Lord of nature that nothing is made of them—they "flash along the chords and go"; and we return to the great lesson which, now that the cautions have been given, can be put in its positive form: "Seek ye first the kingdom of God, and His righteousness; and all these things shall be added unto you" (vi. 33.). Seek ye first *His* kingdom, and *His* righteousness. Already, as we have seen, this lesson has been implied in the Lord's Prayer; but it is well that it should be expressly set down—this will insure that the treasure is above, that the eye is clear, that the life is one: "and all these things shall be added," so that to-morrow need not trouble you. Trouble there must be in the world, but no one need have more than each day brings: "Sufficient unto the day is the evil thereof."

(2) *As regards the evil in the world.* The transition from the good things of the world to the evil that is in it comes quite naturally from the turn the Master's thought has taken in the close of the preceding paragraph. It is important to observe, however, that the whole subject of the evil in the world is not in view at this point. Has not the evil in the world in the large sense been in view from the beginning throughout; and has not the great subject of righteousness had all along as its background the dark subject of sin? The one point here is this: the attitude of the children of the kingdom to the evil which they cannot but see in the people of the world by whom they are surrounded.

Here, as before, there are two warnings, each against a danger lying in opposite directions: the one, the danger of making too much of the evil we see, or think we see, in others; the other, that of making too little of it.

(*a*) As against making too much of it—the danger of censoriousness (vii. 1-5). Here, again, the language is very strong, and the warning given is solemn and earnest—a sure sign that the danger is real and great. Again, too, considerations are urged, one after another, why we should beware. First, there is so much evil in ourselves, that we should be most careful how we condemn it in others, for "with what judgment ye judge ye shall be judged; and with what measure ye mete, it shall be measured to you again." Moreover, severity is a sign not of purity but of the reverse: "Why beholdest thou the mote that is in thy brother's eye, but considerest not the beam that is in thine own eye?" Our severity should be applied to ourselves, our charity to others; especially if we would have any success in the correcting of our neighbour's faults: "How wilt thou say to thy brother, Let me cast out the mote out of thine eye; and lo, the beam is in thine own eye?" (R.V.) Otherwise we are hypocrites, and we must thoroughly reform ourselves before we have any idea even how to begin to improve others: "Thou hypocrite, first cast out the beam out of thine own eye; and then shalt thou see clearly to cast out the mote out of thy brother's eye." Of what exceeding value is this teaching just where it stands! The Saviour has been summoning His people not only to pure morality and true godliness, but to lofty spirituality of mind and heart; and knowing what was in man—knowing that dangers lurked on his path at every turn, and that even the highest spirituality has its special danger, its besetting sin—He points it out, paints it in all its blackness, spares not the sin of the saint any more than the sin of the sinner, calls the man that gathers his skirts about him with the word or the thought "I am holier than thou" by the same ugly name with which He brands the poor fools who disfigure their faces that they may be seen of men to fast. Yet, severe as it is, is it not needed? does not our best judgment approve and applaud? and are we not glad and grateful that our Lord has warned us so earnestly and impressively against a danger it might never have occurred to us to fear?

But there is another side to the subject; so we have another warning, in relation to the evil we see in the men of the world. It is—

(*b*) Against making too little of it (ver. 6). Though we may not judge, we must discriminate. It may be wrong to condemn; but it may be necessary to withdraw, otherwise sacred things may be profaned and angry passions stirred, and thus much harm may be done though only good was intended. Such is the manifest purport of the striking caution: "Give not that which is holy unto the dogs, neither cast ye your pearls before swine, lest they trample them under their feet, and turn again and rend you."

The Saviour is now about to close what He has to say on the Righteousness of the Kingdom in its relation to the Law and the Prophets; and He does it by setting forth in most memorable words a great privilege and a compact, comprehensive, portable rule—a privilege which will keep the heart right with God, a rule which will keep the heart right with man (vv. 7-12). The former is of course the more important of the two, so it comes first and has much the larger space. It is the mighty privilege of prayer. When we think of the height and the depth, the length and the breadth, of the righteousness of the kingdom—when we think of the dangers which lurk on every hand and at every stage in our life-journey—we may well cry, "Who is sufficient for these things?" To that cry of the heart this is the answer: "Ask, and it shall be given you." We have had prayer before; but it was prayer as a part of righteousness, prayer as a religious duty. Now it is prayer as a power, as the one sure and only means of avoiding the terrible evils on every side, and obtaining the unspeakable blessings, the "good things" (ver. 11) of the kingdom of heaven. This being so, it was of the greatest importance that we should have faith to use it. Hence the repeated assurance, and the plain strong language in which it is conveyed; hence, too, the simple, strong and touching arguments to dispel our doubts and encourage our trust (vv. 9-11).

Here, again, of what priceless value are these few words of our blessed Lord! Just where they are needed most they come, bringing "strength to the fainting heart" in view of the seemingly inaccessible heights of God's holy hill, on which the city of His kingdom is set. Why need we faint or fear, now that we can ask and be sure of receiving, can seek and be sure of finding, can knock at door after door of these halls of Sion, and have them, one after another, opened at our touch?

Again as before, prayer to God is closely connected with our behaviour to men. In the model prayer we were taught to say "Forgive us our debts, as we forgive our debtors"; and not only so, but a special warning was added, that if we do not forgive others, we cannot be forgiven. So here too we are reminded that if we are to expect our Father to act in a fatherly way to us by giving us good things, we must act in a brotherly way to our neighbours. Hence the golden rule which follows, and hence its connection with the prayer-charter by the word "therefore." And now that our relations to God and man have been summed up in the filial relation embodied in prayer, and in the fraternal relation embodied in the golden rule, all is complete, and the proof of this is furnished in the appropriate concluding words: "This is the Law and the Prophets."

III. Invitation to enter the Kingdom (vii. 13-29)

The Master has now said everything necessary in order to clear away popular misapprehensions, and place the truth about His kingdom fairly before the minds of His hearers. He has explained its nature as inward and spiritual, setting forth the character of those who belong to it, the blessedness they will enjoy, and the influence they will exert on the world around them. He has set forth clearly and fully the obligations that will rest upon them, as summed up in the comprehensive requirement of righteousness understood in a larger and deeper sense than ever before—obligations of such stringency as to make it apparent that to seek the kingdom of God and His righteousness is no holiday undertaking, that it is no easy thing to be a Christian, but that it requires self-restraint, self-humbling, self-denial; and that therefore His kingdom cannot be attractive to the many, but must appeal to those who are earnest-spirited enough to ask and seek and knock for admittance.

Now that all has been fully and faithfully set forth—now that there is no danger of obtaining disciples under misapprehension—the great invitation is issued: *Enter ye in*. It is the free universal invitation of the Gospel, as large and liberal as that later one, "Whosoever will, let him come," though given in such a way as to keep still prominently before the minds of all comers what they may expect, and what is expected of them: "Enter ye in by the narrow gate: for wide is the gate, and broad is the way, that leadeth to destruction, and many be they that enter in thereby. For narrow is the gate, and straitened the way, that leadeth unto life, and few be they that find it" (R.V.).

The terms of this first invitation are very significant. The motives of fear and hope are appealed to; but not directly or specially. In the background lies, on the one hand, the dark doom of "destruction," and on the other the glorious hope of "life"; but neither the one nor the other is made emphatic. The demand for "righteousness" has been elaborated in full, and warnings against sin have been multiplied and pressed with intensest earnestness; but Christ does not now, as on account of the hardness of men's hearts He felt it needful later on to do, set forth in language that appeals vividly to the imagination the fate of those who take the broad way of easy self-indulgence; nor does He endeavour to picture the things which eye hath not seen, nor ear heard, nor heart conceived, which God hath prepared for them that love Him; He simply suggests in the briefest manner, by the use of a single word in each case—and that word characterised not so much by strength as by suggestiveness what will be the fate of the one, the goal of the other. Suggestive as both words are in the highest degree, they are not emphatic, but lie as it were in the background, while the attention is kept on the present alternative: on the one hand the wide gate, the broad way, the many thronging it; on the other, the narrow gate, the straitened way, the few finding it. Our Lord summons not so much to a choice that will pay, as to a choice that will cost; and in so doing makes His appeal to all that is noblest and highest and best in human nature.

Throughout the whole discourse He has been leading up to this point. He has been setting forth no prospect of happiness "to draw the carnal eye," but an ideal of blessedness to win the spiritual heart. He has been unfolding a righteousness, which, while it cannot but be repulsive to man's natural selfishness, profoundly stirs and satisfies his conscience; and now, in strict keeping with all that has gone before, the appeal is made in such a way as shall commend it, not to the thoughtless, selfish crowd, but to those whose hearts have been drawn and whose consciences have been touched by His presentation of the blessedness they may expect and the righteousness expected of them. From all this there is surely to be learned a most important lesson, as to the manner in which the Gospel should usually be presented — not by sensational descriptions of the glories of heaven or the horrors of hell, nor by the mere reiteration of exhortations to "come to Jesus," but by such information of the mind, awakening of the heart, and stirring of the conscience as are found in perfection in this great discourse of the Master.

It is characteristic of the large view our Lord takes of human life that He speaks of only two paths. There seem so many, leading off in all different directions; and so there are on a limited view of life's horizon; but when eternal issues are in sight, there are but two: the easy path of self-indulgence leading down to death, and the difficult path of duty[7] leading up to life.

It is worthy of remark that there is not a trace of asceticism in our Lord's representation. The straitness referred to is not outward, any more than the righteousness is; so that there is no encouragement given to self-imposed restrictions and limitations, as in the monastic vows of "poverty, chastity, and obedience." The way is strait enough in itself without any effort of ours to make it straiter. It is enough that we set ourselves to keep all the commandments; so shall we have a sufficiency of exercise to toughen our spiritual fibre, to strengthen our moral energies, to make us men and women instead of slaves of lust or tools of mammon. For, be it ever remembered, the way we take leads on naturally and unavoidably to its end. Destruction is no arbitrary punishment for self-indulgence; nor is life an arbitrary reward for self-discipline and surrender to the will of God. The path of self-indulgence "leadeth to destruction," by a law which cannot be annulled or set aside. But the path of self-restraint and self-surrender (for these are what make of us men, and not "blind mouths," as Milton expressively puts it), the path which is entered by the strait gate, and is continued along the narrow way, is one which in the course of natural development "leadeth unto life."

The call to enter is followed by words of solemn warning against certain dangers which might beset even those who wish to enter. First, the danger of false guidance: "Beware of false prophets." The danger lies in the future. Hitherto, while speaking throughout of present duty, there have been backward glances over the past, as our Lord has made it evident, point after point, that the righteousness of His kingdom was not the destruction but the fulfilment of the law and the prophets. Now, however, He anticipates the time when there will be those claiming to speak in the name of God, or in His own name, whose doctrines will not be a fulfilment but a destruction of the Truth, and a constant danger to those who may be exposed to their wolf-like ravages. There is manifestly no reference to such differences of opinion as divide real Christians from each other in these days. The doctrine throughout this manifesto is not speculative, but practical; it nowhere brings into prominence matters of opinion, or what are called theological tenets, but everywhere lays stress on that which immediately and powerfully affects the life. So it is here also, as is evident from the criterion suggested for the detection of false teachers: "By their fruits ye shall know them." Besides, the connection in which the caution occurs makes it evident that our Lord had specially in view those teachers who would lead their disciples astray as to the way of life, especially those who would dare to make that easy which he had shown to be "strait," who would set before their hearers or readers a broad path instead of the narrow one which alone leadeth unto life. This is a danger which besets us in these days. There is so strong a sentiment abroad in favour of liberality—and liberality properly so called is so admirable, and has been so much a stranger in times past—that we are in danger of accepting in its name easy-going representations of the Christian life which amount to a total abolition of the strait gate and the narrow way. Let us by all means be liberal enough to acknowledge all who have entered by the strait gate of genuine repentance, and are walking in the narrow way of faith and obedience, however much they may differ from us in matters of opinion, forms of worship, or modes of work; but let us beware how we give even the smallest encouragement to any on the broad road to imagine that they can continue as they are, and find it all right in the end. So to tamper with truth in the guise of liberality is to play the wolf in sheep's clothing.

The test our Lord gives for "discerning the spirits" is one which requires time for its application, but it is the only sure one; and when we remember that the Master is now looking forward into the future history of His kingdom, we can see why He should lay stress on a test whose operation, though slow, was sure. It is of course assumed that the first criterion is the Word of the Lord Himself. This is the law of the kingdom; but, knowing well what was in man, the Lord could not but foresee that there would be those who could so twist any words that might be spoken on those great subjects as to lay snares for the unwary; and therefore, besides the obvious appeal "to the law and to the testimony," He supplied a practical test which, though less speedy in its application, was perfectly sure in its results.

The announcement of so important a test leads to the development of the general principle on which its validity depends — viz., the vital connection between essential doctrine and life. In the long run the one is always the outcome of the other. In the spiritual as in the natural world every species brings forth fruit "after its kind." "Do men gather grapes of thorns, or figs of thistles? Even so every good tree bringeth forth good fruit; but a corrupt tree bringeth forth evil fruit. A good tree cannot bring forth evil fruit, neither can a corrupt tree bring forth good fruit." The law being so absolute, making it certain, on the one hand, that where there is truth in the inward parts there will be good fruit in the outward life, and on the other, that where there is corrupt fruit in the outward life there must be that which is corrupt in the hidden man of the heart, it follows that the criterion is so sure as to be without appeal: "Every tree that bringeth not forth good fruit is hewn down, and cast into the fire" (ver. 19), and therefore may well determine the question as to who are trustworthy teachers in the Church: "Wherefore by their fruits ye shall know them."

In the development of the principle the Master's thought has been enlarged so as to include not teachers only, but all His disciples; and His range of view has been extended so as to embrace the last things. The great day of Judgment is before him. He sees the multitudes gathered around the throne. He foresees that there will be many on that great day who will discover, when it is too late, that they have allowed themselves to be deceived, that they have not been careful enough to test their spiritual guides, that they have not been careful enough to try themselves and make sure that their fruits were such that the Lord of the vineyard could recognise them as His own. He is filled with sympathy and sorrow at the prospect; so He lifts up His voice in earnest warning, that, if possible, none of those to whom the words will ever come may allow themselves to fall into so fatal an error: "Not every one that saith unto me, Lord, Lord, shall enter into the kingdom of heaven; but he that doeth the will of My Father which is in heaven."

How naturally, and as it were unconsciously and inevitably, He has passed from the Teacher to the Judge! Not as a personal claim. In His earliest teaching He kept personal claims as much in the background as possible. But now it is impossible to avoid some disclosure of His divine authority. He must speak of the Judgment; and He cannot speak of it without making it appear that He is Judge. The force of this is all the greater that He is, as it were, surprised into it; for He is evidently not thinking of Himself at all, but only of those who then were or would afterwards be in danger of making a most fatal mistake, leading to consequences awful and irreparable. We can well imagine that from this point on to the end there must have been a light on His face, a fire in His eye, a solemnity in His tone, a grandeur in His very attitude, which struck the multitude with amazement, especially at the *authority* (ver. 29) with which He spoke: "Many will say to Me in that day, Lord, Lord, did we not prophesy by Thy name, and by Thy name cast out devils, and by Thy name do many mighty works? And then will I profess unto them, I never knew you: depart from me, ye that work iniquity" (R.V.).

Again, observe the form the warning takes, revealing the consciousness that to depart from Him was *doom*—one of the many tokens throughout this discourse that none else than the Lord of life and glory could possibly have spoken it. Yet how many vainly think that they can accept it without acknowledging Him!

The same solemn and regal tone is kept up throughout the impressive passage which closes all, and presses home the great warning against trusting to any experience short of the surrender of the life to do the will of God as set forth in the words of Christ His Son. The two classes He has now in view are not the two great classes who walk, the one in the broad and the other in the narrow way. They are two classes of *hearers*. Most of those that throng the broad way are not hearers at all; they have no desire or intention of seeking any other than the broad way—they would as little think of going up into a mountain and listening to a discourse on righteousness, as they would of wearing a hair shirt or doing any other kind of penance; but those our Lord has now in view all have the idea of seeking the right way: their very attitude as hearers shows it—they are all of the church-going class, to translate into modern phrase; and what He fears is that some of them may deceive themselves by imagining that because they hear with interest and attention, perhaps admiration, therefore they are in the narrow way. Accordingly He solemnly warns them that all this may amount to nothing: there may be attention, interest, admiration, full assent to all; but if the hearing is not followed by doing, all is in vain.

It may almost go without saying that, after what our Lord has just been teaching as to the vital connection between the faith of the heart and the "fruits" of the life (vv. 15-23), there is no "legalism" here. In fact, the doing is not outward; it is a doing of the heart. The righteousness He has been expounding has, as we have seen, been a righteousness of the heart, and the doing of it, as a matter of course, is a heart-work, having its root in faith, which is the beginning of the doing in every case, according to His own word in another place: "This is the work of God, that ye believe on Him Whom He hath sent."

The illustration with which He presses home the warning is in the highest degree appropriate and forcible. The man who not only hears, but does, makes thorough work, digs deep (as St. Luke puts it in his record), and founds the house he is building for time and eternity upon solid rock; while the man who hears but does not, is one who takes no care as to his foundation, but erects his house just where he happens to be, on loose sand or earth, which the first storm will dislodge and sweep away. Meanwhile testing times are coming—rains, floods, winds—the searching trials of life culminating in the final judgment in the life to come. These all test the work of the builder, and render apparent the wisdom of the man who provided against the coming storm by choosing the rock foundation, for his house abides through all; and the folly of the other, who without a foundation carelessly risked all, for his house gives way before the storm, and great is the fall of it.

Alas for many hearers of the Word! Alas for many admirers of the "Sermon on the Mount"! Where will they be when everything turns on the question "Wert thou a doer of it?"

FOOTNOTES

[5] It is true that under the head of oaths comes the duty of reverence, which scarcely seems to fall under this head; but it will be remembered that this point comes in by way of a very natural suggestion in dealing with falsehood and the regulation of conversation, which evidently belongs to righteousness as between man and man.

[6] This complete change of meaning, amounting in fact to the destruction and almost to the inversion of the sense, is one of many illustrations of the absolute need of revision from time to time of translations, not only to make them more correct, but even to keep them as correct as they were at first.

[7] Duty of course in its largest sense—to God and man and self—including all "righteousness" in the Master's sense of the word.

VIII
THE SIGNS OF THE KINGDOM

Matt. viii.-ix. 35.

REFERRING to chapter iv. 23, we find the work of Christ at the beginning of His ministry summarised as teaching and preaching and healing all manner of diseases. Of the teaching and preaching we have had a signal illustration in what is called the Sermon on the Mount; now the other great branch of the work is set before us in a group of miracles, filling up almost the whole of the eighth and ninth chapters.

The naturalness of the sequence will be at once apparent. If men had needed nothing more than counsel, guidance, rules of life, then might the Gospel have ended when the Sermon on the Mount was concluded. There are those who think they need nothing more; but if they knew themselves they would feel their need not only of the Teacher's word, but of the Healer's touch, and would hail with gladness the chapters which tell how the Saviour dealt with the poor leper, the man with the palsy, the woman with the fever, those poor creatures that were vexed with evil spirits, that dead damsel in the ruler's house. We may well rejoice that the great Teacher came down from the mountain, and made Himself known on the plain and among the city crowds as the mighty Healer; that His stern demand for perfect righteousness was so soon followed by that encouraging word, so full of comfort, for such as we: "I came not to call the righteous, but sinners" (ix. 13). The healing, then, is quite as essential as the teaching. The Sermon points out the way, unfolds the truth; but in the touch and word of the King Himself is found the life. The Christ of God had come, not as a mere Ambassador from the court of heaven to demand submission to its laws, but as a mighty Saviour, Friend, and Comforter. Hence it was necessary that He should make full proof of His mission in this respect as well as in the other; and accordingly the noble ethics taught on the mount are followed by a series of heavenly deeds of power and loving-kindness done in the plain.

The group in chapters viii. and ix. is well fitted to give a comprehensive view of Christ's power and willingness to save. If only they were looked at in this intelligent way, how the paltry prejudices against "miracles" (a word, let it be observed, not once to be found in this Gospel) would vanish.

Miracles, wonders, prodigies—how incredible in an age of enlightenment! Yes; if they were introduced as miracles, wonders, prodigies; but they are not. They are signs of the kingdom of heaven—just such signs of it as the intelligent reason demands; for how otherwise is it possible for One Who comes to save to show that He is able to do it? How could the people have been expected to welcome Him as a Saviour, unless He had taken some means to make it evident that He had the power as well as the will to save? Accordingly, in consonance with what enlightened reason imperatively demands of such an One as He claims to be, we have a series of "mighty deeds" of love, showing forth, not only His grace, but His power—power to heal the diseases of the body, power over the realm of nature, power over the unseen world of spirit, power to forgive and save from sin, power to restore lost faculties and conquer death itself. Such are the appropriate signs of the kingdom spread before us here.

Let us look first at that which occupies the foremost place,—power to heal disease. The diseases of the body are the outward symptoms of the deep-seated malady of the spirit; hence it is fitting that He should begin by showing in this region His will and power to save. Yet it is not a formal *showing* of it. It is no mere demonstration. He does not seek out the leper, set him up before them, and say, "Now you will see what I can do." All comes about in a most simple and natural way, as became Him Who was no wonder-worker, no worker of miracles in the vulgar use of that word, but a mighty Saviour from heaven with a heart of love and a hand of power.

The Leper (viii. 1-4)

"And when He was come down from the mountain, great multitudes followed Him. And behold, there came to Him a leper." What will He do with him? Should He say to him, "Poor man, you are too late—the sermon is done"? or should He give him some of the best bits over again? No, there is not a sentence in the whole of it that would be any answer to that cry, "Lord, if Thou wilt, Thou canst make me clean." What does He do, then? "Jesus put forth His hand, and touched him, saying, I will: be thou clean. And immediately his leprosy was cleansed."

Is it, then, a great stumbling-block in your way, O nineteenth-century critic, that you are expected to believe that the Lord Jesus actually did heal this leper? Would it take the stumbling-block away to have it altered? Suppose we try it, amended to suit the "anti-supernaturalism" of the age. "And behold, there came a leper to Him, saying, Lord, if Thou wilt, Thou canst make me clean. And Jesus put out His hand, and motioned him away, saying, Poor man, you are quite mistaken, I cannot help you. I came to teach wise people, not to help poor wretches like you. There are great laws of health and disease; I advise you to find them out, and obey them: consult your doctor, and do the best you can. Farewell." Oh, what nonsense many wise people talk about the difficulty of believing in Divine power to heal! The fact is, that if Christ had not proved Himself a healer, men could not have believed in Him at all.

There could have been no better introduction to the saving work of the Christ of God. Leprosy was of all diseases the most striking symbol of sin. This is so familiar a thought that it need not be set forth in detail. One point, however, must be mentioned, as it opens up a vein of tender beauty in the exquisite simplicity of the story—the rigorous separation of the leprous from the healthy, enforced by the ceremonial law, which made it defilement to touch a leper. Yet "Jesus stretched forth His hand, and *touched* him." "He was holy, harmless, undefiled, separate from sinners;" therefore He could mingle with them, contracting no stain Himself, but diffusing health around Him. He could take no defilement from the leper's touch; the current was all the other way: "virtue" went out of Him, and flowed in healing streams through the poor leper's veins. O lovely symbol of the Saviour's relation to us sinners! He has in His holy Incarnation touched our leprous humanity; and remaining stainless Himself, has set flowing a fountain of healing for all who will open to Him hearts of faith and let Him touch them with His pure heart of love. Those were most wonderful words spoken on the mount: they touch the conscience to the quick and fire the soul with heavenly aspiration; but this touch of the leper goes to our hearts, for it proves to us that, though the time is coming when He shall sit as Judge and say to all the sinful, "Depart from Me," as yet He is the loving Saviour, saying, "Come unto Me, ye weary," and touching the leprous into health.

That our Saviour was totally averse to anything at all sensational, and determined rather to repress than encourage the mere thirst for marvels, is evident from the directions given to the leper to say nothing about what had happened to him, but to take the appointed method of giving thanks to God for his recovery, at the same time registering the fact, so that while his cure should not be used to gather a crowd, it might be on record with the proper authorities as a witness to the truth of which it was a sign.

The Centurion's Servant (5-13)

This case, while affording another valuable illustration of the Master's willingness and power to save, differs in several important points from the first, so that the lesson is widened. First and chiefly, the application was from a Gentile; next, it was not on his own behalf that the centurion made it, but on behalf of another, and that other his servant; and, further, it was a request to heal a patient out of sight, out of knowledge even, as it would seem. Each of these particulars might suggest a doubt. He has healed this Jew; but will He listen to that Gentile? He has responded to this man's own cry; but will He respond when there is no direct application from the patient? He has cured this man with a touch; but can he cure a patient miles away? The Saviour knew well the difficulties which must have lain in the way of this man's faith. He has evidence, moreover, that his is genuine faith, and not the credulity of superstition. One could readily imagine an ignorant person thinking that it made no difference whether the patient were present, or a thousand miles away: what difference does distance make to the mere magician? But this man is no ignorant believer in charms or incantations. He is an intelligent man, and has thought it all out. He has heard of the kingdom of heaven, and knows that this is the King. Reasoning from what he knows of the Roman kingdom, how orders given from a central authority can be despatched to the outskirts, and be executed there with as great certainty as if the Emperor himself had gone to do it, he concludes that the King of the spiritual world must in like manner have means of communication with every part of His dominion; and just as it was not necessary, even for a mere centurion, to do personally everything he wanted done, having it in his power to employ some servant to do it, so it was unreasonable to expect the King of heaven Himself to come in person and heal his servant: it was only necessary, therefore, that He should speak the word, and by some unseen agency the thing would be done. At once the Saviour recognises the man's thoughtful intelligence on the subject, and, contrasting with it the slowness of mind and heart of those of whom so much more might have been expected, "He marvelled, and said to them that followed, Verily I say unto you, I have not found so great faith, no, not in Israel."

The thought of this immediately suggests to Him the multitudes that shall exercise a similar faith in ages to come, and in lands far off; and, as on the mount, when He looked forward to the great future, His heart yearned over the mere hearers of the word shut out at last; so here He yearns with a great yearning over His unbelieving countrymen, whose exclusion at last from the heavenly kingdom would be felt with all the sharper pain that such multitudes from far less favoured lands were safe within—at home with the patriarchs of the chosen nation—while they, the natural heirs of the kingdom, were exiles from it for evermore. Hence the wail and warning which follow His hearty appreciation of the centurion's faith: "And I say unto you, that many shall come from the east and the west, and shall sit down with Abraham, and Isaac, and Jacob, in the kingdom of heaven: but the sons of the kingdom shall be cast forth into the outer darkness: there shall be weeping and gnashing of teeth."

How fared it with the centurion's appeal? Was it any hindrance that he was a foreigner, that he made it not for himself but for a servant, and that the patient was so far away? None whatever. As he rightly judged, the King of heaven had resources in abundance to meet the case. Without the least hesitation, Jesus said to the centurion, "Go thy way: and as thou hast believed, so be it done unto thee. And his servant was healed in the selfsame hour."

The Fever Patient (14, 15)

The leprosy and palsy were symbols of sin wholly possessing its victims: the one suggestive of the state of those who are positively defiled by sin, the other of the condition of those who, though sound to all outward appearance, are simply wanting in inward life, paralysed in that part of their being which constitutes life. These two cases, then, were most suitable for setting forth the saving power of the Christ of God as regards the unconverted, be they Jew or Gentile. This third cure is within the circle of the disciples. It is a case of fever in the home of Peter. It therefore fitly suggests the diseases to which those are still liable who have come to Christ and been healed of their leprosy or palsy, the chronic disease which defiled or paralysed them in time past; but who are still liable to contagion, still exposed to attacks of fever, acute diseases which, though temporary, are most dangerous, and, just as certainly as the others, need the touch of the Great Physician for their healing. These fevers separate us from Christ and unfit us for His service; but they need not continue to do this, for if only we allow Him to enter the house and touch us, the fever will cease; and, like this patient in the home of Peter, we may at once arise and minister unto Him.

The three specific cases which have been so appropriately selected and given in detail are followed by a general enumeration of a number of similar ones dealt with in like manner, "when the even was come"—the whole experience of that eventful day leading to the joyful recognition of the fulfilment of a grand prophetic word spoken long ago of the Messiah that was to come: "Himself took our infirmities, and bare our sicknesses."

The quotation is most suggestive. It raises the question of our Lord's personal relation to disease. We have seen reason to believe that disease could not contaminate His holy flesh; and certainly we never read of His suffering from any sickness of His own. Did He then know nothing personally of disease and fleshly infirmity? If not, how could He be tempted in all points like as we are? The solution seems to lie in this most interesting quotation. It is not a literal citation from the Septuagint, but it is a thoroughly fair and true reproduction of the idea of the prophet; and it clearly suggests to the mind that the Christ's relation to human sickness was of the same kind as

His relation to human sin. Though personally He had no sin, yet "He was made sin for us," so that He felt the intolerable weight pressing Him down as in the garden, and the awful darkness wrapping Him round as on the cross. In the same way, even though His flesh may never actually have been subjected to physical disease, He nevertheless could not remove diseases from others without bearing them Himself. Ah! it cost Him far more than we are apt to think, to say, "I will, be thou clean." It was only by the sacrifice of His life that He could take away the sin of the world; and we believe that it was only by the sacrifice of a part of His life that He could take away the disease of a sufferer. When He said, "Somebody hath touched Me, for virtue has gone out of Me," we may be sure it was no mere jostling of the crowd; it was an outflow of His life, a partial shedding, so to speak, of His precious blood. Just as later, in the words of St. Peter, "He bare our sins in His own body on the tree," so already "Himself took our infirmities and bare our sicknesses."

The Impulsive Scribe (18-20)

The two incidents which follow, though at first sight apparently different in character from the great majority of the group, are quite in place among the mighty deeds of the Master, manifesting, as they do, His penetrating insight into character. To all appearance there could have been no better offer than that of the impulsive scribe—"Master, I will follow Thee whithersoever Thou goest"; and, had it been made with a full understanding of all it meant, it would beyond all question have been at once accepted; but He Who "knew what was in man" saw at once what manner of man this was—how he was quite unprepared for the hardships he would have to undergo; and therefore, while by no means declining the offer, He gives him fair warning of what he might expect, in these memorable words: "The foxes have holes, and the birds of the air have nests; but the Son of man hath not where to lay His head." There is infinite pathos in the words. Moreover, the form in which the truth is put, while fitted effectually to deter the selfish and faint-hearted, would be no discouragement to a truly devoted and courageous soul, but would rather fire it with a holier ardour to follow the Son of man anywhere, at whatever cost, rejoicing to be "counted worthy to suffer shame" and loss "for His name."

The Hesitating Disciple (21, 22)

This case is one of the opposite description. Judging from the way in which the scribe had been dealt with, it might have been expected that when this disciple asked to be excused for a time, in order to discharge a duty which seemed so urgent, the answer would have been one not only allowing but even enforcing the delay. But no. Why the difference? Again, because the Master saw "what was in man." This was no impulsive, impetuous nature which needed a word of caution; but one of those hesitating natures which need to be summoned to immediate decision. It would seem also, from the peculiar expression, "Leave *the dead* to bury their own dead" (R.V.), that he belonged to an ungodly family, to associate again with whom at such a critical time in his history would be most prejudicial; and it must be remembered that it would not have been the mere attending of the funeral; there were the laws of uncleanness, which would oblige him, if he went, to stay many days; and meantime the golden opportunity might be gone.

Thus are we guarded against the two opposite dangers—the one besetting the eager and impulsive, the other the halting and irresolute. In neither case are we told what the result was. We may surmise that the scribe disappeared from view, and that the other joined the party in the boat; but "something sealed the lips of that Evangelist"; from which we may perhaps infer that his main object in relating the two incidents was, not to give information of them, but to show forth the glory of the Master as the Searcher of hearts, to signalise the fact that He was no less Master of the minds than of the bodies of men.

The Storm Stilled (23-27)

It was not enough that the Saviour of mankind should have power to grapple with disease and skill to search the hearts of men: He must be Master not only of life, but of its environment too. That He is becomes apparent before the boat which carries the little company reaches the other side of the lake. One of those tempests which often lash the Sea of Galilee into sudden fury has burst upon them, and the little boat is almost covered with the waves. Here is a situation beyond the reach even of the Great Physician, unless indeed He be something more. He is something more. He is Lord of nature, Master of all its forces!

Must He not be? He has come to reveal the unseen God of nature; must He not then make it manifest, now that the occasion calls for it, that winds and waves are "ministers of His, that do His pleasure"? Again, it is no mere "miracle," no mere marvel which He works in the salvation of His terrified disciples—it is a sign, an indispensable sign of the kingdom of heaven.

The story is told with exquisite simplicity, and with all the reality of manifest and transparent truthfulness. "He was asleep"—naturally enough after the fatigues of the day, notwithstanding the howling of the storm; for why should He fear wind or wave? Is there not a promise here for all His followers when tempest-tossed: "So He giveth His beloved sleep"?

His disciples let Him sleep as long as they dare; but the peril is too imminent now. So they come to Him and awake Him, saying, "Save, Lord; we perish!" Though no concern for Himself would ever have disturbed His slumber, the first cry of His disciples rouses Him at once to action. The resources of His human nature, beyond which He never went for the purpose of meeting His own personal needs, had been completely exhausted; but there is no diminution of His power to save those who call upon Him. Without any trace remaining of weariness or weakness, He hastens to relieve them. First,[8] He quiets the tempest in the disciples' hearts, rebuking their unbelief and calming their fears; then He stills the storm without, rebuking the winds and the sea; "and there was a great calm." It reads like the story of creation. No wonder the astonished disciples exclaimed: "What manner of man is this, that even the winds and the sea obey Him?"

Demons cast out (28-34)

Visible nature is not man's sole environment. There is an unseen universe besides; and He Who would be Saviour of mankind must be Master there as well. That this also is sure is now proved beyond a doubt. For it is important to observe that this is not an ordinary case of healing, otherwise its true place would have been with the group of bodily diseases at the beginning of this series. When we consider its salient features, we see that it is just in its right place, closely following, as it does, the stilling of the storm. There are storms in the spiritual world, more terrible by far than any in the realm of nature; and it is necessary that these darker storms be also subject to the control of the Saviour of mankind. "The prince of the power of the air" and all his legions must be subject to the "Son of man." And this subjection, rather than the cure of the individual sufferers, is the salient feature of the passage. It is not the men, but the demons possessing them, who cry out, "What have we to do with Thee, Jesus, Thou Son of God? art Thou come hither to torment us before the time?" Well did these evil spirits know who He was; and well, also, did they know that He was mightier than they, and that the time was coming when they would be put entirely under His feet: "Art Thou come to torment us *before the time*?"

The sequel has been the occasion of much cavil. It has been represented as entirely beyond the bounds of rational belief; but why? The whole subject of demoniacal possession is a most difficult one; but many of the calmest and deepest thinkers, quite apart from the testimony of the Gospel, have found themselves unable to explain a multitude of dark facts in history and experience apart from the reality of demoniacal influence. If a spirit can exercise a malign influence on a man, why not on an animal? Moreover, seeing that the keeping of these swine was an open breach of the law, what difficulty is there in supposing that Christ should allow their destruction, especially when we consider that this transference of the malign influence not only made more apparent His absolute control over the spirits of evil, but taught a most striking and instructive lesson as to their affinities? For certain persons there is no more instructive and no more needful passage in Scripture than this. The difficulty is, that those who prefer to keep their swine will not welcome the mighty Exorcist, but, like these people of old, beseech Him to "depart out of their coasts."

Sins Forgiven (ix. 1-13)

Master of disease—Searcher of hearts—Master of the forces of nature—Master of the powers of the Unseen: is not this enough? Not yet; He must make it evident that "the Son of man hath power on earth to forgive sins." To heal the diseases of the body was a great and blessed thing to do, but it was not thorough work; for what are all these varied diseases—leprosy, fever, palsy—but symptoms of one great disorder which has its roots, not in the flesh, but in the soul, a disease belonging to that region of the unseen, in which He has now made manifest His power—the dark disease of sin. The time has now come to show that He can deal effectually with it; and immediately on His return to His own side of the lake, an opportunity presents itself. "They brought to Him a man sick of the palsy, lying on a bed."

As a case of palsy, it is not new. The centurion's servant was a palsy case; and though from His treatment of it, as of the leprosy and fever, it might fairly have been inferred that He could deal also with that which was deeper, it was not enough to leave it to inference—it must be made manifest. It may have been that the disease of this man had been in some special manner connected with previous sins, so that his conscience may have been the more exercised as he looked back over his past life; but whether this was so or not, it is obvious that his conscience was at work,—that much as his palsy may have troubled him, his guilt troubled him much more. Why, otherwise, should the Saviour have addressed him as He did, making no reference to the disease, but dealing directly with his spiritual condition? Moreover, the special affection shown in the Saviour's mode of address seems to indicate His recognition of that broken and contrite spirit with which the Lord is well pleased. It would scarcely be too strong to translate it thus: "My dear child, be of good cheer; thy sins are forgiven."

The Saviour is coming closer and closer to human need, dealing more and more thoroughly with the world's want and woe. If we look at it aright, we cannot but recognise it as really a greater thing to heal the deep disease of the soul, than to heal any or all of the diseases of the body, greater even than to still the storm or rule by superior power the spirits of evil. For here there is something more needed than power or skill, even though both be infinite. We have already had a glimpse of the need there was, even in taking away human sickness, that the Healer Himself should suffer. But deeper far is this necessity if the disease of the soul is to be reached. It is only the Lamb of God that can take away the sin of the world. These scribes were right for once when they made more of this claim than of any that had gone before, saying within themselves, "This man blasphemeth;" ... "Who can forgive sins but God only?"

How could He prove to them His power actually to forgive the man's sins? A demonstration of this is quite impossible; but He will come as near to it as may be. He has already recognised the faith of the bearers, and the penitence of the man himself; just as quickly He discerns the thoughts of the scribes, and gives them proof that He does so by asking them, "Wherefore think ye evil in your hearts?" Then, answering their thought (which was, "He is only saying it"), He replies in effect, "It is indeed as easy to say one thing as another, if saying is all; but that you may be sure that the saying of it is not all, I shall not repeat what I said before, the result of which from the nature of the case you cannot see, but something else, the result of which you shall see presently"; whereupon, turning to the sick of the palsy, He said: "Arise, take up thy bed, and go unto thine house. And he arose, and departed to his house." With characteristic reticence, the sacred historian says nothing of the feelings of the happy man as he hied him home with a double blessing beyond the power of words to tell.

Is it possible to imagine any better proof that could have been given of Christ's authority to forgive sins? Let those who have a horror of anything extraordinary suggest some way in which this assurance could have been given without any manifestation of superhuman power. If they cannot, why continue those unreasoning objections to the kind of proof He did give, when no other proof can be even suggested that would have at all suited the purpose?

The purpose was accomplished, so far at least as the people were concerned. Whether the scribes found some way of evading the conclusion, the Evangelist does not say; but he does say that "when the multitudes saw it, they marvelled," or, as the probably more correct version of the Revisers gives it, "they were afraid." This is true to nature, for now they knew that they stood in the presence of One Who could look them through and through, and touch them in their sorest spot; so it was natural that their first feeling should be one of awe. Still, they could not but be thankful at the same time that there was forgiveness within their reach; so quite consistently the narrative proceeds—And they "glorified God, which had given such power unto men."

Now that His power to deal with sin is made so apparent, it is time to let it be known that all sinners are welcome. Hence most appropriately there follows the call of one from among the most despised class to take a place among His closest followers. We can well understand how the modest Matthew, who never mentions anything else about himself, was glad to signalise the grace of the Master in seeking out the hated and despised publican. Not only does Christ welcome him, but consents to sit at meat with his former associates (ver. 10); and when the self-righteous Pharisee complains, He takes occasion to speak those memorable words, so full of warning to those who think themselves righteous, so full of comfort to those who know themselves sinners: "They that be whole need not a physician, but they that are sick.... I am not come to call the righteous, but sinners to repentance."

Death Vanquished (14-26)

The focal point of the passage is the chamber of death in the house of Jairus. There we learn that He Who had shown Himself to be Lord of nature and of human nature, Master of the spirits of evil, and Saviour from sin, is also Conqueror of Death. He needs no preparation for the encounter. The summons comes to Him in the midst of a discourse, yet He asks not a moment's delay, but sets out at once; on the other hand, He is in no haste, for He has time to attend to another sufferer by the way; and there is no exhaustion afterwards, for He deals with another case, and still another, on His way back.

The question with which He was engaged when the summons came was one raised by the disciples of John, who, as we learn from the other accounts, were prompted by the Pharisees in the hope of exciting antagonism between the followers of John and of Jesus. Perhaps also they had the hope of setting Him at variance with Himself, for had he not declared that one jot or one tittle should not pass from the law till all was fulfilled? Why, then, did not His disciples fast? To this it might have been answered that the frequent fasts observed by Pharisees, and also by the disciples of John, were not really appointed by the law, which prescribed only one day of fasting in the year—the great atonement day. But the Saviour gives an answer of much wider scope and farther-reaching significance. There was involved, not the question of fasting only, but of the entire ceremonial law; and He disposes of it all by a series of characteristic illustrations, each of them as good as a volume on the subject could have been.

The first of these illustrations sets the true principle of fasting in full, clear light by a simple question—"Can the children of the bridechamber mourn, as long as the bridegroom is with them? But the days will come, when the bridegroom shall be taken away from them, and then shall they fast." There is here much more to think of besides the answering of the question. There is a treasury of valuable suggestion in His calling Himself the Bridegroom, thus applying to Himself the rich imagery of the Old Testament on this theme; while at the same time He adopts the very figure which John himself had used in order to mark his relation to Jesus as the Bridegroom's friend (cf. John iii. 29); and it is especially worthy of note how this keeps up the *Gospel* idea,—the great joy, as of a marriage, in the yielding of the heart to Christ. No less striking is His touching reference to the dark days coming, the first distinct foreshadowing of the Cross. It has been well said by a German writer, "What man has ever looked so calmly, so lovingly (*lieblich*), from such a height into such an abyss!" from the position of the Bridegroom of humanity to that of the outcast on the Cross. Ah! the shadow of that Cross is never off Him, not even when He is exulting in His bridegroom joy. But these are only incidental suggestions; the main idea is the true principle of fasting, which, like all the observances of the New Testament, must be the expression of that which is in the heart. Let the heart only be true, and when the Bridegroom of the heart is present, fasting will be entirely out of the question; but when He is absent no rule will be needed—they will fast as the natural expression of their sorrow.

The two companion illustrations which follow set in the clearest light the large subject of the relation of the new dispensation to the old in respect of forms. As to substance, He had already made it plain that the old was not to be destroyed, nor even superseded, but fulfilled, to its last jot and tittle, as harvest fulfils seed-time. But as to form, the case was entirely different. The new life, while losing nothing which was in the old, was to be larger and freer, and therefore must have new garments to match. To try to piece out and patch the old would be no improvement, but much the reverse, for a worse rent would be the only result. The second illustration, suggested like the first by the associations of the marriage feast (the Saviour's illustrations are never far-fetched—He always finds exactly what He needs close at hand, thus proving Himself Master of the imagination as of all else), is to the same purpose. The new wine of the kingdom of heaven, though it retains all the excellence of the old vintage, yet having fresh properties of its own, must have fresh skins to hold it, that its natural expansion be not hindered; for to attempt to confine it in the old vessels would be to expose them to destruction and to lose the wine.

What a striking illustration of these suggestive words of warning has been the history of doctrine and of form in those churches which cling to the worn-out ritualism of the Old Testament! Old Testament forms were good in their time; but they are not good to hold the new wine of spiritual life; and to attempt to combine them, as modern ritualists do, is to injure both, to do violence to the forms by subjecting them to a strain for which they were never intended, and to lose the greater part of the life by trying to put it in moulds which were never intended for it. There is now no longer the excuse which our Lord was so ready to make, at that time of transition, for those who were slow to recognise the superiority of the new—a point which is brought out in the pendant to this illustration which the Evangelist Luke records: "No man also having drunk old wine straightway desireth new: for he saith, The old is better;" or rather, according to the more correct reading, "the old is good." Thus, while the true principle was laid down for all time, excuse was made on behalf of John and his disciples, for clinging with a natural fondness to that which had done good service in the past. A very needful lesson this for too ardent reformers, not considerate enough of what is in many respects wholesome and praiseworthy conservatism.

It was in the midst of these important teachings that the message came from the chamber of death, to which we must now again direct our thoughts: "While He spake these things unto them, behold, there came a ruler, and worshipped Him, saying, My daughter is even now dead: but come and lay Thy hand upon her, and she shall live. And Jesus arose, and followed him, and so did His disciples." This promptness is a most precious revelation of the Divine readiness to help at any moment. No need of waiting for a convenient time. Any moment is convenient for Him, to Whom the affairs even of the infinite universe are no burden.

The same lesson is still more strikingly taught by His manner of dealing with the case which met Him on the way to the ruler's house. So hastily had He set out, in response to the ruler's appeal, that one would have thought this of all times the most inconvenient—especially for a chronic invalid—to gain a hearing. Here is a woman who has had a disease for twelve years, and who therefore might surely be asked to wait a few hours at least, till the Physician should be at leisure! And the case is not at all forced on His attention; she does not stand in front of Him, so that He cannot pass without noticing her,—she only "came behind Him"; nor does she take any means that seem likely to arrest His attention,—she only "touched the hem of His garment." But it is enough. Slight as the indication is that some one needs His help, He at once observes it; nor does He exhibit the least sign of impatience or of haste; He turns round, and speaks in the kindest manner, assuring her, as it were, of her right to enjoy the great blessing of health, which had just come to her, for as soon as she had touched Him He had cured her of her long and weary ailment. What encouragement to the most timid soul! and what a revelation of the large sympathy and ever-ready helpfulness of our Saviour Christ, and of our heavenly Father Whom He so gloriously reveals!

The scene is now changed to the chamber of death. There are most interesting details given in the fuller account by the Evangelist Mark, but our scope is large enough here without endeavouring to bring them all in. The maid had been at the point of death when the father left the house; now it is all over, and the room is full of noisy mourners. These clamorous demonstrations were evidently very painful to the sensitive heart of Christ, not only, perhaps, on account of their unreality, but also because of their inappropriateness in view of the better hope which He was bringing into light. For we take it that in these words "Give place: for the maid is not dead, but sleepeth," there was not only a reference to His intention at once to bring the dead one back to life, but to the true nature of death in His kingdom. In it death was to be death no longer—only a sleep, with the prospect of a speedy and blessed awaking. Therefore such heathenish lamentations were to be henceforward out of place. Perhaps, too, He wished to set these people thinking on the great subject of death—what it is, what it means, and whether after all it need be death in the sense in which alone the noisy mourners thought of it. But "they laughed Him to scorn," so they must be "put forth." The Lord of life cannot reveal Himself to such as these. Only the faithful disciples, and the parents whose hearts have been prepared for such a revelation by the discipline of genuine grief, are permitted to be present. It is probable that both parents had their hearts fully opened to the Lord; for though the mother had waited by the daughter's bedside, she had no doubt gone with her husband in spirit on his hopeful errand; and the father's faith must have been greatly confirmed by what had happened on the way back—there was nothing lost by that delay, even though in the meantime the message had come from the house that it was too late. It was not too late: it was well that the damsel had died; for now the Saviour has the opportunity to show that He is no less Master of the last great enemy than of all the other enemies of man. "He took her by the hand, and the maid arose."

Lost Faculties Restored (27-34)

The raising of the dead may be regarded as the culminating point of the series; yet there is a special value in the two that follow in close succession before the series is complete. We have seen already that, occurring, as they do, immediately after, they show that His power is not at all exhausted—a token this of the exhaustlessness of the Divine love and helpfulness. But, besides this, are they not resurrections too—the raising again of faculties that had long been dead? Vision is a large part of our natural life; and to lose it is to descend, so far, into the darkness of death. And as the eye is to impression, so is the tongue to expression. The one is the crown of life on its receptive side, the other on its communicative side (cf. Psalm lvii. 8; cviii. 1, 2). The eye, then, may well represent life on the one side of it and the tongue on the other; while the two together represent it as completely as it is possible to do. Thus these two cases really come nearer to the idea of spiritual resurrection than even the raising of the dead damsel. In the case of the daughter of Jairus there was no part left alive to make its appeal to the Lifegiver on behalf of the rest; but with the others it was different: the blind men, for example, were able to cry for mercy (ver. 27); and it was possible for the Saviour to say to them, as He touched their eyes, "According to your faith be it unto you" (ver. 29), which He could not have said to the damsel.

Had the series ended with the raising of the daughter of Jairus, it had been made sufficiently apparent that Christ was able and willing to raise the dead; but it had still remained unrevealed by what means a man spiritually dead could secure for himself the resurrection of his lost spiritual powers. Now it is clear. The death of the spirit is parallel, not to the total death of the damsel, but to the partial death of the blind; for though the spirit of a man be dead, his mind remains alive, his heart too, his conscience even, and his body of course; there remains enough of him, so to speak, to imitate the example of these two blind men, to ask the Son of David for mercy, to follow Him till he finds it, to allow Him first to draw out the dormant faculty of faith, and then, having prepared him for the mighty boon, to pour celestial light upon his soul, bestowing on him a life so new and fresh and blessed, that it will seem to him as if it were, and it will in point of spiritual fact really be, life from the dead.

It seems more than likely that it was because He wished to subordinate the physical to the spiritual that He strictly charged them, saying, "See that no man know it." If the main thing had been the restoration of bodily sight, the more who heard of it the better. But His great purpose was far higher, — even to put an end to spiritual blindness and death; therefore He must limit His dealings with natural blindness to those who were prepared to receive the lower blessing without injuring them in their higher nature; and to make known such a case in the way of advertisement through the country-side would have been to descend from His lofty position as Saviour of men and Herald of the kingdom of heaven to that of oculist for the neighbourhood. But, though we can readily see why the Saviour should forbid the publication of the cure, it was natural enough that the men should disobey the order. They probably attributed His injunction to modesty, and thought they were showing a proper appreciation of what had been done for them by publishing it abroad. Blameworthy they certainly were; but not inexcusable.

The other case—the cure of the dumb demoniac—comes, if possible, still closer to the spiritual condition with which it was the work of the Saviour especially to deal. Like the former, it was the loss of a faculty; but, unlike it, it was not the natural loss of it, but the eclipsing of it by the malign presence of a spirit of evil. How closely parallel is this to the case of the spiritually dead. What is it that has destroyed the great faculty by which God is known and worshipped? Is it not sin? Let that demon be cast out, and not only will the eye see, but the tongue will speak; there will be a new song in the mouth, even praise to the Most High.

Furthermore, as the cure of the blind men brought into prominence the power of faith, this brings into prominence the power of Christ to save to the uttermost. For what more helpless case could there be? He could not cry, for he was dumb. He could not follow Christ as the blind men had done, for he had not control of himself; so he must be brought by others. Yet for him, as well as for them, there is full salvation, as soon as he comes into the presence of the Lord of life. No wonder the multitudes marvelled, and said, "It was never so seen in Israel"! and no wonder that the Pharisees, unable in any other way to evade the force of such a succession of manifest signs of the kingdom of heaven, should be driven to the contradictory and blasphemous suggestion, "He casteth out devils through the prince of the devils" (ver. 34).

The series is now complete; and, long as it has been, we could not dispense with a single case. There has been no repetition. Each case reported in detail has had its own special and peculiar value: the leper, the centurion's servant, the mother-in-law of Peter, the dealings with the impulsive scribe and the hesitating disciple, the stilling of the storm and mastery of the unseen legions of evil, the forgiving of sin, and welcoming of repentant sinners, the healing of the chronic invalid by the way, the raising of the dead damsel, and the restoring of sight to the blind and speech to the dumb, — all different, all most precious, all needed to bring out some aspect of the truth concerning Jesus as the Saviour of mankind, all together giving us a most comprehensive presentation of the signs of the kingdom of heaven. And now that the nature of His work has been so fully set forth in its two great departments of teaching and of healing, the rest is left unrecorded, except in the general statement that "Jesus went about all the cities and villages, teaching in their synagogues, and preaching the gospel of the kingdom, and healing every sickness and every disease among the people" (ver. 35).

FOOTNOTE

[8] The order is different in the second and third Gospels; but here only is the order of events noted: "And He saith unto them, Why are ye fearful, O ye of little faith? *Then* He arose."

IX
THE KING'S AMBASSADORS

Matt. ix. 36-x. 42.

I.—The Mission (ix. 36-x. 5)

SO far the King Himself has done all the work of the kingdom. But it has grown upon Him, so that He can no longer do it without assistance; He must therefore provide Himself with deputies. His doing so will be the first step in the organisation of His world-wide kingdom. He reveals, however, no plan laid down to meet all possible emergencies. It is enough to provide for necessities as they develop themselves. He constructs no mechanism beforehand into the different parts of which life may be afterwards guided or forced; His only care is about the life, knowing well that if only this be full and strong, the appropriate organisation will be ready when it is needed.

In conformity with this principle He does not make His arrangements, necessary as they manifestly are, without first providing that they shall not be mechanical but vital, that they shall originate, not as a contrivance of mind but as an outflow of soul. First, we are informed by the Evangelist that the soul of the Master Himself was stirred with compassion as He looked upon the multitude, and thought how much they needed in the way of shepherding, and how little it was possible for them to have. It was no matter of planning for the extension of His kingdom; it was a great yearning over the sheep that were scattered, and torn (ver. 36, Gk. of oldest MSS.), and lost (x. 6). But it is not enough that the Master's heart should be touched: the disciples also must be moved. So He turns their thoughts in the same direction, urging them to observe how plenteous the harvest, how few the labourers; and therefore to pray that the lack may be speedily supplied. He sets them thinking and praying about it—the only way to lay foundations for that which shall be true and lasting. Let it be observed further, that the two emblems He uses present most strikingly the great motives to missionary work: compassion for the lost, and zeal for the Divine glory. "Sheep having no shepherd,"—this appeals to our human sympathies; the Lord of the harvest deprived of His harvest for want of labourers to gather it in,—this appeals to our love and loyalty to God.

The result of their thought and prayer presently appears; for we read in the next sentence of the setting apart of the twelve disciples to the work. It does not follow, because the narrative is continuous, that the events recorded were; it is probable that an interval elapsed which would be largely spent in prayer according to the word of the Master.

This is the first mention of the Twelve in this Gospel; but it is evident that the number had been already made up, for they are spoken of as "His twelve disciples." It would appear from the second and third Gospels that, immediately before the delivery of the Sermon on the Mount, the Twelve were chosen from the whole number of disciples to be constantly with Him, as witnesses of His works and learners of His doctrine. By this time they had been so far instructed and trained by their companionship with Christ, that they could be safely entrusted with a mission by themselves; accordingly He for the first time gives them power to do deeds of mercy of the same sort as those which He Himself had been doing, as signs of the kingdom of heaven.

As the apostles have not been mentioned before, their names are appropriately given here. The number "twelve" was no doubt significant, as suggestive of the twelve tribes of Israel; but there was plainly no attempt to have the tribes represented separately. It would seem as if all were Galileans, except one, and that one was Judas Iscariot (*i.e.*, the man of Kerioth, supposed to be a town in Judæa). The reason of this almost exclusive choice of Galileans is in all probability to be found in the simple fact that there were none other available. There had been those, in the course of His Judæan ministry, who had after a certain fashion believed on Him; but there was not one of them whom He could trust with such work as this (John ii. 23-5). It may be thought, indeed, that surely there might have been some better representative—at least, than Judas proved himself to be—of the southern tribes; but why should we think so? We have no reason to suppose that Judas was a traitor at heart when he was chosen. Perhaps there was in him at that time the making of as grand an apostle as the best of them. It was not long, indeed, before the demon in him began to betray itself to the searching glance of the Master (John vi. 70); but had he only, in the power of the Master he followed, cast that demon out of his own heart, as possibly enough he may have helped in this very mission to cast demons out of others, all would have been well. The subsequent fall of the traitor does not by any means show that Christ now made a mistaken choice; it only shows that the highest privileges and opportunities may, by the tolerance of sin in the heart, be not only all in vain, but may lead to a condemnation and ruin more terrible by far than would have been possible without them.

Not only was the apostolate Galilean,—it was plebeian, and that without a solitary exception. It seems to include not a single person of recognised rank or position. Again, we believe that this is to be accounted for by the simple fact that there were none of these available. We cannot suppose that if there had been a disciple like Paul in the ranks, the Master would have hesitated to give him a place in the sacred college; but, seeing there was none, He would not go out of His way to secure a representative of the learned or the great. Had Nicodemus been bold enough to come out decidedly on the Lord's side, or had Joseph of Arimathæa developed earlier that splendid courage which he showed when the Master's work on earth was done, we can scarcely doubt that their names might have been included in the roll. But there is no such name; and now, as we look back, was it not better so? Otherwise there could not have been such a wonderful illustration of the great fact that "God hath chosen the weak things of the world to confound the things which are mighty"; there could not otherwise have been the same invincible evidence that the work these men did was not the work of men, but was indeed and in truth the doing of God.

Though they were all from the lower ranks of life, they were characterised by great varieties of gifts and dispositions. Some of them, indeed, are scarcely known to us at all. It may be that they were more or less ordinary men who made no special mark; but it would be rash to set this down as certain, or even as probable, seeing that our records of the time are so scanty, and are manifestly constructed with the idea, not of giving to every man his due—as would be the poor ideal of a mere writer of history—but of making nothing of the men, and everything of the cause and of the Master in Whose great Personality theirs was merged. But those of them who do appear in the records are men of such varied dispositions and powers that the Twelve might after all have been a fair miniature of the Church at large. Some of the selections seem very strange. We have already referred to Judas the traitor. But there were those among them who must have been far less likely men than he. There were two in particular, the choice of whom seemed to violate all dictates of wisdom and prudence. These were Matthew the publican and Simon the Cananæan or Zealot. To have a publican, hated as the whole class was, among the apostles, was apparently to invite the hostility and contempt of the great majority of the nation, and especially of those who were strongly national in feeling. On the other hand, to invite one who was known as a Zealot, a radical and revolutionist in politics, a man who had identified himself with the wildest schemes for the overthrow of the Government, was to provoke the opposition of all the law-abiding and peace-loving people of the time. Yet how could the heavenly King have more effectually shown that His kingdom was not of this world, that the petty party spirit of the day had no place in it whatever, that it mattered not what a man had been, if now he was renewed in the spirit of his mind, and consecrated in heart and soul and life to do the will of God and serve his Master Christ?[9]

So it has come to pass that, though these twelve men had nothing at all to recommend them to the favour of the world, and though there was very much from every worldly point of view to create the strongest prejudices against them and to militate against their influence, yet they have, by the grace of their Divine Master, so triumphed over all, that when we think of them now, it is not as fishermen, nor as publican or Zealot—even the traitor has simply dropped out of sight—we see before us only "the glorious company of the apostles"!

II.—The Commission (x. 5-42)

"These twelve Jesus sent forth" (in pairs, as we learn elsewhere, and as is indicated here, perhaps, by the grouping in the list), "and charged them." This leads us to look at their commission. It begins with a limitation, which, however, was only to be temporary. The time had not yet come for the opening of the door to the Gentiles. Besides this, we must remember that the Saviour's heart was yearning over His own people. This appears in the tender way He speaks of them as "the lost sheep of the house of Israel." Moreover, the apostles were by no means ready, with all their national prejudices still rank in them, to be entrusted with so delicate and difficult a duty as getting into communication with an alien race. Accordingly their field is strictly limited to their own countrymen.

There seems to have been a limitation also in their message. They had themselves been to some extent instructed in regard to the nature of the kingdom, its blessedness, its righteousness, its leading principles and features; but, though they may have begun to get some glimpse of the truth in regard to these great matters, they certainly had not yet made it their own; accordingly they are given, as the substance of their preaching, only the simple announcement, with which the Baptist had begun his ministry, and with which Christ also commenced His: "The kingdom of heaven is at hand." Though there seems to have been a limitation on the teaching side, there was none on the side of healing, for their Lord empowers them to do the very same things for the relief of their suffering fellow-countrymen as they had seen Himself doing. We have already seen how much teaching there was in these signs of the kingdom; and we can well believe that it was far better, considering the stage of advancement the apostles had reached, that reliance should be placed on the light such deeds of mercy would necessarily throw on the nature of the kingdom, than on any exposition which, apart from their Master, they could at that time have been able to give. Above all it is to be clear that the privileges of the kingdom are free to all; its blessings are to be dispensed without money and without price: "Freely ye have received, freely give."

How, then, were they to be supported? About this they were to give themselves no concern. They were now to put in practice the great command, "Seek ye first the kingdom of God, and His righteousness," relying on the promise, "all these things shall be added unto you." But in no miraculous way are they to look for the provision of their wants. They are to be maintained by those among whom and for whom they labour. This was to be no burden, but a privilege, reserved for those who were found "worthy" (ver. 11). Nor was it to be divided among as many as possible. They were to stay on with the same person who first received them, as the one whom the Master had chosen for the honour; while, if any refused to recognise it as a privilege, there was to be no weak solicitation, but a dignified withdrawal. The regulations throughout are manifestly intended to keep most vividly before their minds that they went not in their own names, nor on their own strength, nor at their own charges, — that they were ambassadors of a King, clothed with His authority, armed with His power, vested with His rights; so that there is a manifest appropriateness in the solemn words with which this part of the commission closes: "Verily I say unto you, It shall be more tolerable for the land of Sodom and Gomorrha in the day of judgment, than for that city" which rejects you (ver. 15).

The part of the charge which follows, and which the limitation of our plan will not allow us to illustrate point by point, bears not so much on the work more immediately before them as on the whole work of their apostolate. It may have been spoken, as some suppose, later on, and only put here as germane to the occasion; for, as we have seen, the arrangement of this gospel is not chronological, but is largely topical. Still there seems no very strong reason for supposing that the entire discourse was not spoken at this very time; for why should not the apostles in the very beginning of their way have some idea of what it would cost them to accept the work to which they were now called?

The leading thoughts are these: They must expect to be exposed to trial and suffering in the prosecution of their mission. The Master Himself was sorely tried, and the servant must not expect exemption. He is not indeed to court trials, or to submit to persecutions which are not inevitable: "When they persecute you in this city, flee ye into another." On the other hand, when the path of duty lies evidently through trial or danger, he must not shirk it, but face it boldly; and in all emergencies he is to place implicit confidence in Him Whose servant he is: "When they deliver you up, be not anxious how or what ye shall speak: for it shall be given you in that hour what ye shall speak" (R.V.). "The very hairs of your head are all numbered. Fear ye not, therefore." There is no way of avoiding the cross; and they would be quite unworthy of their Master should they seek to avoid it. Yet there is a great reward for those who bravely take it up and patiently bear it to the end. It is the way to higher honour (ver. 32), and to the only life that is worthy of the name (ver. 39); while to turn away from it is to choose a path which leads to shame (ver. 33) and death (ver. 39).

The passage, taken up, as so much of it has been, with the anticipations of ill-treatment which the apostles will receive in setting out as sheep in the midst of wolves, closes most appropriately and beautifully with a series of blessings on those who will treat them well, ending with the encouraging assurance that even a cup of cold water given to a thirsty disciple will not be forgotten of God.

The lessons on Christian work with which this passage abounds are so numerous that it would be vain to attempt to unfold them. It is not merely a record of facts; it is an embodiment of great principles which are to govern the disciples of Christ in their service to the end of the world. If only the Church as a whole were to think and pray as Christ taught His disciples to think and pray before this great event; and then if the labourers whom God has sent, or would, in answer to the prayers of the Church, immediately send, into His harvest were to act—not necessarily according to the letter, but in every part according to the spirit of these instructions,—using their own faculties with all the wisdom of the serpent, and trusting to Divine grace and power with all the simplicity of the dove—it would not be long before all the scattered sheep were gathered into the fold, all the ripe sheaves garnered for the Lord of the harvest!

FOOTNOTE

[9] It is interesting to notice that, though Matthew here calls himself Matthew the publican, no one else does. To others the publican is lost in the apostle—it is only himself who will not forget the hole of the pit whence he was digged.

X
THE SHADOW OF THE CROSS

Matt. xi., xii.

I.—Discouragements (xi)

HITHERTO almost everything has been hopeful and encouraging in our Evangelist's record of the Saviour's ministry. It began like daybreak on the shores of the sea of Galilee. Great multitudes followed Him wherever He went; and those whom He called to be with Him cheerfully responded to the summons. When He preached the Gospel of the kingdom, the people were astonished at His doctrine, and recognised that He "taught them as one having authority, and not as the scribes." His works of healing were warmly welcomed, and to a large extent appreciated by the people generally, though already it was apparent that those whose selfish interests were touched by the progress of the truth were ready to cavil and complain. Notwithstanding this, the work has grown upon Him so, that He has found it necessary to arm His twelve disciples with powers like His own, and send them forth as heralds of His kingdom through the land.

But the path of the King is not to be a triumphal progress. It is to be a *via dolorosa*, leading to a cross and a grave. Many prophecies had been already fulfilled, as our Evangelist has shown again and again; but there are others of a different sort which can as little fail of their fulfilment,—like that which speaks of the Messiah as "despised and rejected of men, a man of sorrows, and acquainted with grief." It is not at all to be wondered at, then, that the Evangelist should now give his readers some idea of the discouragements which met the King in the setting up of His kingdom on the earth. The first of these which he mentions comes from a quarter from which least of all it might have been expected.

1. *John in doubt* (vv. 1-15)

It was, indeed, not at all unnatural that John should be in doubt. Think of his character: stern, uncompromising, severe, and bold to rashness. Think of his circumstances: languishing in prison for the truth's sake, without any prospect of rescue;—after all, was Jesus King, or Herod? Remember, too, in what terms he had predicted the coming One: "Now also the axe is laid unto the root of the trees;" ... "He that cometh after me is mightier than I;" ... "Whose fan is in His hand, and He will thoroughly purge His floor, and gather His wheat into the garner; but He will burn up the chaff with unquenchable fire." Did not this betoken a work which would be swift, severe, thorough,—very different from anything of which he could hear in his prison cell? The coming of the kingdom was too gentle and too slow for the stern, impatient Baptist. Accordingly, "offended" (see ver. 6, R.V.: "finding occasion of stumbling") in his Master, he sends this message, in the hope possibly that it may constrain Him to avow Himself and to bring matters to a crisis: "Art thou He that should come, or do we look for another?"

Though it was natural enough that John should doubt, it was none the less trying to Jesus. The disciples were only children yet. Not one of them could enter into full sympathy with Him. John, the forerunner, was the one strong man, on whom He had reason thoroughly to rely, who had been tried again and again, and always found brave and true. Yet it is he who sends the doubting message. What a shock it must have been to the sensitive heart, what a trial to the faith, of the Man Christ Jesus!

The message must have been a very disturbing and disconcerting one, and fitted, if widely known, to neutralise to a large degree in the minds of the people the witness John had borne to Jesus. It is the last thing the Evangelist would have thought of mentioning, if he had been actuated in the selection of his material by motives of policy; and the fact that this incident is published in two of the Gospels is a striking illustration of what is manifest throughout—the perfect simplicity and candour of the sacred historians.

Have we not reason to be most thankful that they did record it? To the truly thoughtful mind it is no weakening of the testimony of John; while it is full of comfort for the honest doubter, giving him the assurance that even when the most serious questions trouble him—even though the very foundations of his faith seem to be shaken—"there hath no temptation taken" him "but such as is common to man," such as even a brave and true soul like John had to face; full of encouragement also to do just as he did,— go straight to the Master Himself with the doubts, and let Him deal with them—wisely, faithfully, tenderly—as He does here.

How, then, does He deal with them? By a miracle, opening the prison doors, and so making it perfectly plain to him that not Herod, but Jesus, is King? By a sudden outburst of vengeance, destroying hosts of unrepentant sinners and alarming all the country side, and so satisfying the sternest thoughts of the Baptist in his cell? Not at all. He deals with them as He intends to deal with doubters always: points him quietly to the many tokens of His Divine mission—not in the way of judgment wrought on sinners, nor of any grand demonstration which will astonish the nation, but in the quiet progress of His helpful, healing, comforting work: "Go, and show John again those things which ye do hear and see: the blind receive their sight, and the lame walk, the lepers are cleansed, and the deaf hear, the dead are raised up, and the poor have the gospel preached to them." Then He encourages him to hold fast the beginning of his confidence firm unto the end, by adding the significant words, "Blessed is he, whosoever shall find none occasion of stumbling in Me" (R.V.). It was far better for John himself that he should be allowed to rally, than that anything special should be done to meet his doubts. He did rally; he did secure the blessing his Master set before him; he was satisfied without any open demonstration, satisfied to wait on and suffer in faith and patience, till at last he sealed the testimony of his magnificent life by a martyr's death.

Those are in some respects to be envied who in childlike simplicity believe without doubt or question; but there is a special blessing for those who by the very force of their nature must wrestle with doubt, yet in the trying hour find no occasion of stumbling in Him. They come out of the conflict more than conquerors through Him that loved them.

The answer sent to John was kind; but there was no flattery in it—not even a word of commendation of his heroic endurance. The Master knew the strength of His disciple, and He dealt with him accordingly. But as soon as the messengers are gone He tells the people what He thinks of him. He in effect deprecates the thought of judging John by a message sent in an hour of weakness and despondency. "Do not imagine for a moment," He seems to say, "that the man you went out into the wilderness to see is feeble as a reed, or soft as a courtier. He is all, and more than all, you took him to be. He is a prophet indeed; and much more, for he is a herald of the heavenly King. Among them that are born of woman there hath not risen a greater than John the Baptist; and though he has not the advantages of even the little ones in the kingdom of heaven, inasmuch as he belongs to the old dispensation, yet, as herald of the new, he occupies a peculiarly honoured place—he stands between the old and the new; for all the prophets and the law prophesied until John; while from the days of John the Baptist until now the kingdom of heaven is preached, and men are pressing into it. He is, in fact, if only you had ears to hear, if only your minds were open to read the Scriptures according to the spirit of them, that very Elijah whose coming your prophet has taught you to expect" (vv. 7-14).

So far we have followed what seems to be the drift of our Saviour's words in regard to John; but there is more than this in them. He is contrasting the feebleness and fickleness of the multitude with the strength and stability of John. There is before His mind, throughout, the thought of the transcendent importance of the events of the time as compared with the thoughtlessness of the people of the time. The question "What went ye out for to see?" was intended not merely to bring into relief the greatness of John, but to search their hearts. The important events of the time had circled first around John the Baptist, then around Himself. The people had not the least idea of the transcendent greatness of John and still less of the infinite greatness of Him to Whom he had borne witness. Jesus did not wish as yet fully to assert His own claims, yet He desired to bring the inconsiderate multitudes to some conception of the things which their eyes saw, to rebuke and, if possible, to correct their thoughtlessness and indifference.

It is to the presence of this underlying thought that some forms of expression are due which otherwise are difficult to understand. This applies in particular to ver. 12, which has been a terrible stumbling-block to expositors. So far as the position of John was concerned, it was enough to say that from his time the kingdom of God was preached (the form found in St. Luke); but in view of the levity and thoughtlessness of the multitudes it is put in such a way as to suggest that it is not your thoughtless, fickle, reed-hunting, sight-seeing people, that get the kingdom, but eager, earnest, "violent" men. The same thought accounts for the manner in which the paragraph closes, indicating that that which had been spoken ought to lead to more serious thought, more intelligent appreciation both of the herald and of the kingdom which in the spirit and power of the Great Elijah he has heralded: *"He that hath ears to hear, let him hear."*

But would they hear? Alas! no; and this accordingly must be put down as a second and most serious discouragement.

2. *The unreasonableness of the people* (vv. 16-19).

Unable to recognise the true significance of the events of the time, with deaf ears to the heavenly message which first the herald and then the King had brought them, they fastened their attention on that which was merely incidental: the asceticism of John, the social friendliness of Jesus. Of the first they complained, because it was not like the second; of the second they complained, because it was not like the first. Any excuse for a complaint; no ear to hear nor soul to appreciate the message of either. To what can He liken them? To a set of children, sitting in the market-place indeed, but with no thought of business in their heads: they are there only to amuse themselves; and even in their games they are as unreasonable as they can be. One set proposes to play a wedding, and the rest say, "No, we want a funeral"; then, when the others take it up and start the game of funeral, they change their tune, and say, "No, we prefer a wedding." Nothing will please those who have no intention to be satisfied. Caring nothing for the kingdom which John heralded, the multitude only noticed the peculiarity of his garb, and the stern solitariness of his life, and said he must be a lunatic. When the King Himself comes with no such peculiarity, but mingling on familiar and friendly terms with the people, still caring nothing for the kingdom which He preached, they find fault with Him for the very qualities the absence of which they deprecated in John. If they had acted, not as foolish children, but as wise men, they would have recognised that both were right, inasmuch as each was true to himself and to the position he filled. It was right and fitting that the last of the old prophets should be rugged and stern and solitary, even as the great Elijah, in whose spirit and power he came. It was no less right and fit that the Saviour-King of men should set out on new lines and introduce the new dispensation in a manner suited to its distinctive features of freedom and familiar friendliness. Thus, in the one case, and in the other, "wisdom is justified of her children."

3. *The Unbelief of the Cities* (vv. 20-24).

Though the multitudes which had flocked to hear John might be fickle and thoughtless, surely better things might be expected of those favoured towns by the lake of Galilee, where the signs of the kingdom had been so abundantly exhibited and the truth of the kingdom so earnestly and frequently preached. But no: even they "repented not." They would bring their sick in crowds to get them healed; but they hid as it were their faces from Him. They had not indeed treated Him as the people of Nazareth had done; for Nazareth had cast Him out, and Capernaum had taken Him in. Yet His lamentation is not over Nazareth, but over Capernaum. We can readily see why. What He suffered at Nazareth was a personal indignity. He was so summarily ejected that He had not time or opportunity to set before them the signs of the kingdom. But in Capernaum the time and opportunity had been ample. The truth had been fully told; the signs had been fully wrought. The people had seemed to listen; and all betokened a happy issue. We can imagine the Saviour waiting and hoping and longing (for again, let it be remembered that He was very man, and that this experience discouraged Him as it would discourage any of us), and then tasting all the bitterness of hope deferred, ending in crushing disappointment.

For a long time He continues silent, bearing the heavy burden in His heart, till the fountain of grief could be pent up no longer: "Then began He to upbraid the cities wherein most of His mighty works were done, because they repented not." The words He speaks are very awful; but it is in the last resort. Love and mercy have been His theme from day to day; and it is only because these are obstinately rejected that wrath and judgment must now find a voice. It is not a wrathful voice: there are tears in it. What must it have cost Him to speak these awful words about Capernaum's impending doom! To think that those who were nearest His heart of all, to whom He devoted the freshness of His first days of service, the dew of His youth, so to speak—that they would have none of Him, but preferred to remain in sin with all the woe it necessarily entailed,—oh! it must have been torture to that loving heart. And we may be sure there was no less pathos in this last appeal to Bethsaida, Chorazin and Capernaum, than there was in the later lamentation over the city of the South.

How does the Saviour bear Himself under these repeated discouragements? The passage which follows will show (vv. 25-30). Some have found a difficulty in the word "answered," because there appears no question with which it is connected. But did not these discouragements require an answer? As we read, first of the doubts of John, then of the thoughtlessness of the multitudes, and then of the impenitence of the favoured cities by the lake, is there not a question in our hearts, becoming more and more urgent as each new discouragement appears, What will He say to this? What can He answer? Thus our minds are well prepared for that which immediately follows: "At that time Jesus answered and said, I thank Thee, O Father." Is it to be a thanksgiving, then, after such a series of disappointments and vexations? Even so. As He has looked to the cities of the plain, His voice has been a wail; now that He looks up to His Father, wailing ceases, and thanksgiving takes its place. So will it always be to faith which is genuine and deep enough. It is only when we look below and around that we are depressed. When we look up we are strong. "I will lift up mine eyes unto the hills, from whence cometh my help. My help cometh from the Lord Who made heaven and earth." Was it the remembrance of this passage at the time of need which suggested the form of His thanksgiving: "I thank Thee, Father, *Lord of heaven and earth*"?

Surely we have here the living original of that grand apostolic word, "In everything give thanks"; for if "at that season" (R.V.) the Saviour of men found occasion for thanksgiving, we may well believe that at any season, however dark, we may find something to stir our hearts to gratitude; and the very exercise of thanksgiving will bring a deep spiritual joy to set against the bitterest sorrow, even as it was with our Lord, Who, as St. Luke informs us, "rejoiced in spirit" as He lifted up His soul in thanks to God that day.

What, then, does He find to be thankful for? First, He discovers a cause for gratitude in the very limitation which occasions His sorest disappointments: "I thank Thee, ... because Thou hast hid these things from the wise and prudent, and hast revealed them unto babes." There is of course the cheering thought that amid the general unbelief and rejection there are some childlike souls who have welcomed the truth. Some are fain to make this the sole cause of thankfulness, as if He meant to say, "I thank Thee, that *though* Thou hast hid these things from the wise and prudent, Thou hast revealed them unto babes." But there is no authority for introducing this little word. The Saviour gives thanks, not merely in spite of this hiding, but because of it. It is true, indeed, that He uses the language of resignation, "Even so, Father: for so it seemed good in Thy sight," which makes it evident that the fact that so many of the wise and intelligent rejected His gospel presented a real difficulty to His mind, as it has done to earnest souls in all ages. But while it was no doubt enough for Him to feel sure that it was right in the sight of God, we are not without indication in what follows, that His faith not only led to resignation, but enabled Him to see for Himself that it was wisely ordered. For what is the great object of the Gospel? Is it not to dethrone self and enthrone God in the hearts of men? It is clear, then, that, if it had in any way appealed to pride and self-sufficiency, it would have defeated its own end. Suppose the revealing of things had been to the wise and prudent as such, what would have been the result? The kingdom of heaven would have become a mere scholarship prize. And, however good a thing scholarship may be, and however important that it be encouraged, this is not the work of the Christ of God. His Gospel is for all; so it is addressed not to the great in intellect, which would confine it to the few, but to the lowly in heart, which brings it within reach of all,—for the very wisest and greatest in intellect may be, and ought to be, meek and lowly in heart.

Indeed, is it not to the meek and lowly heart that even the truths of science are disclosed? A man who approaches nature with a preconceived theory, about which his mind is already made up, is sure to miss the mark. To enter into its secrets, prejudices and prepossessions must be laid aside, and things observed with open mind and simple receptiveness. In this connection one sees the special appropriateness of the reference to "the Lord of heaven and earth." The principle is one which is not restricted in its range: it runs all through nature. Still more appropriate is the appeal to the fatherhood of God. It is not for the Father to be partial to his clever children, and leave the less favoured ones to shift for themselves. To Him they are all "babes"; and to them He must be not examiner, nor prize-giver, but above all *Father*, if they would understand and feel His love. So the more one thinks of it, the more in every point of view does it seem good and necessary that these things should not be made known to the "wise and understanding" (R.V.) as such, but should be revealed to "babes," to those of childlike spirit. It is well. The wisest and most learned may join in the thanksgiving, for it is far better for them to take their places with the rest, as many happily do, and receive the same loving welcome; and those of us who cannot call ourselves wise and learned should surely be most devoutly thankful that, however impossible it may be to compete with these highly favoured ones in obtaining the prizes of earth, we are at no disadvantage in striving for "the prize of the high calling of God in Christ Jesus."

The next great thought which comes to the relief of the Saviour in His discouragement is that, while there are barriers in the heart of man, there is no barrier in the heart of God, no limit whatever to the outpouring of Divine love and grace: "All things are delivered unto Me of My Father." Even at the time when it is borne in upon Him that men will have none of Him, He exults in the thought that He has everything for them. If only they could see it! If only they knew the boundless treasure there was for them in God! If only they knew that God had put all within their reach by sending them His Son! But the Son is unknown except to the Father, Who sent Him; and the Father is unknown except to the Son, Who has come to reveal Him. But He *has* come to reveal Him; and with the revealing the way will be opened for all good things to follow. As He thinks of it His heart yearns over the orphaned children of men, and He exults in the thought that He has for them the revelation of the Father's heart and home, with enough and to spare for all His children (ver. 27).

Then follows such an outpouring of heart as there never has been before. He knows that only in the Father can the children of men find rest, and so He says "Come unto Me," and I will lead you to the Father, Who alone knows Me, as I alone know Him; and you, finding Him in Me, shall know Him too, and your hearts shall be at rest.

It is beautiful and most touching to observe how our Lord is, as it were, compelled to make His appeal more personal than He has ever done before. We look in vain through His previous utterances as reported in this Gospel for such reduplication of the personal pronouns as there is here. What is the reason of it? We can see it when we read between the lines. Hitherto His great subject has been the kingdom of heaven. This kingdom He has been preaching through all the country-side, setting forth its purity and blessedness, unfolding its unspeakable riches, and entreating all to enter in by the strait gate, which He has thrown open to receive them. But they will not enter. These things, in spite of all He can say, are hid from them. Well He knows what is the difficulty: it is the hardness of their hearts. If He could only get at these hearts! How can He do it? It can only be by the opening out of all His heart to them; so He will make His pleading a personal entreaty now. Hence the peculiarly winning form His invitation now assumes. It is no longer "Enter ye in at the strait gate"; it is not even, "I have come to call sinners to repentance"; it is the cry of a loving, yearning heart, "Come unto Me." And how tenderly He thinks of them!—no more upbraiding now, no more reproof. He will try to reach the conscience through the heart, and so He does not even think of them as sinners now—He forgets everything but their weariness and woe: "Come unto Me, all ye that labour and are heavy laden, and I will rest you."[10]

We shall not, however, dwell on the precious words with which this chapter ends. They are as rich and suggestive as they are simple and heart-thrilling; but for this very reason we must not attempt to do more than place them in their setting, which is often missed, for the words themselves have attracted so much attention, and so filled the minds and hearts of those who have looked at them that too little has been made of their surroundings. Observe only how nobly the Son of man comes out of this ordeal of disappointment and discouragement. See the grandeur of His faith. "At that season," when we should expect to see Him in the depths, He rises to the very height of His dignity and majesty. This passage above all others has been cited as an example of the self-assertion of Jesus—say rather His sublime consciousness of divine dignity, prerogative and power; yet so entirely natural and unassuming is it all, that in the very same breath He can say, without conveying to the most thoughtful mind the least feeling of incongruity: "I am meek and lowly in heart." Then, behold what manner of love! These chilling blasts of doubt, indifference, and unbelief, only fan it into a warmer, steadier flame. The sweetest of all His invitations, the most touching of all His appeals, comes from a heart which has just been wounded in its tenderest place, and has tasted the bitterness of cruel disappointment. Who can measure the patient love which "at that season" finds such utterance?

II.—The Contradiction of Sinners (xii.)

The darkness deepens on the Saviour's path. He has now to encounter direct antagonism. There have been, indeed, signs of opposition before. When the man sick of the palsy was forgiven, "certain of the scribes said within themselves, This man blasphemeth" (ix. 3); but it was only "within themselves," they did not venture to speak out. Again, after the feast in the house of Levi, the Pharisees complained, but not to Christ Himself; "they said unto His disciples, Why eateth your Master with publicans and sinners?" (ix. 11). And when the dumb demoniac was cured, the Pharisees muttered, "He casteth out devils through the prince of the devils" (ix. 34), but did not yet say it to His face. But now they are emboldened to attack Him directly. Possibly they saw as clearly as any the discouraging aspect of affairs for the new kingdom. They had, in all probability, heard of the doubts of John, had taken note of the fault-findings of the people (if, indeed, these had not been first suggested by themselves), had observed that even "the cities where most of His mighty works were done repented not" (xi. 20); and having therefore less occasion to fear consequences, they might think it safe to attack one who stood for a rapidly failing cause.

1. Observe, first, the spirit in which our Lord meets the repeated attacks of which the record is given in this chapter. There are four in close succession. The first is the charge of Sabbath-breaking made against the disciples, because they rubbed a few ears of corn in their hands as they passed through the fields on the Sabbath day; and following it, the entangling question put to the Master in the synagogue. Then there is the accusation founded on the healing of the blind and dumb demoniac: "This man doth not cast out devils, but by Beelzebub the prince of the devils" (ver. 24). The third attack is the hypocritical application, "Master, we would see a sign from Thee" (ver. 38), the word "Master" being evidently used in mockery, and the request for "a sign" a scornful way of suggesting that all the signs He was giving were worth nothing. These three attacks were made by the Pharisees, and were most irritating and vexatious, each in its own way. The first was annoying on account of its pettiness, the second because of its bitter malice, while the third was a studied insult; and yet, galling as these repeated attacks must have been, we may well suppose that the keenest wound of all to the gentle spirit of the Son of man would be the last, inflicted by the members of His own family, who seemed at this time as unsympathetic and unbelieving as the Pharisees themselves; for the untimely interruption recorded at the close of the chapter was intended, as we learn from the account in the second gospel, to put Him under restraint as a madman. This last interruption, in which even His mother joined, must have been gall and wormwood to that tender heart.

Now "consider Him that endured such contradiction of sinners against Himself" (Heb. xii. 3). How does He bear Himself through these storms of calumny and insult? He bears Himself so that out of this dark chapter of His history there comes to us one of the loveliest portraits of Him to be found anywhere. It had been sketched by one of the old masters as an ideal portrait, and is now at last matched in real life: "Behold My servant, Whom I have chosen; My Beloved, in Whom My soul is well pleased: I will put My spirit upon Him, and He shall show judgment to the Gentiles. He shall not strive, nor cry; neither shall any man hear His voice in the streets. A bruised reed shall He not break, and smoking flax shall He not quench, till He send forth judgment unto victory. And in His name shall the Gentiles trust" (vv. 18-21). What gentleness and tenderness, yet what strength and majesty!— for, though "He strives not," nor lifts up His voice in angry altercation, while He will not break the bruised reed, nor quench the smoking flax, He will nevertheless declare judgment, and secure victory, and make His name such a power in the earth, that the Gentiles shall hope in Him and the world go after Him. We can fancy the glow on the Evangelist's face as he pauses in the midst of the sad record of these cruel assaults, to look at, and show to us, that lovely portrait of the Son of man. And is it not all the lovelier that it shines out from such a background? Does it not give new significance to the tender words which linger in our ears from the chapter of discouragement before: "Learn of Me; for I am meek and lowly in heart: and ye shall find rest unto your souls"?

2. It would have been a great thing if our Lord had only borne in dignified silence these repeated provocations; but He is too good and kind to leave these misguided people to their own devices without an effort to enlighten their dark minds and arouse their sleeping consciences. How patiently He reasons with them! We may glance at each attack in succession as an illustration of this.

On the charge of Sabbath-breaking He endeavours to set them right by citing appropriate scriptures (vv. 3, 4); appealing to the law itself (ver. 5); furnishing them with a great principle laid down by one of the prophets, the key of the whole position (ver. 7); and concludes by an illustrative act, accompanied by a simple and telling argument, which appeals to the universal conscience and heart (vv. 9-13). Again, how patiently He answers the malicious charge of collusion with Satan, showing them in the clearest manner, and with amazing power, how far they are astray, and what a dangerous path they are treading (vv. 25-37). So, too, in meeting the third attack: though He cannot but sternly rebuke the hypocritical application for "a sign," He yet does it in such a way as to prepare for them in due time, when perhaps they may be ready to appreciate it, a new sign—His death and resurrection—overcoming the difficulty arising from the fact that He could not yet speak of it in plain terms (for it was at a later period than this that He began to speak plainly of it even to His disciples) by veiling it under the figure of "the sign of the prophet Jonas": a way of putting it which had the advantage of being memorable, and at the same time enigmatical enough to veil its meaning till the event should lighten it all up, and bring out its deep suggestiveness; and while thus preparing them for the new sign when it should come, He warns them against that evil state of mind and heart which threatened to render even it of no avail (vv. 38-45). And then, with what marvellous readiness does He use the painful interruption with which the chapter ends for the teaching of truth of the highest and purest and tenderest quality! What patience, what long-suffering, what meekness of wisdom, what faithfulness, what strength and tenderness! Every line of the likeness drawn by the inspired hand of the old master is more than justified (vv. 46-50).

3. Observe, further, that in all His dealings with His bitterest foes He never in the least degree lowers His dignity, but rather asserts it in the boldest and strongest terms. It may be questioned, indeed, if there is any chapter in all the history in which this is more marked. This, again, may be illustrated from all the four occasions.

In the argument on the Sabbath question hear Him as He draws Himself up, in presence of His accusers, and says: "In this place is One greater than the temple" (ver. 6); and again: "The Son of man is Lord even of the Sabbath day" (ver. 8). Must there not have been something heavenly-majestic in His look and bearing when words like these were allowed to pass unchallenged by such men? This consciousness of dignity appears no less in the argument by which the second charge is met. In proof of this we may point to verses 28 and 30; and the same impression is produced by the solemnly repeated "I say unto you" (vv. 31, 36), in each case introducing one of those declarations of judgment to which reference is made in the passage quoted from the prophet (vv. 18, 20). Quite as conspicuous is the same feature in the third remonstrance, in which He asserts His superiority to the great ones of the old covenant in language which acquires, from the connection in which it occurs, a strength far beyond the mere terms employed: "Behold, a greater than Jonas, ... behold, a greater than Solomon, is here" (vv. 41, 42). And in the last of the four sad encounters the same lofty consciousness of peerless dignity is manifest. Son of Mary is He? brother of James and Joses? See Him lift His eyes to heaven, and speak of *"My* Father," and look down the ages, and out to the uttermost bounds of earth, and say, "Whosoever shall do the will of My Father which is in heaven, the same is My brother, and sister, and mother" (ver. 50).

4. We have seen how kindly and patiently the Saviour deals with these cavillers, so as to give them every opportunity of seeing their folly and wickedness and the beauty and excellence of the truth they are resisting. But He does much more than this. He speaks not only so as to meet their objections, and give them the opportunity of being set right, but so as to provide instruction, warning and encouragement for all succeeding ages. To show in any satisfactory way how this is done would require separate treatment for each of the four instances; but it may be possible in a very brief way to suggest it.

The first attack gave Him the opportunity of speaking on the Sabbath law. As we have seen, He began to treat the subject from the strictly Jewish standpoint, using the example of David and the ritual of the Temple to correct the misapprehensions and misrepresentations of those with whom in the first instance He had to do. But He does not leave it as a mere Jewish question; He broadens His view, and shows that the day of rest is for humanity at large—not, however, as a burden, but as a blessing, the principle which underlies it being "mercy, and not sacrifice." Thus, out of this conflict there has come to us the Magna Charta of the people's Sabbath, the full text of which is given in the corresponding passage of the second gospel: "The Sabbath was made for man, and not man for the Sabbath: therefore the Son of man is Lord also of the Sabbath." Here we have, on the one hand, the vindication of our rights against those who would deprive us of the day of rest, as if the privilege had been intended only for the Jews, and was abolished when the dispensation closed; and, on the other, the assertion of our liberty against those who, by their petty regulations and restrictions, would make God's precious gift a burden instead of a blessing. And how wisely and beautifully does He confirm to us our privileges by following the charter with an argument, which, though coming still under the head of the great principle ("Mercy, and not sacrifice"), is no mere repetition, but illustrates the wider aspect just unfolded, by its freedom from Jewish colour, and its appeal to the conscience and heart of mankind at large: "What man shall there be among you, that shall have one sheep, and if it fall into a pit on the Sabbath day, will he not lay hold on it, and lift it out? How much, then, is a man better than a sheep?" (vv. 11, 12).

The second attack gave Him the opportunity of bringing out with great distinctness and vividness the witness of the Spirit of God to His work as Saviour of mankind. These Pharisees regarded His miracles as mere displays of power, apart altogether from the spirit of purity, mercy and grace so manifest in them all. It was only this narrowness of view that made it possible for them to imagine that the Spirit of evil, to whom of course no one could deny a certain measure of mere power, was behind them. How completely He answers their blasphemous suggestion by showing that the works He did, judged, not by the mere power they displayed, but by their whole spirit and tendency, were at the very opposite pole from the works of Satan, we plainly see; but the point now is the permanent value of His reasoning. At first sight it may seem to be quite out of date. Whoever dreams now of disposing of the works of Christ by attributing them to Satan? Let us not be over-hasty, however, in concluding that old objections are out of date. If we look closely at those regarded as the newest, we may find that they are but old ones in a new dress. What of the position taken by some intelligent men in our day, who candidly admit the power of Christianity to elevate and sanctify men, and yet set it down as false?

As an illustration of this, we cannot do better than refer to a recent production[11] of the Agnostic School, in which there is the most emphatic testimony to the blessed power of Christianity in particular instances, followed by these most candid and generous words: "What needs admitting, or rather proclaiming, by agnostics who would be just, is that the Christian doctrine has the power of elevating and developing saintliness, which has had no equal in any other creed or philosophy." Yet the book in which that sentence occurs assumes throughout that this doctrine, which has had no equal in producing saintliness—a quality which in another place is described as "so lofty, so pure, so attractive, that it ravishes men's souls"—is untrue! Is, then, the argument of our Lord out of date? and is it too late to ask the old question, "Can Satan cast out Satan?"

It does not always follow, of course, that that which is good in its effects in particular cases, is thereby proved to be true. Truth and falsehood are to be determined fundamentally on other grounds than those of proved utility—this applies alike to truth and duty; there is an absolute truth and falsehood quite irrespective of utility, and there is an absolute right and wrong quite irrespective of utility,—but though we cannot in particular cases prove that to be true which appears to be beneficial, yet we cannot but believe that in the end, the true, the good, and the beautiful will be found to coincide; and we maintain that, seeing the effects of genuine Christianity on human character have been tested for nearly two thousand years, and have been found to "make for righteousness," nobility, purity, all that is good and gracious, high and holy, it is too late in the day to set it down to the father of lies. We may be mistaken in our passing judgments, may be misled into accepting as eternally true and right some measure or doctrine which has not yet had time to develop its real nature and character, which may produce good results at first, and then by degrees develop other results of quite a contrary kind—take the history of Monasticism as a case in point; but when there has been ample time and opportunity for testing the fruits of a system, as there has been in the case of Christianity; when we observe that the gospel of Christ has had these wonderful effects through eighteen successive centuries among all ranks and classes, nations and races of men— it ought surely to require something stronger than Agnosticism (which at the worst can only say, "I do not know") to make us believe the outrageously improbable supposition that it is false, and therefore presumably of the kingdom of lies and of unclean things. There have been too many devils cast out of human hearts to make it at all doubtful that in very deed "the kingdom of God has come" among us (ver. 28). There has been too much spoiling of "the strong man's goods" to make it at all doubtful that "a stronger than he" has mastered him and is spoiling his house. "The Son of God was manifested, that He might destroy the works of the devil" (1 John

iii. 8); and wherever He has been admitted into human hearts He has done it, setting up His kingdom of "righteousness and peace and joy in the Holy Ghost." The argument is as fresh to-day as the day it was propounded; and it has now all the added strength of centuries of confirmation.

The third attack gave our Lord the opportunity of laying bare the root of unbelief, and setting forth the important truth that, when the heart is estranged from God, mere signs are unavailing. The signs He had given in abundance should have been enough, especially when the only way of evading their force the ingenuity of scepticism could devise had been closed by the powerful argument just delivered. Besides this there was the crowning sign of the resurrection still to come; yet He knew that even that would fail to satisfy—not for reasons intellectual, but because of the spirit of the age, as He points out in that striking and powerful parable (vv. 43-45), and hints in the suggestive term, "an evil and adulterous generation" (ver. 39), the word "adulterous" referring to the well-known, and at that time thoroughly understood, language of the Old Testament, according to which estrangement of heart from God is branded as spiritual adultery. (See Jeremiah iii., Hosea i., ii., and many other passages.)

Herein we see a sufficient explanation of the widespread unbelief of the age in which we live. It is because the heart of this generation is so far estranged from God, so wedded to the earthly and material, so taken up with selfish aggrandisement and the multiplication of the luxuries of life. In many cases of unbelief the individual is not so much to blame as the spirit of the age of which he is the representative. Observe that the Lord does not say, "Ye evil Pharisees," but, "An evil and adulterous generation"; thus making it evident that the spirit of scepticism was not peculiar to themselves, but a something diffused throughout society. Hence it comes that many men, of blameless lives—of whom it would be a breach of charity to say that they loved darkness rather than light, because their deeds were evil— nevertheless declare themselves unsatisfied with the signs of the divine mission of Christ our Lord. Why is this? It is because they are infected with the spirit of the age, engrossed with the material, the sensible, the secular; while their hearts, "swept and garnished" though they be, are "empty" of God: "The god of this world hath blinded the minds of the unbelieving, that the light of the gospel of the glory of Christ, Who is the image of God, should not dawn upon them" (2 Cor. iv. 4, R.V.).

Such persons not only cannot recognise the signs of the kingdom of heaven, but are in a state of heart and mind to which no sign can possibly be given. We are indebted to the fine candour of the late Mr. Darwin for a striking illustration of this. In his Life there is an interesting correspondence with Professor Asa Gray, the great botanist, who, wondering how Darwin could remain unconvinced by the innumerable evidences of design in nature, took the liberty of asking him if he could think of any possible proof which he would consider sufficient. To this Mr. Darwin replied: "Your question, 'What would convince me?' is a poser. If I saw an angel come down to teach us so, and I was convinced, from others seeing him, that I was not mad, I should believe." If he had left it there, it might have been pertinent to ask him whether Christ is not just such an angel come down from heaven to teach us, and whether a sufficient number of persons did not see Him in the flesh, to say nothing of the multitudes who know Him in the spirit, to convince us that we are not mad in believing it. He did not, however, leave it there, but went on to say: "If man was made of brass and iron, and in no way connected with any other organism which had ever lived, I should perhaps be convinced." Nothing could be more candid, or more in keeping with the transparent honesty of this great man. But what an acknowledgment! Man must cease to be man, and become a metal machine, and the universe must cease to be a harmonious whole, before there can be evidence enough for so simple and elementary a principle as design in the universe; and then only a "perhaps"! If all this were done for me, "I should *perhaps* be convinced." Is our Lord's answer to the seekers after a sign out of date? "Verily I say unto you, There shall no sign be given unto this generation" (Mark viii. 12). How could there be?

What will He make of the distressing interruption caused by the interference of His mother and brethren? Knowing their motives and intentions as He did, He could not for a moment yield; and how was it possible to deal with them without a public rebuke, from which, seeing that His mother was involved in it, His heart would instinctively shrink? It was a most painful position; and the more we think of it, and try to imagine possible ways of extrication, the more we must admire the wisdom and kindness shown in the way in which He confronted the difficulty. He makes use of the opportunity for giving a new and most winning view of the kingdom of heaven as a happy family, united each to Himself, and all to the Father by the holiest bonds; thus opening out the paradise of a perfect home to all who choose to enter it, taking the sacred ties involved in the sweet words "brother" and "sister" and "mother," and giving them a range, a dignity, and a permanence they never had before.

In all this there was no word of direct censure; yet the sadly mistaken conduct of His kindred did not pass without implied rebuke; for the effect of His words was to make it clear that, sacred as were, in His eyes, the ties of earth, their only hope of permanence was in alliance with the higher ties of heaven. He has come in the loving Father's name to gather in His wandering children; and if His mother and brethren according to the flesh attempt to hinder Him, He cannot listen to them for a moment, but must steel His heart against their blind appeals, and that, not only for His works' sake, but for theirs also. They are slow to believe; but the least likely way to bring them to faith would be to yield to their unbelief. He will prosecute the path of duty, though it involve the sacrifice of all that cheers and comforts His heart; He must set His face as a flint to finish the work His Father has given Him to do, and they will understand Him by-and-by. There is no doubt they would go home with sore hearts that day; but no very long time would elapse till they would all be most grateful that their foolish, however well meant, interference had failed of its intent.

The course of events in later times has proved that the gentle rebuke involved in our Lord's reception of the message from His mother was not only necessary at the time and for her, but for the ages to come as well. We have seen that, in each of the attacks recorded before, our Saviour replies in such a way that His words not only meet the objection of the moment, but continue of permanent value to meet similar objections and gainsayings in ages to come. So is it here. It certainly is no fault of Mary herself, whose name should ever be held in the highest respect by all who love the Lord, that a corrupt Church, reversing all the teaching of the Church's Head, not only elevated the earthly relationship far above the spiritual, but in virtue of this relationship put the mother in the place of the Son, and taught an ignorant people to worship her and trust in her as a mediator. But the fact that this was done, and is persisted in to this day, shows that when our Lord set aside the mere earthly relationship as one that must be merged in the spiritual, He was correcting not only a pardonable error of Mary, but a most unpardonable error that afterwards, without any encouragement whatever from her, should be committed in her name.

After all, however, it is not the setting aside of the claims of Mary and the lowering of the earthly relationship in comparison with the heavenly, which is the great thing in the passage; but the Gospel of the Family of God. We have had the Gospel of the Kingdom of God, and glad tidings it has been indeed; but have we not here something even better? It is much to be permitted to hail the Son of God as our King; is it not better still to be encouraged to hail Him as a Brother, to know that all that is sweetest and tenderest in the dear words "brother," "sister," "mother," can be imported into our relation to Him? How it endears the heavenly relationship, and hallows the earthly!

Again, how it rebukes all sectarianism! He "stretches out His hand towards His disciples," and then to all the world by that word "*whosoever.*" And it is not the mere promise of salvation with which this "whosoever" is connected. There are Christians in the present day who can scarcely allow themselves to be sectarian enough to deny that there is salvation out of the Church to which they happen to belong: they are good enough to think that these people, who do not follow with them may somehow or other be saved; but the idea of fraternising with them! that is quite another thing. Now listen to the Saviour Himself: "Whosoever shall do the will of My Father which is in heaven" (no question of what Church he belongs to, or anything of that sort), "the same is My brother, and sister, and mother." No arm's-length recognition there; He takes all true disciples to His heart.

Observe, moreover, the emphasis on *doing*, with which we are already familiar. In setting forth the Gospel of the Kingdom, our Lord was careful to warn His hearers: "Not every one that saith unto Me, Lord, Lord, shall enter into the kingdom of heaven; but he that doeth the will of My Father" (vii. 21); and now that He is setting forth the Gospel of the Family the emphasis is still in the same place. It is not "Whosoever shall connect himself with this church or that church;" it is not "Whosoever shall be baptised, and take the sacrament;" it is "Whosoever shall do the will of My Father in heaven." This emphasis on doing, in connection with these endearing relations, is most significant. There must be love among the members of the family; and what else than love is the characteristic of the family ties? But how is love to be shown? How are we to distinguish it from mere sentiment? Our Saviour is careful to teach us; and never is He more careful than in those passages where tender feeling is most prominent—as, for example, in His parting words in the upper room, where again and again He reminds His disciples that obedience is the only sure test of love: "If ye love Me, keep My commandments;" "He that hath My commandments, and keepeth them, he it is that loveth Me" (John xiv. 15, 21). For the same reason obedience is here set forth as the only certain mark of the true disciple: "Whosoever shall do the will of My Father which is in heaven, the same is My brother, and sister, and mother."

FOOTNOTES

[10] This is the literal translation, which means more than "give you rest." It is not as if rest were a blessing He could bestow, as a friend would make a present which might be retained after the giver had gone. Rest is not so much what He gives to us as what He is to us; and so He says, not "I will give you rest," but "I will rest you" (*i.e.*, I will *be* your rest).

[11] "The Service of Man," by J. Cotter Morrison.

XI

THE PARABLES OF THE KINGDOM

Matt. xiii.

"THE same day went Jesus out of the house, and sat by the sea side." We can well imagine that, after such a series of discouragements and mortifications, the weary and heavy-laden Saviour would long to be alone, to get away from the abodes of men, to some lonely place where silent nature around Him would calm His spirit and furnish a temple in which He might lift up His soul to God. How long He was allowed to be alone we cannot tell; but possibly He may have contrived for a time to remain unobserved. How burdened His spirit must have been! What strength of faith it must have needed to look forward with any hope to the future of His work at such a time of crushing disappointment! We must remember that He was true man, and therefore His heart must have been very sore as He dwelt on the painful experiences through which He had just been passing. The obstacles which lay right in His path must have seemed well-nigh insuperable; and it would have been no wonder if at such a time He had despaired of the prospects of the kingdom of righteousness and peace and joy He had come to set up on the earth. He did not despair; but He did most deeply ponder; and the result of His thinking appears in the series of parables recorded in this chapter, which set forth, on the one hand, the nature of the obstacles the kingdom must meet, and the reason why it must meet them, and on the other, its certain prospect, notwithstanding these, of growth and development onward to its final consummation.

If He was permitted to enjoy His seclusion, it was only for a short time. "He could not be hid," His quiet retreat was discovered; and presently there came to Him great multitudes, so many that the only convenient way to address them all was to get into a boat, and speak to the people gathered on the shore. It is a lovely picture: the multitudes on the shore with the green fields around and the hills behind, and the Master speaking from the little boat. Viewed apart from the sorrowful experience of the past, it would have been full of cheer and hope. What more encouraging sight than such a throng gathered to hear the words of light and hope He had for them? But how can He view it apart from the sorrowful experience of the past? Have not these crowds been around Him day after day, week after week; and what has come of it all?

It is one thing to sow the seed of the kingdom; it is quite another to gather the harvest. The result depends on the soil. Some of it may be hard, so that the seed cannot enter; some of it, though receptive on the surface, yet so rocky underneath, that the fairest shoots will wither in a day; some of it so filled with seeds of thorns and weeds, that plants of grace are choked as they attempt to grow; while only a portion, and it may be a small proportion of the whole, can yield a fair or full return. Such were His thoughts as He looked on the field of men before Him, and glanced from it to the fields of the plain of Gennesaret around, in the foreground of which as in a picture the multitudes were set. As He thought, so He spoke, using the one field as a parable of the other, thus veiling, and at the same time beautifully revealing, His thought in a figure, which, simple as it was, demanded some degree of spiritual understanding for its appreciation; and accordingly after speaking the parable He adds the suggestive word, "Who hath ears to hear, let him hear."

There is something very touching in that word. It thrills with the pathos of these preceding chapters of disappointment. He had such a message for them—good tidings of great joy, rest for the weary and heavy laden, words of life and light and hope eternal—if only there were ears to hear. But that sad passage of Isaiah is running in His mind: "By hearing ye shall hear, and shall not understand; and seeing ye shall see, and shall not perceive: for this people's heart is waxed gross, and their ears are dull of hearing, and their eyes they have closed; lest at any time they should see with their eyes, and hear with their ears, and should understand with their heart, and should be converted, and I should heal them." That is the great obstacle, the one hindrance. Oh! if only men would hear; if only they would not close the ears of their souls! "Who hath ears to hear, let him hear."

I.—The Principle of Parabolic Instruction

The parable is a new style of teaching as compared with that of which the "Sermon on the Mount" was so notable an example. That discourse was not by any means lacking in illustration; still its main lines of thought were of the nature of direct spiritual instruction. But here there is no direct spiritual teaching. It is all indirect; it is parabolic through and through. No wonder the disciples noticed the difference, and came to the Master with the question, "Why speakest Thou unto them in parables?" The answer He gives is a revelation of the thoughts which have been passing in His mind. Of this disclosure we have already availed ourselves in our attempt to picture the scene; but it remains to look at this weighty passage as answering the disciples' question, and so explaining the rise of that form of instruction in which, as in all that He did, He showed himself a perfect Master.

The whole thing turns on the distinction between earnest inquirers and careless hearers. There must have been many of the latter in His audience, for this was no selected company, like that which listened to the Sermon on the Mount. The earnest inquirer has ears to hear; the other has not. The difference this makes is most strikingly set forth in the strong declaration: "Whosoever hath, to him shall be given, and he shall have more abundance: but whosoever hath not, from him shall be taken away even that he hath," — that is, instead of being the better for what he has heard, he is the worse; not apprehending the truth, he is only perplexed and confused by it, and instead of going away enriched, he is poorer than ever.

What, then, is to be done? If, instead of doing the people good, it only does them harm, why try to teach them at all? Why not let them alone, till they come with ears to hear, ready to receive? Happily this sad alternative is not the only resource. The truth may be put in such a way that it has both a shell and kernel of meaning; and the kernel may be so inclosed in the shell that it can be kept safely there, ready for the time when the inner fruit, which is the true food of the soul, can be used. For this purpose the parable is pre-eminently serviceable. The shell of meaning is so simple and familiar, that even a child can understand it; being of the nature of a story, it is very easily remembered; and connected as it is with that which is frequently observed, it will come up again and again to the minds of those in whom the thought has been lodged; so that, even if, on first hearing it, there is no possibility of understanding its deep spiritual significance, the time may come when it will flash upon the spirit the light which has been concealed within and so preserved from waste.

Take this parable of "The Sower" as an illustration. The disciples, having ears to hear, were ready to get the good of it at once, so to them He expounds it (vv. 18-23) on the spot. The rest were not ready to receive and apply it. Having ears (but not ears to hear), they heard not; but did it follow from this that it was useless, even worse than useless, to give it them? Had the teaching been direct, it would have been so; for they would have heard and rejected, and that would have been the last of it. But put as it was in parabolic form, while they were not prepared to understand and apply it then, they could not but carry it away with them; and, as they walked the fields, and observed the birds picking the seeds from the trodden field-paths, or the tiny plants withering on the rocky ledges, or the springing wheat strangled with rank growths of thorns, or the healthy growing wheat plant, or later in the season the rich golden grain on the good soil, they would have opportunity after opportunity of getting a glimpse of the truth, and finding that which at the first they were so unprepared to receive.

In this we can see the harmony of the passage before us, with its parallels in the second and third Gospels, where the object of speaking in parables is represented as being "that seeing, they might not see, and hearing they might not understand" (see Mark iv. 12, and Luke viii. 10). It is true that the object of the parable was to veil as well as to reveal; and the effect, which was also an intended effect, was to veil it from the unprepared heart and reveal it to the heart prepared; but inasmuch as the heart which is unprepared to-day may be prepared to-morrow, or next month, or next year, the parable may serve, and was intended to serve, the double purpose of veiling it and revealing it to the same person—veiling it from him as long as his heart was gross, but revealing it to him as soon as he should turn to the Lord and be willing to use his spiritual powers of apprehension for the purpose for which they had been given him. Thus, while this method of instruction was of the nature of judgment on the hard-hearted for the moment, it was really in the deepest sense a device of love, to prolong the time of their opportunity, to give them repeated chances instead of only one. It was judgment for the moment, with a view to mercy in the time to come. So we find, as always, that even when our Saviour seems to deal harshly with men, His deepest thoughts are thoughts of love; and in His recourse to the parabolic veil, He is once more illustrating the truth of the prophet's description of Him cited in the foregoing chapter: "A bruised reed shall He not break, and smoking flax shall He not quench, till He send forth judgment unto victory."

How many difficulties might have been avoided if expositors had used less of the mere "dry light" of the understanding, and tried more to lay their hearts alongside the beating heart of Christ! "Is not my word like as a fire? saith the Lord." Had this been remembered, and the fire of love in such a passage as this brought to bear upon the heart, before it was used "like a hammer that breaketh the rock in pieces," how different in many cases would have been the result! It is sad to think that this very passage as to the object of the parables has been used as if it simply taught predestination in its hardest sense, dooming the poor misguided soul to hopelessness for ever; whereas, if we enter at all into sympathy with the Saviour's heart in the sad and trying circumstances in which the words were spoken, we find in it no harshness at all, but the yearning of a patient love, seeking if by any means He may reach and gain the lost.

We have, indeed, the evidence on every side that the Saviour's heart was greatly moved at this time. We have already recognised the pathos of the cry, "Who hath ears to hear, let him hear." We have seen the sorrow of His heart in the sad quotation from the prophet Isaiah. On the other hand, what joy He has in those who do see and hear!—"But blessed are your eyes, for they see; and your ears, for they hear. For verily I say unto you, That many prophets and righteous men have desired to see those things which ye see, and have not seen them; and to hear those things which ye hear, and have not heard them." The same satisfaction appears later (ver. 51), when, after finishing the series, He asks His disciples, "Have ye understood all these things?" and they say unto Him, "Yea, Lord." He adds, "Therefore every scribe which is instructed unto the kingdom of heaven is like unto a man that is an householder, which bringeth forth out of his treasure things new and old." The Saviour evidently rejoices in the thought that these disciples, having ears to hear, are making real progress,—so much so that in due time they will be ready to be teachers of others, each having a treasury of his own; and not only will they be in possession of the old, but will have power to strike out new views of sacred truth, and so be prepared with freshness and variety to set forth the glad tidings of the kingdom of heaven. How fully these hopes were realised we have only to look forward to the epistles to see. There we have things old, the very truths the Master taught in the days of His flesh; and not the old alone, for there are things new as well, fresh settings of the old, new aspects, varied applications of the truth—a treasury indeed for the ages to come. The Saviour, then, had good reason to take comfort that some of the seed He was sowing in tears was falling on good soil, and promising a rich and blessed harvest.

But the dark and discouraging side is never long out of sight. Returning to His own country, and teaching in their synagogue, He so impressed the people that they could not but ask certain questions, which, if they had only pondered them, would have led them to the truth: "Whence hath this man this wisdom, and these mighty works?" But the mere outside things that met their eyes so engrossed their attention, that their heads and hearts remained as empty as ever. Instead of pressing the question *Whence?* which would have led them up to heaven and to God, they dwelt upon "*this man*," this common man, this carpenter's son, with a mother called Mary, and brothers with the common names, James and Joseph, Simon and Judas; so, proving themselves to be of the earth earthy, they closed their ears and were "offended in Him." It was very evident that the only hope of reaching people of that kind was to speak in parables, which they could remember without understanding in the meantime, with the hope that by-and-by as they thought of the subject without such prejudices as these which now cause them to stumble, they may at last understand, and receive the truth and inherit eternal life.

II.—The Group of Seven

So far we have dealt with the parabolic method of teaching, and in doing so have glanced at only one of the seven parables the chapter contains, every one of which invites special study; but inasmuch as our plan will not admit of this, we shall attempt nothing more than a general view of the entire group; and to this we restrict ourselves the more willingly that there is a unity in the cluster which is apt to escape notice when they are considered apart, and because by letting go the details we get the prominent features more vividly before our minds.

The arrangement seems to be in three pairs, with a single concluding parable. The first pair—"The Sower" and "The Tares"—set forth the manner of the establishment of the kingdom of heaven, and the obstacles it must encounter. The sphere from which both parables are taken is admirably suited to bring out the radical distinction in regard to the manner of its establishment between the new kingdom and those with which the people were already familiar. They were founded by the sword; this kingdom by the Word. Not force, but persuasion, is to be the weapon; and accordingly there is placed before the mind, not a warrior hasting to battle, but a sower sowing seed. "The field is the world," we are told—the world of men, of human hearts; and the seed is "the word of the kingdom." It is "good seed," and therefore it ought to be welcome; but there are serious obstacles in the way.

The first parable sets forth the obstacles encountered in the soil itself. Sometimes the seed falls on *hard soil*, where it cannot penetrate the surface, and presently birds come and carry it away—representing those hearers of the word, who, though they remember it for a short time, have their hearts hardened against it, so that it does not enter, but is presently snatched away by trifling worldly thoughts which come fluttering into the mind. Then there is the *shallow soil*, a little loose earth on the surface, and close under it the hard rock, harder even than the trodden wayside—a kind of soil in which the seed will rapidly take root and spring up, and as rapidly wither away in the noonday heat, and which therefore fitly represents those who are easily impressed, but whose impressions do not last; who make many resolutions indeed, but in so half-hearted and impulsive a way that they are destined to be blighted by the first blast of temptation. Finally, there is the *preoccupied soil*, where thorns and thistles hold the ground and choke the springing plants of grace, representing those who "are choked with cares, and riches and pleasures of this life, and bring no fruit to maturity."

The *good soil* is marked by characteristics which are simply the negatives of these: it is not hard, so the seed enters; not shallow, so it takes root; not preoccupied, so it holds the ground, and springs up and brings forth fruit, "in some thirty, in some sixty, in some a hundredfold."

There are, however, other obstacles than those found in the nature of the soil. There is the diligence of the enemy, and the impossibility of getting rid of those who have come under his influence, as set forth in the second parable, that of "The Tares of the Field." In this parable the good seed is no longer the word, but "the children of the kingdom"; as if to suggest that Christians themselves are to be to the world what the word has been to them; while the bad seed—sown when men sleep, sown when Christians are asleep—does not remain as mere seed, but embodies itself in "children of the wicked one," who take their places side by side with the true children of the kingdom, and whom it is so difficult to distinguish from them, that the separation may not be attempted till the time of the harvest, when it shall be complete and final, and "the righteous shall shine forth as the sun in the kingdom of their Father."

The second pair—"The Mustard Seed" and "The Leaven"—set forth the growth of the kingdom notwithstanding the many obstacles it must encounter, the one indicating its growth as recognisable to the observant eye, the other its pervasive power as permeating society. This twofold view of the development of the kingdom is in the same line of thought as the illustrations of the light and the salt in the Sermon on the Mount. The prophecy these parables infold is most marvellous, spoken as it was in a time of so deep discouragement. There is true pathos in the thought of the grain of mustard seed, *the least of all seeds,*" and in the little word "hid," which comes in so significantly in the parable of the Leaven; and there is great strength of faith in the readiness of mind to recognise the hopeful thought of the inherent life and energy hidden in the tiny germ, and working all unseen in the little leaven which literally disappeared in the at first unaltered mass.

The parables of "The Hid Treasure" and "The Pearl" form a third pair, shadowing forth the unsearchable riches of Christ. The reduplication of the thought adds greatly to its impressiveness, and moreover affords the opportunity of suggested variation in the experience of those who find the treasure. The merchantman we naturally think of as representing the rich, and the man finding the treasure in the field as one of the poor in this world's goods. Both alike, however, "buy" their prize at the price of all that they possess, on the principle which underlies all our Lord's teaching as to the way of life: "Whosoever he be of you that forsaketh not all that he hath cannot be My disciple." The one comes upon his treasure unexpectedly; the other finds it in the course of diligent search. Both alike, however, recognise its exceeding value as soon as it is seen; and it is under no constraint, but willingly and gladly—"for joy thereof," as it is put in the case of the man who from his not seeking it might have been thought indifferent to it—that each one sells all that he has and buys it.

The last parable, according to the arrangement we have suggested, stands alone. It is the parable of "The Net," and its subject is the consummation of the Kingdom. Its teaching is indeed to a great extent anticipated in the parable of the tares of the field; but in that parable, though "the end of the world" is pictured in the most impressive imagery, it is not the main thought, as it is here, where the one lesson is, that the present mixed state of things cannot continue for ever, that there must come a time of separation, when those in whose hearts God reigns shall be gathered to a place by themselves, where they shall be satisfied for ever, with their treasure no longer hid, but open in all its immeasurable fulness; while those who refused to allow God to reign in their hearts, and preferred their own selfishness and sin, shall be cast away and consumed, with "wailing and gnashing of teeth."

XII
THE CRISIS IN GALILEE

Matt. xiv.-xvi. 12.

THE lives of John and of Jesus, lived so far apart, and with so little intercommunication, have yet been interwoven in a remarkable way, the connection only appearing at the most critical times in the life of our Lord. This interweaving, strikingly anticipated in the incidents of the nativity as recorded by St. Luke, appears, not only at the time of our Saviour's baptism and first introduction to His Messianic work, but again at the beginning of His Galilean ministry, which dates from the time when John was cast into prison, and once again as the stern prophet of the desert finishes his course; for his martyrdom precipitates a crisis, to which events for some time have been tending.

The period of crisis, embracing the facts recorded in the two chapters following and in part of the sixteenth, is marked by events of thrilling interest. The shadow of the cross falls so very darkly now upon the Saviour's path, that we may look for some more striking effects of light and shade,—Rembrandt-like touches, if with reverence we may so put it,—in the Evangelist's picture. Many impressive contrasts will arrest our attention as we proceed to touch briefly on the story of the time.

I.—The Banquet of Herod and the Feast of Christ (xiv. 1-21)

"Among them that are born of woman there hath not risen a greater than John the Baptist." Such was the Saviour's testimony to His forerunner in the hour of his weakness; and the sequel fully justified it. The answer which came to John's inquiry brought him no outward relief. His prison bolts were as firmly fastened as before, Herod was as inexorable, the prospect before Him as dark as ever; but he had the assurance that Jesus was the Christ, and that His blessed work of healing the sick and preaching the gospel to the poor was going on; and that was enough for him. So he was quite content to languish on, resting in the Lord and waiting patiently for Him. We learn from St. Mark that Herod was in the habit of sending for him at times, evidently interested in the strange man, probably to some extent fascinated by him, and possibly not without some lingering hope that there might be some way of reconciling the preacher of righteousness and securing the blessing of so well-accredited a messenger of Heaven. There is little doubt that at these times the way was open for John to be restored to liberty, if only he had been willing to lower his testimony against Herod's sin, or consent to say no more about it; but no such thought ever crossed his noble soul. He had said, "It is not lawful for thee to have her;" and not even in the hour of deepest depression and darkest doubt did he for a moment relax the rigour of his requirements as a preacher of righteousness.

As he had lived, so he died. We shall not dwell on the details of the revolting story. It is quite realistic enough in the simple recital of the Evangelist. One cannot help recalling in this connection four hideous pictures of Salome with the head of John the Baptist recently displayed, all on the line, in the *Salon* at Paris. Of what possible use are such representations? To what sort of taste do they minister? There was no picture of John looking with flashing eyes at the guilty monarch as he said, "It is not lawful for thee to have her." That is the scene which is worthy of remembrance: let it abide in the memory and heart; let the tragic end serve only as a dark background to make the central figure luminous, "a burning and a shining light."

The time of Herod's merciful visitation is over. So long as he kept the Baptist safe (Mark vi. 19, 20) from the machinations of Herodias, he retained one link with better things. The stern prisoner was to him like a second conscience; and so long as he was there within easy reach, and Herod continued from time to time to see him and hear what he had to say, there remained some hope of repentance and reformation. Had he only yielded to the promptings of his better nature, and obeyed the prophet, the way of the Lord would have been prepared, the preacher of righteousness would have been followed by the Prince of Peace; and the gospel of Jesus, with all its unspeakable blessing, would have had free course in his court and throughout his realm. But the sacrifice of the prophet to the cruelty of Herodias and the folly and wickedness of his vow put an end to such prospects; and the fame of Christ's deeds of mercy, when at last it reached his ears, instead of stirring in him a living hope, aroused the demon of a guilty conscience, which could not rid itself of the superstitious fear that it was John the Baptist risen from the dead. Thus passed away for ever the great opportunity of Herod Antipas.

The disciples of John withdrew in sorrow, but not in despair. They had evidently caught the spirit of their master; for as soon as they had reverently and lovingly taken up the mortal remains and buried them, they came and told Jesus.

It must have been a terrible blow to Him,—perhaps even more than it was to them, for they had Him to go to, while He had none on earth to take counsel with: He must carry the heavy burden of responsibility all alone; for even the most advanced of the Twelve could not enter into any of His thoughts and purposes; and certainly not one of them, we might indeed say not all of them together, had at this time anything like the strength and steadfastness of the great man who had just been taken away. We learn from the other accounts that at the same time the Twelve returned from their first missionary journey; so that the question would immediately come up, What was to be done? It was a critical time. Should they stir up the people to avenge the death of their prophet? This would have been after the manner of men, but not according to the counsel of God. Long ago the Saviour had set aside, as quite apart from His way of working, all appeals to force; His kingdom must be a kingdom of the truth, and on the truth He will rely, with nothing else to trust to than the power of patient love. So He takes His disciples away to the other side of the lake, outside the jurisdiction of Herod, with the thoughtful invitation: "Come ye yourselves apart into a desert place, and rest awhile."

What are the prospects of the kingdom now? Sin and righteousness have long been at strife in the court of Galilee; now sin has conquered and has the field. The great preacher of righteousness is dead; and the Christ, to Whom he bore such faithful witness, has gone to the desert. Again the sad prophecy is fulfilled: "He is despised and rejected of men; a man of sorrows, and acquainted with grief." That little boat crossing from the populous shores of Gennesaret to the desert land on the other side—what does it mean? Defeat? A lost cause? Is this the end of the mission in Galilee, begun to the music of that majestic prophecy which spoke of it as daybreak on the hills and shores of Naphtali and Zebulun, Gennesaret and Jordan? Is this the outcome of two mighty movements so full of promise and hope? Did not all Jerusalem and Judæa go after John, confessing their sins and accepting his baptism? And has not all Galilee thronged after Jesus, bringing their sick to be healed, and listening, at least with outward respect and often expressed astonishment, to His words of truth and hope? Now John is dead, and Jesus is crossing with His own disciples and those of John in a boat—one boat enough to hold them all—to mourn together in a desert place apart. Suppose we had been sitting on the shore that day, and had watched it getting ever smaller as it crossed the sea, what should we have thought of the prospects? Should we have found it easy to believe in Christ that day? Verily "the kingdom of God cometh not with observation."

The multitudes will not believe on Him; yet they will not let Him rest. They have rejected the kingdom; but they would fain get as much as they can of those earthly blessings which have been scattered so freely as its signs. So the people, noticing the direction the boat has taken, throng after Him, running on foot round the northern shore. When Jesus sees them, sad and weary as He is, He cannot turn away. He knows too well that it is with no pure and lofty devotion that they follow Him; but He cannot see a multitude of people without having His heart moved with a great longing to bless them. So He "went forth, and healed their sick."

He continued His loving work, lavishing His sympathy on those who had no sympathy with Him, till evening fell, and the disciples suggested that it was time to send the people away, especially as they were beginning to suffer from want of food. "But Jesus said unto them, They need not depart: give ye them to eat. And they say unto Him, We have here but five loaves, and two fishes. He said, Bring them hither to Me."

The miracle which follows is of very special significance. Many things point to this. (1) It is the one miracle which all the four Evangelists record. (2) It occurs at a critical time in our Lord's history. There has been discouragement after discouragement, repulse after repulse, despite and rejection by the leaders, obstinate unbelief and impenitence on the part of the people, the good seed finding almost everywhere hard or shallow or thorny soil, with little or no promise of the longed-for harvest. And now a crowning disaster has come in the death of John. Can we wonder that Christ received the tidings of it as a premonition of His own? Can we wonder that henceforth He should give less attention to public preaching, and more to the training of the little band of faithful disciples who must be prepared for days of darkness coming on apace—prepared for the cross, manifestly now the only way to the crown? (3) There is the significant remark (John vi. 4) that "the Passover was nigh." This was the last Passover but one of our Saviour's life. The next was to be marked by the sacrifice of Himself as "the Lamb of God that taketh away the sin of the world." Another year, and He will have fulfilled His course, as John has fulfilled His. Was it not, then, most natural that His mind should be full, not only of thoughts of the approaching Passover, but also of what the next one must bring. This is no mere conjecture; for it plainly appears in the long and most suggestive discourse St. John reports as following immediately upon the miracle and designed for its application.

The feeding of the five thousand is indeed a sign of the kingdom, like those grouped together in the earlier part of the Gospel (viii., ix.). It showed the compassion of the Lord upon the hungry multitude, and His readiness to supply their wants. It showed the Lordship of Christ over nature, and served as a representation in miniature of what the God of nature is doing every year, when, by agencies as far beyond our ken as those by which His

Son multiplied the loaves that day, He transmutes the handful of seed-corn into the rich harvests of grain which feed the multitudes of men. It taught also, by implication, that the same God Who feeds the bodies of men with the rich abundance of the year is able and willing to satisfy all their spiritual wants. But there is something more than all this, as we might gather from the very way it is told: "And He commanded the multitude to sit down on the grass, and took the five loaves, ... and looking up to heaven, He blessed, and brake, and gave the loaves to the disciples, and the disciples to the multitude." Can we read these words without thinking of what our Saviour did just a year later, when He took bread and blessed it, and brake it, and gave it to the disciples and said, "Take, eat, this is My body" (xxvi. 26)? He is not, indeed, instituting the Supper now; but it is very plain that the same thoughts are in His mind as when, a year later, He did so. And what might be inferred from the recital of what He did becomes still more evident when we are told what afterwards He said—especially such utterances as these: "I am the bread of life;" "The bread which I will give you is My flesh, which I will give for the life of the world;" "Verily I say unto you, Except ye eat the flesh of the Son of man, and drink His blood, ye have no life in you."

We have, then, here, not a sign of the kingdom only, but a parable of life eternal, life to be bestowed in no other way than by the death to be accomplished at Jerusalem at the next passover, life for thousands, life ministered through the disciples to the multitudes, and not diminished in the ministering, but growing and multiplying in their hands, so that after all are fed there remain "twelve baskets full,"—far more than at the first: a beautiful hint of the abundance that will remain for the Gentile nations of the earth. That passover parable comes out of the anguish of the great Redeemer's heart. Already, as He breaks that bread and gives it to the people, He is enduring the cross and despising the shame of it, for the joy set before Him of giving the bread of life to a hungry world.

One can scarcely fail at this point to contrast the feast in honour of Herod's birthday with the feast which symbolised the Saviour's death. "When a convenient day was come, Herod on his birthday made a supper to his lords, high captains, and chief estates of Galilee; and— —" the rest is well known,—the feasting, mirth and revelry, ending in the dark tragedy, followed by the remorse of a guilty conscience, the gnawing of the worm that dieth not, the burning of the fire that is not quenched. Then think of that other feast on the green grass in the pure air of the fresh and breezy hillside—the hungry multitudes, the homely fare, the few barley loaves and the two small fishes; yet by the blessing of the Lord Jesus there was provided a repast far more enjoyable to these keen appetites than all the delicacies of the banquet to the lords of Galilee—a feast pointing indeed to a death, but a death which was to bring life and peace and joy to thousands, with abundance over for all who will receive it. The one is the feast to which the world invites; the other is the feast which Christ provides for all who are willing to "labour not for the meat that perisheth, but for that which endureth unto eternal life."

II.—Calm on the Mountain and Trouble on the Sea

We learn from the fourth Gospel that the immediate result of the impression made by our Lord's miraculous feeding of the five thousand was an attempt on the part of the people to take Him by force and make Him a king. Thus, as always, their minds would run on political change, and the hope of bettering their circumstances thereby; while they refused to allow themselves to think of that spiritual change which must begin with themselves, and show itself in that repentance and hunger and thirst after righteousness, which He so longed to see in them. Even His disciples, as we know, were not now, nor for a long time subsequent to this, altogether free from the same spirit of earthliness; and it is quite likely that the general enthusiasm would excite them not a little, and perhaps lead them to raise the question, as they were often fain to do, whether the time had not at last come for their Master to declare Himself openly, put Himself at the head of these thousands, take advantage of the widespread feeling of irritation and discontent awakened by the murder of John the Baptist, whom all men counted for a prophet (Mark xi. 32), hurl Herod Antipas from the high position he disgraced, and, with all Galilee under His control and full of enthusiasm for His cause, march southward on Jerusalem. This was no doubt the course of action they for the most part expected and wished; and, with One at their head Who could do such wonders, what was there to hinder complete success?

May we not also with reverence suppose that this was one of the occasions on which Satan renewed those assaults which he began in the wilderness of Judæa? A little later, when Peter was trying to turn Him aside from the path of the Cross, Jesus recognised it, not merely as a suggestion of the disciple, but as a renewed temptation of the great adversary. We may well suppose, then, that at this crisis the old temptation to bestow on Him the kingdoms of the world and the glory of them—not for their own sake, of course (there could have been no temptation in that direction), but for the sake of the advancement of the interests of the heavenly kingdom by the use of worldly methods of policy and force—was presented to Him with peculiar strength.

However this may have been, the circumstances required prompt action of some kind. It was necessary that the disciples should be got out of reach of temptation as soon as possible; so He constrained them to enter into a boat, and go before Him to the other side, while He dispersed the multitude. And need we wonder that in the circumstances He should wish to be entirely alone? He could not consult with those He trusted most, for they were quite in the dark, and anything they were at all likely to say would only increase the pressure put upon Him by the people. He had only One for His Counsellor and Comforter, His Father in heaven, Whose will He had come to do; so He must be alone with Him. He must have been in a state of great physical exhaustion after all the fatigue of the day, for though He had come for rest He had found none; but the brave, strong spirit conquers the weary flesh, and instead of going to sleep He ascends the neighbouring height to spend the night in prayer.

It is interesting to remember that it was after this night spent in prayer that He delivered the remarkable discourse recorded in the sixth chapter of St. John, in which He speaks so plainly about giving His flesh for the life of the world. It is evident, then, that, if any question had arisen in His mind as to the path of duty, when He was suddenly confronted with the enthusiastic desire of the multitudes to crown Him at once, it was speedily set at rest: He now plainly saw that it was not the will of His Father in heaven that He should take advantage of any such stirring of worldly desire, that He must give no encouragement to any, except those who were hungering and thirsting after righteousness, to range themselves upon His side. Hence, no doubt, the sifting nature of the discourse He delivered the following day. He is eager to gather the multitudes to Himself; but He cannot allow them to come under any false assumption;—He must have spiritually-minded disciples, or none at all: accordingly He makes His discourse so strongly spiritual, directs their attention so far away from earthly issues to the issues of eternity ("I will raise him up at the last day" is the promise He gives over and over again, whereas they wanted to be raised up then and there to high places in the world), that not only did the multitude lose all their enthusiasm, but "from that time many of His disciples went back, and walked no more with Him," while even the Twelve themselves were shaken in their allegiance, as seems evident from the sorrowful question with which He turned to them: "Will ye also go away?" We may reverently suppose, then, that our Lord was occupied, during the early part of the night, with thoughts like these—in preparation, as it were, for the faithful words He will speak and the sad duty He will discharge on the morrow.

Meantime a storm has arisen on the lake—one of those sudden and often terrible squalls to which inland waters everywhere are subject, but which are greatly aggravated here by the contrast between the tropical climate of the lake, 620 feet below the level of the Mediterranean, and the cool air on the heights which surround it. The storm becomes fiercer as the night advances. The Saviour has been much absorbed, but He cannot fail to notice how angry the lake is becoming, and to what peril His loved disciples are exposed. As the Passover was nigh, the moon would be nearly full, and there would be frequent opportunities, between the passing of the clouds, to watch the little boat. As long as there seems any prospect of their weathering the storm by their own exertions He leaves them to themselves; but when it appears that they are making no progress, though it is evident that they are "toiling in rowing," He sets out at once to their relief.

The rescue which follows recalls a former incident on the same lake (viii. 23-27). But the points of difference are both important and instructive. Then He was with His disciples in the ship, though asleep; in their extremity they had only to rouse Him with the cry, "Save, Lord, or we perish!" to secure immediate calm and safety. Now He was not with them; He was out of sight, and beyond the reach even of the most piercing cries. It was therefore a much severer trial than the last; and, remembering the special significance of the miracle of the loaves, we can scarcely fail to notice a corresponding suggestiveness in this one. That one had dimly foreshadowed His death; did not this, in the same way, foreshadow the relations He would sustain to His disciples after His death? May we not look upon His ascent of this mountain as a picture of His ascension into heaven—His betaking Himself to His Father now as a shadow of His going to the Father then—His prayer on the mount as a shadow of His heavenly intercession? It was to pray that He ascended; and though He, no doubt, needed, at that trying time, to pray for Himself, His heart would be poured out in pleading for His disciples too, especially when the storm came on. And these disciples constrained to go off in a boat by themselves,—are they not a picture of the Church after Christ had gone to His Father, launched on the stormy sea of the world? What will they do without Him? What will they do when the winds rise and the waves roar in the dark night? Oh! if only He were here, Who was sleeping in the boat that day, and only needed to be roused to sympathise and save! Where is He now? There on the hilltop, interceding, looking down with tenderest compassion, watching every effort of the toiling rowers. Nay, He is nearer still! See that Form upon the waves! "It is a spirit," they cry; and are afraid, very much as, a little more than a year afterward, when He came suddenly into the midst of them with His "Peace be unto you," they were terrified and affrighted, and supposed that they had seen a spirit (Luke xxiv. 37). But presently they hear the familiar voice: "Be of good cheer: it is I; be not afraid." There can be no doubt that the remembrance of that night on the lake of Galilee would be a wondrous consolation to these disciples during the storms of persecution through which they had to pass after their Master had ascended up to heaven; and their faith in the presence of His Spirit, and His constant readiness to help and save, would be greatly strengthened by the memory of that apparently spectral Form they had seen coming across the troubled sea to their relief. Have we not some reason, then, for saying that here, too, we have not only another of the many signs of the kingdom showing our Lord's power over nature and constant readiness to help His people in time of need, but a parable of the future, most appropriately following that parable of life through death set forth in the feeding of the thousands on the day before?

There seems, in fact, a strange prophetic element running all through the scenes of that wondrous time. We have already referred to the disposition on the part even of the Twelve, as manifested next day at the close of the discourse on the "bread of life," to desert Him—to show the same spirit which afterward, when the crisis reached its height, so demoralised them that "they all forsook Him, and fled"; and have we not, in the closing incident, in which Peter figures so conspicuously, a mild foreshadowing of his terrible fall, when the storm of human passion was raging as fiercely in Jerusalem as did the winds and waves on the lake of Galilee that night? There is the same self-confidence: "Lord, if it be Thou, bid me come unto Thee on the water;" the same alarm when he was brought face to face with the danger the thought of which he had braved; then the sinking, sinking as if about to perish, yet not hopelessly (for the Master had prayed for him that his faith should not fail); then the humble prayer, "Lord, save me"; and the gracious hand immediately stretched out to save. Had the adventurous disciple learnt his lesson well that day, what it would have saved him! May we not say that there is never a great and terrible fall, however sudden it seems, which has not been preceded by warnings, even long before, which, if heeded, would have certainly averted it? How much need have the disciples of Christ to learn thoroughly the lessons their Lord teaches them in His gentler dealings, so that when darker days and heavier trials come they may be ready, having taken unto themselves the whole armour of God, to withstand in the evil day, and having done all, to stand.

There are many other important lessons which might be learnt from this incident, but we may not dwell on them; a mere enumeration of some of them may, however, be attempted. It was faith, in part, at least, which led the apostle to make this venture; and this is, no doubt, the reason why the Lord did not forbid it. Faith is too precious to be repressed; but the faith of Peter on this occasion is anything but simple, clear and strong: there is a large measure of self-will in it, of impulsiveness, of self-confidence, perhaps of love of display. A confused and encumbered faith of this kind is sure to lead into mischief,—to set on foot rash enterprises, which show great enthusiasm, and perhaps seem to rebuke the caution of the less confident for the time, but which come to grief, and in the end bring no credit to the cause of Christ. The rash disciple's enterprise is not, however, an entire failure: he does succeed so far; but presently the weakness of his faith betrays itself. As long as the impulse lasted, and his eye was fixed on his Master, all went well; but when the first burst of enthusiasm was spent, and he had time to look round upon the waves, he began to sink. But how encouraging it is to observe that, when put to extremity, that which is genuine in the man carries it over all the rest!—the faith which had been encumbered extricates itself, and becomes simple, clear and strong; the last atom of self-confidence is gone, and with it all thought of display; nothing but simple faith is left in that strong cry of his, "Lord, save me!"

Nothing could be imagined better suited than this incident to discriminate between self-confidence and faith. Peter enters on this experience with the two well mixed together,—so well mixed, that neither he himself nor his fellow-disciples could distinguish them; but the testing process precipitates one and clarifies the other,—lets the self-confidence all go, and brings out the faith pure and strong. Immediately, therefore, his Lord is at his side, and he is safe;—a great lesson this on faith, especially in revealing its simplicity. Peter tried to make a grand thing of it: he had to come back to the simple, humble cry, and the grasping of his Saviour's outstretched hand.

The same lesson is taught on a larger scale in the brief account of the cures the Master wrought when they reached the other side, where all that was asked was the privilege of touching His garment's hem, "and as many as touched were made perfectly whole;" not the great ones, not the strong ones, but "as many as touched." Only let us keep in touch with Him, and all will assuredly be well with us both in time and in eternity.

III.—Israel after the Flesh, and Israel after the Spirit (xv.)

Issue is now joined with the ecclesiastical leaders at Jerusalem, who send a deputation to make a formal complaint. When Jerusalem was last mentioned in our Gospel, it was in connection with a movement of quite a different character. The fame of the Saviour's deeds of mercy in Galilee had then just reached the capital, the result being that many set out at once to find out what new thing this might be: "There followed Him great multitudes of people from Galilee, and from Decapolis, and from Jerusalem, and from Judæa, and from beyond Jordan" (iv. 25). That wave of interest in the south had now died down; and instead of eager multitudes there is a small sinister band of cold, keen-witted, hard-hearted critics. It was a sad change, and must have brought new distress to the Saviour's troubled heart;

but He is none the less ready to face the trial with His wonted courage and unfailing readiness of resource.

Their complaint is trivial enough. It is to be remembered, of course, that it was not a question of cleanliness, but of ritual; not even of ritual appointed by Moses, but only of that prescribed by certain traditions of their fathers which they held in superstitious veneration. These traditions, by a multitude of minute regulations and restrictions, imposed an intolerable burden on those who thought it their duty to observe them; while the magnifying of trifles had the natural effect of keeping out of sight the weightier matters of the law. Not only so, but the most trivial regulations were sometimes so managed as to furnish an excuse for neglect of the plainest duties. Our Lord could not therefore miss the opportunity of denouncing this evil, and accordingly He exposes it in the plainest and strongest language.

The question with which He opens His attack is most incisive. It is as if He said, "I am accused of transgressing *your* tradition. What is your tradition? It is itself transgression of the law of God." Then follows the striking illustration, showing how by their rules of tradition they put it within the power of any heartless son to escape entirely the obligation of providing even for his aged father or mother—an illustration, be it remembered, which brought out more than a breach of the fifth commandment; for by what means was it that the ungrateful son escaped his obligation? By taking the name of the Lord in vain; for surely there could be no greater dishonour to the name of God than meanly to mark as dedicated to Him (*Corban*) what ought to have been devoted to the discharge of an imperative filial duty. Besides, it was not at all necessary that the money or property should be actually dedicated to sacred uses; it was only necessary to say that it was, only necessary to pronounce over it that magic word Corban, and then the mean hypocrite could use it for the most selfish purposes—for any purpose, in fact, he chose, except that purpose for which it was his duty to use it. It is really difficult to conceive such iniquity wrapped up in a cloak of so-called religion. No wonder our Lord was moved to indignation, and applied to His critics the strong language of the prophet: "Ye hypocrites, well did Isaiah prophesy of you, saying, This people honoureth Me with their lips; but their heart is far from Me, ... teaching as their doctrines the precepts of men" (R.V.). No wonder that He turned away from men who were so deeply committed to a system so vile, and that He explained, not to His questioners, but to the multitude who had gathered round, the principle on which He acted.

There seems, however, to have been more of sorrow than of anger in His tone and manner. How else could the disciples have asked Him such a question as that which follows: "Knowest thou that the Pharisees were offended, after they heard this saying?" Of course the Pharisees were offended. They had most excellent reason. And the disciples would have known that He had no intention of sparing them in the least, and no concern whether they took offence or not, if His tone had been such as an ordinary person would naturally have put into such an invective. It is probable that he said it all calmly, earnestly, tenderly, without the slightest trace of passion; from which it would not be at all unnatural for the disciples to infer that He had not fully realised how strong His language had been, and into what serious collision He had brought Himself with the leaders in Jerusalem. Hence their gentle remonstrance, the expression of those feelings of dismay with which they saw their Master break with one party after another, as if determined to wreck His mission altogether. Was it not bad policy to give serious offence to persons of such importance at so critical a time?

The Saviour's answer is just what was to be expected. Policy had no place in His plan. His kingdom was of the truth; and whatever was not of truth must go, be the consequences what they might. That system of traditionalism had its roots deeply and firmly fastened in the Jewish soil; its fibres were through it all; and to disturb it was to go against a feeling that was nothing less than national in its extent. But no matter: firmly, deeply, widely rooted though it was, it was not of God's planting, and therefore it cannot be let alone: "Every plant, which My heavenly Father hath not planted, shall be rooted up." It is for all ritualists, ancient and modern, all who teach for doctrines what are only commandments of men, seriously to ponder this most radical utterance by One Whose right it is to speak with an authority from which there is no appeal.

Having thus condemned the ritualistic teaching of the day, He disposes next of the false teachers. This He does in a way which ought to have been a warning to those persecutors and heresy-hunters who, by their unwise use of force and law, have given only larger currency to the evil doctrines they have tried to suppress. He simply says "Let them alone: they be blind leaders of the blind. And if the blind lead the blind, both shall fall into the ditch." Expose their error by all means; root it out, if possible; but as for the men themselves, "let them alone."

The principle He sets forth as underlying the whole subject is the same as that which underlies His teaching in the Sermon on the Mount—viz., that "out of the heart are the issues of life." The ritualist lays stress on that which enters into the man—the kind of food which enters his mouth, the objects which meet his eye, the incense which enters his nostril; Christ sets all this aside as of no consequence in comparison with the state of the heart (vv. 16-20). Such teaching as this was not only irreconcilable with that of the scribes and Pharisees from Jerusalem, but it lay at the very opposite pole.

Was it on this account that after this interview Jesus withdrew as far as possible from Jerusalem? He is limited, indeed, in His range to the Holy Land, as He indicates in His conversation with the woman of Canaan; but just as after the death of John He had withdrawn out of the jurisdiction of Herod to the east, so now, after this collision with the deputation from Jerusalem, He withdraws to the far north, to the borders of Tyre and Sidon. And was it only a coincidence that, just as Jerusalem had furnished such sorry specimens of dead formalism, the distant borders of heathen Tyre and Sidon should immediately thereafter furnish one of the very noblest examples of living faith? The coincidence is certainly very striking and most instructive. The leaders from Jerusalem had been dismissed with the condemnation of their own prophet: "This people honoureth Me with their lips, but their heart is far from Me;" while out of far-away heathendom there comes one whose whole heart is poured out to Him in earnest, persevering, prevailing prayer. It is one of those contrasts with which this portion of our Lord's history abounds, the force of which will appear more clearly as we proceed.

The suppliant was "a woman of Canaan," or, as she is described more definitely elsewhere, a Syro-Phœnician woman. Yet she has learned of Jesus—knows Him as the Christ, for she calls Him "Son of David"—knows Him as a Saviour, for she comes to ask that her daughter may be healed. Her application must have been a great solace to His wounded heart. He always loved to be asked for such blessings; and, rejected as He had been by His countrymen, it must have been a special encouragement to be approached in this way by a stranger. That it was so may be inferred from what He said on similar occasions. When the Roman centurion came to have his servant healed, Jesus commended his wonderful faith, and then added: "I say unto you, That many shall come from the east and west, and shall sit down with Abraham, and Isaac, and Jacob, in the kingdom of heaven." So, too, when it was announced to Him that some Greeks desired to see Him, the first effect was to sharpen the agony of His rejection by His own countrymen; but immediately He recovers Himself, looks beyond the cross and the shame to the glory that shall follow, and exclaims, "I, if I be lifted up from the earth, will draw all men unto Me." There can be no doubt that at this time of rejection in Galilee it must have been a similar consolation to receive this visit from the woman of Canaan.

How, then, can we explain His treatment of her? First, He answered her not a word. Then He reminded her that she did not belong to Israel, as if she therefore could have no claim on Him. And when she still urged her suit, in a manner that might have appealed to the hardest heart, He gave her an answer which seems so incredibly harsh, that it is with a feeling of pain one hears it repeated after eighteen hundred years. What does all this mean? It means "praise and honour and glory" for the poor woman; for the disciples, and for all disciples, a lesson never to be forgotten. He Who knew what was in man, knew what was in this noble woman's heart, and He wished to bring it out—to bring it out so that the disciples should see it, so that other disciples should see it, so that generation after generation and century after century should see it, and admire it, and learn its lesson. It cost her some minutes' pain: Him also,—how it must have wrung His heart to treat her in a way so foreign to every fibre of His soul! But had He not so dealt with her, what a loss to her, to the disciples, to countless multitudes! He very much needs a shining example of living faith to set over against the dead formalism of these traditionalists; and here it is: He must bring it out of its obscurity, and set it as a star in the firmament of His gospel, to shine for ever and ever. He tested her to the uttermost, because He knew that at the end of all He could say: "O woman, great is thy faith: be it unto thee even as thou wilt." The heart of the Saviour was never filled with a deeper tenderness or a wiser and more far-seeing love than when He repulsed this woman again and again, and treated her with what seemed at the moment most inexcusable and unaccountable harshness.

The lessons which shine out in the simple story of this woman can only be touched in the slightest manner. We have already referred to the contrast between the great men of Jerusalem and this poor woman of Canaan; observe now how strikingly is suggested the distinction between Israel according to the flesh and Israel according to the spirit. The current idea of the time was that lineal descent from Abraham determined who belonged to the house of Israel and who did not. The Saviour strikes at the root of this error. He does not indeed attack it directly. For this the time has not yet come: the veil of the Temple has not yet been rent in twain. But He draws aside the veil a little, so as to give a glimpse of the truth and prepare the way for its full revealing when the time shall come. He does not broadly say, "This woman of Canaan is as good an Israelite as any of you;" but He says, "I am not sent but unto the lost sheep of the house of Israel"—and heals her daughter notwithstanding. Was it not, then, evident that this poor woman after all did in some sense belong to the lost sheep of the house of Israel whom Jesus came to save?

The house of Israel?—what does Israel mean? Learn at Peniel. See Jacob in sore distress at the brook Jabbok. A man is wrestling with him,—wrestling with him all the night, until the break of day. It is no mere man, for Jacob finds before all is over that he has been face to face with God. The man who wrestled with him indeed was the same as He Who wrestled with this woman of Canaan. The Divine Man struggles to get away without blessing the patriarch. Jacob cries, in the very desperation of his faith, "I will not let Thee go, except Thou bless me!" The victory is won. The blessing is granted, and these words are added: "What is thy name?" "Jacob." "Thy name shall be called no more Jacob, but Israel" (i.e. prince with God): "for as a prince hast thou power with God and with men, and hast prevailed."

Was this woman, then, or was she not, "a prince" with God? Did she, or did she not, belong to the true house of Israel? Let us now look back to vv. 8 and 9: "This people" (i.e. the children of Israel according to the flesh) ... "honoureth Me with their lips; but their heart is far from Me. But *in vain* they do worship Me." In vain do they worship: are they, then, princes with God? Nay, verily; they are only actors before Him, as the Saviour plainly says. Truly they are not all Israel who are of Israel; and just as truly they are not the only Israel who are of Israel, for here is this woman of Canaan who earns the name of Israel by as hard a contest and as great a victory as that of Jacob at the brook Jabbok, when first the name was given.

Another instructive contrast is inevitably suggested between the foremost of the apostles and this nameless woman of Canaan. The last illustration of faith was Peter's venture on the water. What a difference between the strong man and the weak woman! To the strong, brave man the Master had to say "O thou of little faith! wherefore didst thou doubt?" To the weak woman, "O woman, great is thy faith." What an encouragement here to the little ones, the obscure, unnoticed disciples! "Many that are first shall be last, and the last first."

The encouragement to persevering prayer, especially to parents anxious for their children, is so obvious that it need only be named. That silence first, and then these apparent refusals, are trials of faith, to which many earnest hearts have not been strangers. To all such the example of this woman of Canaan is of great value. Her earnestness in making the case of her daughter her own (she does not say, "Have mercy on my daughter;" but, "Have mercy on *me*;" and again, "Lord, help *me*"), and her unconquerable perseverance till the answer came, have been an inspiration ever since, and will be to the end of the world.

The lesson taught by our Lord's dealing with the woman of Canaan is conveyed again on a larger scale by what happened in the region of Decapolis, east of the Sea of Galilee; for it was in that region, as we learn from the more detailed account in the second Gospel, that the events which follow came to pass.

The distance from the one place to the other is considerable, and the route our Lord took was by no means direct. His object at this time seems to have been to court retirement as much as possible, that He might give

Himself to the preparation of His disciples—and we may, with reverence add, His own preparation also—for the sad journey southward to Jerusalem and Calvary. Besides, His work in the north is done: no more circuits in Galilee now; so He keeps on the far outskirts of the land, passing through Sidon, across the southern ridge of Lebanon, past the base of mighty Hermon, then southward to Decapolis—all the way on border territory, where the people were more heathen than Jewish in race and religion. We can imagine Him on this long and toilsome journey, looking in both directions with strange emotion—away out to the Gentile nations with love and longing; and (with what mingled feelings of pain and eagerness who can tell?) to that Jerusalem, where soon He must offer up the awful sacrifice. When, after the long journey, He came nigh to the Sea of Galilee, He sought seclusion by going up into a mountain. But even in this borderland He cannot be hid; and when the sick and needy throng around Him, He cannot turn away from them. He still keeps within the limits of His commission, as set forth in His reply to the woman of Canaan; but, though He does not go to seek out those beyond the pale, when they seek Him, He cannot send them away; accordingly, in these heathen or semi-heathen regions, we have another set of cures and another feeding of the hungry multitude.

We need not dwell on these incidents, as they are a repetition, with variations, of what He had done at the conclusion of His work in Galilee. As to the repetition,—strange to say, there are those who cavil, whenever similar events appear successively in the story of the life and work of Christ. As if it were possible that a work like His could be free from repetition! How often does a physician repeat himself in the course of his practice? Christ is always repeating Himself. Every time a sinner comes to Him for salvation, He repeats Himself, with variations; and when need arose in Decapolis— like that which had previously arisen at Bethsaida, only more urgent, for the multitude in the present case had been three days from home, and were ready to faint with hunger—must their wants go unrelieved merely to avoid repetition? As to the telling of it—for this of course might have been avoided, on the ground that a similar event had been related before—was there not most excellent reason for it, in the fact that these people were not of the house of Israel in the literal sense? To have omitted the record of these deeds of mercy would have been to leave out the evidence they afforded that the love of Christ went out not to Jews only, but to all sick and hungry ones.

Sick and hungry—these words suggest the two great needs of humanity. Christ comes to heal disease, to satisfy hunger; in particular, to heal the root disease of sin, and satisfy the deep hunger of the soul for God and life in Him. And when we read how He healed all manner of disease among the multitudes in Decapolis, and thereafter fed them abundantly when they were ready to faint with hunger, we see how He is set forth as a Saviour from sin and Revealer of God beyond the borders of the land of Israel.

It is worth noticing how well this general record follows the story of the woman of Canaan. Just as she—though not of Israel after the flesh—proved herself to be of Israel after the spirit, so these heathen or semi-heathen people of Decapolis forsake their paganism when they see the Christ; for of no heathen deity do they speak: they "glorified the God of Israel" (ver. 31). Thus we have a contrast similar to that which we recognised in the case of the woman of Canaan, between those scribes and Pharisees of Jerusalem—who drew near to the God of Israel with their lips while the heart was far away—and these people of Decapolis, who, though "afar off" in the estimation of these dignitaries of Jerusalem, are in truth "nigh" to the God of Israel. Is there not in the events of the chapter a wondrous light cast on the true meaning of the name Israel, as not according to the flesh, but according to the spirit?

IV.—The Culmination of the Crisis (xvi. 1-12)

All this time Jesus has been keeping as much out of the way of His ungrateful countrymen as the limits of His commission would permit, hovering, as it were, around the northern outskirts of the land. But when in the course of this largest circuit of all His northern journeys, He reaches Decapolis, He is so near home that He cannot but cross the lake and revisit the familiar scenes. How is He received? Do the people flock around Him as they did before? If it had been so, we should no doubt have been told. There seems to have been not a single word of welcome. Of all the multitudes He had healed and blessed, there is no one to cry, "Hosanna to the Son of David!"

His friends, if He has any, have gone back, and walk no more with Him; but His old enemies the Pharisees do not fail Him; and they are not alone now, nor, as before, in alliance only with those naturally in sympathy with them, but have actually made a league with their great opponents, the two rival parties of Pharisee and Sadducee, finding in their common hatred of the Christ of God a sinister bond of union.

This is the first time the Sadducees are mentioned in this Gospel as coming in contact with Jesus. Some of them had come to the baptism of John, to his great astonishment; but, beyond this, they have as yet put in no appearance. They were the aristocracy of the land, and held the most important offices of Church and State in the capital. It is therefore the less to be wondered at that up to this time the Carpenter of Nazareth should have been beneath their notice. Now, however, the news of His great doings in the north has at last compelled attention; the result is this combination with the Pharisees, who have already been for some time engaged in the attempt to put Him down. There is indication elsewhere (Mark viii. 15) that the Herodians had also united with them; so we may look upon this as the culmination of the crisis in Galilee, when all the forces of the country have been roused to active and bitter hostility.

The Pharisees and Sadducees, as is well known, were at opposite poles of thought; the one being the traditionalists, the other the sceptics, of the time, so that it was quite remarkable that they should unite in anything. They did, however, unite in this demand for a sign from heaven. Neither of them could deny that signs had been given,—that the blind had received sight, lepers had been cleansed, the lame healed, and deeds of mercy done on every side. But neither party was satisfied with this. Each was wedded to a system of thought according to which signs on earth were of no evidential value. A sign from heaven was what they needed to convince them. The demand was practically the same as that which the Pharisees and scribes had made before (xii. 38), though it is put more specifically here as a sign *from heaven*. The reason why the Pharisees adopted the same method of attack as before is not far to seek. Their object was not to obtain satisfaction as to His claims, but to find the easiest way of discrediting them; and, knowing as they did from their past experience that the demand of a special sign would be refused, they counted on the refusal beforehand, to be used by their new allies as well as themselves as a weapon against Him. They were not disappointed, for our Lord was no respecter of persons; therefore He spoke just as plainly and sternly when the haughty Sadducees were present as He had done before they made their appearance.

The words are stern and strong; but here again it is "more in sorrow than in anger" that He speaks. We learn from St. Mark that, as He gave His answers, "He sighed deeply in His spirit." There had been so many signs, and they were so plain and clear—signs which spoke for themselves, signs which so plainly spelt out the words, "The kingdom of heaven is among you"—that it was unspeakably sad to think that they should be blind to them all, and find it in their heart to ask for something else, which in its nature would be no sign at all, but only a portent, a barren miracle.

We can see in this how determined our Lord was not to minister to the craving for the merely miraculous. He would work no miracle for the mere purpose of exciting astonishment or even of producing conviction, when there was quite enough for all who were at all willing to receive it, in the regular, natural and necessary development of His work as the Healer of the sick, the Shepherd of the people, the Refuge of the troubled and distressed.

Had there been no signs of the times, there might have been some reason for signs in the heavens; but when there were signs in abundance of the kind to appeal to all that was best in the minds and hearts of men, why should these be discredited by resorting to another kind of sign much inferior and far less adapted to the securing of the special object for which the King of heaven had come into the world? The signs of the times were after all far more easily discerned than those signs in the heavens by which they were accustomed to anticipate both fine and stormy weather. There were signs of blessing enough to convince any doubter that the summer of heaven was easily within His reach; on the other hand, in the state of the nation, and the rapidly developing circumstances which were hastening on the fulfilment of the most terrible of the prophecies concerning it, there were signs enough to give far more certain indication of approaching judgment, than when the red and lowering morning gave token of the coming thunderstorm (vv. 2, 3). So He tells them, convicting them of wilful blindness; and then repeats in almost identical terms the refusal He had given to the scribes and Pharisees before: "A wicked and adulterous generation seeketh after a sign; and there shall no sign be given unto it, but the sign of the prophet Jonas" (see xii. 39, and remarks on it on pp. 166-8).

"And He left them, and departed." How sad for Him; how awful for them! Had there been in their hearts one single aspiration for the true and good, He would not have left them so. Where are these Pharisees and Sadducees now? What do they now think of the work of that day?

"He left them, and again entering into the boat departed to the other side" (Mark viii. 13). Did He ever cross the lake again? If He did, there is no record of it. He passed in sight of it in that sorrowful southward journey to Jerusalem which He must presently commence; and He will visit the same shore again after His resurrection to cheer the apostles at their toil; but this seems to have been the last crossing. What a sad one it must have been!— after a beginning so bright that it was heralded as daybreak on Gennesaret's shore, after all His self-denying toil, after all the words of wisdom He has spoken and the deeds of mercy He has done upon these shores, to leave them, as He does now, rejected and despised, an outcast, to all outward appearance a failure. No wonder He is silent in that crossing of the lake; no wonder He is lost in saddest thought, turning over and over in His mind the signs of the times forced so painfully on His attention!

The disciples with Him in the boat had no share in these sad thoughts. Their minds, as it would seem, were occupied for the most part with the mistake they had made in provisioning the boat. Accordingly, when at last He broke silence, He found them quite out of touch with Him. He had been thinking of the sad unbelief of these Pharisees and Sadducees, and of the awful danger of allowing the spirit which was in them to dominate the life; hence the solemn caution: "Take heed, and beware of the leaven of the Pharisees and of the Sadducees." The disciples meantime had been counting their loaves, or rather, looking sadly on the one loaf which, on searching their baskets, they found to be all they had; and when the word *leaven* caught their ear, coupled with a caution as to a particular kind of it, they said one to another, "It is because we have taken no bread!" Another cause of sadness to the Master. He had been mourning over the blindness of Pharisees and Sadducees; He must now mourn over the blindness of His own disciples; and not blindness only, but also forgetfulness of a thrice-taught lesson: for why should the mere supply of bread be any cause of anxiety to them, after what they had seen once and again in these very regions to which they were going?

But these hearts were not shut against Him; theirs was not the blindness of those that will not see; accordingly, the result is very different. He did not leave them and depart; nor, on the other hand, did He explain in so many words what He meant. It was far better that they should find out for themselves. The riddles of nature and of life are not furnished with keys. They must be discerned by thoughtful attention; so, instead of providing them a key to His little parable, He puts them in the way of finding it for themselves by asking them a series of questions which convinced them of their thoughtlessness and faithlessness, and led them to recognise His true meaning (vv. 8-12).

XIII
THE NEW DEPARTURE

(FOUNDING OF THE CHURCH.)

Matt. xvi. 13-xvii. 21.

THIS conversation at Cæsarea Philippi is universally regarded as marking a new era in the life of Christ. His rejection by "His own" is now complete. Jerusalem, troubled at His birth, had been troubled once again when He suddenly came to His Temple, and began to cleanse it in His Father's name; and though many at the feast were attracted by His deeds of mercy, He could not commit Himself to any of them (John ii. 24): there was no rock there on which to build His Church. He had passed through Samaria, and found there fields white unto the harvest, but the time of reaping was not yet. Galilee had given better promise: again and again it had appeared as if the foundation of the new kingdom would be firmly laid in the land of "Zebulun and Naphtali"; but there had been bitter and crushing disappointment,—even the cities where most of His mighty works were done repented not. The people had eagerly welcomed His earthly things; but when He began to speak to them of heavenly things they "went back, and walked no more with Him." And though opportunity after opportunity was given them while He hovered on the outskirts, ever and anon returning[12] to the familiar scenes, they would not repent; they would not welcome or even receive the kingdom of God which Christ came to found. The country has been traversed from the wilderness of Judæa, in the far south, even unto Dan; and as there had been no room for the Infant King in the inn, so there was none in all the land for the infant kingdom.

Thus it comes to pass that, with the very small band He has gathered around Him—called in the land indeed, but now of necessity called to come out of it—He withdraws to the neighbourhood of the Gentile town of Cæsarea Philippi; not for seclusion only, but, as the event shows, to found an *Ecclesia*—His Church. The scenery in this region is exceptionally beautiful, and the place was in every way suited for a season of quiet communion with nature and with nature's God. It was, moreover, just outside the land; and in the place and surroundings there was much that must have been suggestive and inspiring. Is not this great mountain, on one of the southern flanks of which they are now resting, the mighty Hermon, the great landmark of the north, rearing its snowy head on high to catch the precious clouds of heaven, and enrich with them the winds that shall blow southward over Palestine? And are not these springs which issue from the rock beside them the sources of the Jordan, the sacred river? As the dew of Hermon, and as the flowing of the water-springs, shall be that Church of the living God, which, as the sequel will unfold, had its first foundation on this rocky hillside and by these river sources.

Into this remote and rocky region, then, the Master has retired with the small band of faithful disciples, on whom alone He can depend for the future. But can He depend even on them? Have they not been tainted with the general apostasy? Does He not already know one of them to be in heart a traitor? (cf. John vi. 70). And have not all of them just needed the caution themselves to beware of the leaven of the Pharisees and Sadducees? Are they really strong men of faith, like "faithful Abraham," or are they to be like reeds shaken by the wind? The time has come to test it. This He does, first by asking them what they think of Himself, and then by showing them what they must expect if they still will follow Him. First there must be the test of faith, to ascertain what they have learned from their intercourse with Him in the past; then the test of hope, lest their attachment to Him should be based on expectations doomed to disappointment.

I.—The Christ (xvi. 13-20)

The faith test is a strictly personal one. We have seen how the Master has, so to speak, focussed His gospel in Himself. He had begun by preaching the Gospel of the Kingdom, and calling men to repentance; but as time passed on He found it necessary to make a more personal appeal, pressing His invitations in the winning form, "Come unto Me." When things came to a crisis in Galilee, He first in symbol and then in word set Himself before the people as the bread of life, which each one must receive and eat if he would live. Thus He has been making it more and more evident that the only way to receive the kingdom of God is to welcome Himself as the Son of the living God come to claim the hearts of men for His Father in heaven. How is it with the little band? Is theirs the popular notion, which classes the Son of God as only one among other gifted sons of men, or do they welcome Him in the plenitude of His divine prerogative and power? Hence the first inquiry, which brings out the answer: "Some say that Thou art John the Baptist; some, Elias; and others, Jeremias, or one of the prophets." This is manifestly the popular idea at its highest and best. There were, no doubt, among the people those whose thought already was "Away with Him! away with Him!" But it might well go without saying that the disciples had no sympathy with these. It did, however, remain to be seen whether they were not content, like the best of the people, to accept Him as a teacher sent from God, a great prophet of Israel, or at most a John the Baptist, the mere herald of the coming King. We can imagine, then, with what intensity of feeling the Master would look into the disciples' eyes as He put the testing question, "But whom say *ye* that I am?" and with what joy He would hail the ready response of their spokesman Peter, when, with eyes full of heavenly light and heart glowing with sacred fire, he exclaimed, "Thou art the Christ, the Son of the living God!"

It would be beyond belief, were it not so sadly familiar a fact, that some, professing honestly to interpret this passage, resolve the answer of the apostle into little or nothing more than the popular idea, as if the Sonship here referred to were only what any prophet or righteous man might claim. He surely must be wilfully blind who does not see that the apostolic answer which the Lord accepts is wide as the poles from the popular notions He so decisively rejects; and this is made peculiarly emphatic by the striking words with which the true answer is welcomed—the Saviour's first personal beatitude (as if to suggest, His is the kingdom of heaven—cf. Matt. v. 3, 10): "Blessed art thou, Simon Bar-jona: for flesh and blood hath not revealed it unto thee, but My Father which is in heaven." It will be remembered that, in asserting His own personal relation to the Father, Christ had said: "No man knoweth the Son, but the Father; neither knoweth any man the Father, save the Son, and he to whomsoever the Son will reveal Him" (xi. 27); and now that to one at least the Father has been revealed in the Son, He recognises the fact with joy. These notions of the people about Him were but earth-born notions, the surmisings of "flesh and blood": this faith of the true apostle was born from above; it could have come only from heaven.

Now at last, therefore, the foundation is laid, and the building of the spiritual temple is begun. The words which follow (ver. 18) are quite natural and free from most, if not from all, the difficulties in which perverse human ingenuity has entangled them, if only we bear in mind the circumstances and surroundings. The little group is standing on one of the huge rocky flanks of mighty Hermon, great boulders here and there around them; and in all probability, well in sight, some great stones cut out of the rock and made ready for use in building, like those still to be seen in the neighbourhood of Baalbec, to the north of Hermon; for this region was famous for its great temples. Now, when we remember that the two words our Lord uses (πέτρος and πέτρα) for "rock" in our version have not precisely the same meaning—the one (Petros, Peter) signifying a piece of rock, a stone, the other (Petra) suggesting rather the great bed-rock out of which these stones are cut and on which they are lying—we can understand that, while the reference is certainly in the first place to Peter himself, the main thing is the great fact just brought out that he is resting, in the strength of faith, on God as revealed in His Son. Thus, while Peter is certainly the piece of rock, the first stone which is laid upon the great underlying foundation on which all the faithful build, and therefore is in a sense—the common popular sense, in fact—the foundation stone, yet the foundation of all is the Bed-Rock, on which the first stone and all other stones are laid. Bearing this well in mind, we further see that there is no inconsistency between this and those other scriptures in which God is represented as alone the Rock of our salvation. The Bed-Rock, "the Rock of Ages," is here, as elsewhere, God as revealed in His Son, and Peter is the first stone "well and truly laid" upon it.

If the surroundings suggest the use of the words *Petros* and *Petra*, stone and rock, the circumstances suggest the use of the word Ecclesia, or Church, which is here employed by our Lord for the first time. Up to this time He has spoken always of the kingdom, never of the church. How is this to be explained? Of course the kingdom is the larger term; and now it is necessary that that portion of the kingdom which is to be organised on earth should be distinguished by a specific designation; and the use of the word "church" in preference to the more familiar "synagogue" may be accounted for by the desire to avoid confusion. Besides this, however, the word itself is specially significant. It means an assembly "called out," and suggests the idea of separateness, so appropriate to the circumstances of the little band of outcasts.

To see into this more fully, let us recall the recent teaching as to the true Israel (chap. xv.), no longer to be found in the old land of Israel. If there is to be an Israel at all, it must be reconstituted "outside the camp." In view of this, how strikingly significant is it that just as Abraham had to leave his country and go to a strange land to found the old theocracy, so Christ has to leave His country and go with His followers to these remote northern regions to constitute *"the Israel of God,"* to inaugurate His Church, the company of those who, like these faithful ones, come out and are separate to be united by faith to Him! Christ with the Twelve around Him is the Israel of the New Testament; and we can imagine that it was on this occasion especially that in the prayers which we know from St. Luke's Gospel He offered in connection with this very conversation, He would find these words of devotion especially appropriate: "Behold, I and the children which God hath given Me" (Heb. ii. 13). The family of God (see chap. xii. 49) are by themselves apart, disowned by those who still bear unworthily the name of Israel; and most appropriate it is that on this occasion our Lord should begin to use that great word, which means first "called out" and then "gathered in": "on this rock I will build My Church."

When we think of the place and the scene and the circumstances, the sad memories of the past and the gloomy forebodings for the future, what sublimity of faith must we recognise in the words which immediately follow: "The gates of hell shall not prevail against it"! Oh! shame on us who grow faint-hearted with each discouragement, when the Master, with rejection behind Him and death before Him, found it encouragement enough after so much toil to make a bare beginning of the new temple of the Lord; and even in that day of smallest things was able to look calmly forward across the troubled sea of the dark future and already raise the shout of final victory!

But that day of victory is still far off; and before it can even begin to come, there must be a descent into the valley of the shadow of death. He is about to tell His disciples that He must go up to Jerusalem and die, and leave them to be the builders of the Church. He cannot continue long to be the Keeper of the keys; so He must prepare them for taking them from His hand when the time shall come for Him to go. Hence the words which follow, appropriately addressed in the first place to the disciple who had first confessed Him: "I will give unto thee the keys of the kingdom of heaven." "Honour to whom honour is due:" the first member of the Church is to be its prime minister as well. When the Master's voice shall be silent, the voice of the rock-disciple (and of the other disciples as well, for the same commission was afterwards extended to them all) shall have the same authority to bind, to loose, to regulate the administration of Church affairs as if He Himself were with them. It was not yet time to tell them how it would be—viz., by the coming and indwelling of His Spirit; it is enough now to give them the assurance that the infant Church shall not be left without authority from above, without power from on high.

The Church is founded; but for a time it must remain in obscurity. The people are not ready; and the gospel, which is to be the power of God unto salvation, is not yet complete, until He shall go up to Jerusalem and suffer many things and die. Till then all that has passed in this sacred northern retreat must remain a secret: "He charged His disciples that they should tell no man that He was the Christ" (R.V.).

II.—The Cross (xvi. 21-28)

A still more searching test must now be applied. It is not enough to discover what they have learned from their intercourse with Him in the past; He must find out whether they have courage enough to face what is now impending in the future. Their faith in God as revealed in Christ His Son has been well approved. It remains to be seen whether it is strong enough to bear the ordeal of the cross, to which it must soon be subjected: "From that time forth began Jesus to show unto His disciples, how that He must go unto Jerusalem, and suffer many things of the elders and chief priests and scribes, and be killed."

Already from time to time He had darkly hinted what manner of death He should die; but it was only from this time that He began to *show* it unto them, to put it before them so that they could not fail to see it. Herein see the wisdom and tender considerateness of "the Son of man." So dark and difficult a lesson would have been too much for them before. The ordeal would have been too severe. Not until their faith has begun with some firmness to grasp His true and proper divinity, can their hope live with such a prospect. There must be some basis for a faith in His rising again, before He can ask them even to look into the dark abyss of death into which He must descend. That basis is found in the confession of the rock-apostle; and relying on it He can trust them by-and-by, if not at once, to look through the darkness of the suffering and death to the rising again, the prospect of which He sets before them at the very same time: "and be raised again the third day." Besides, there was no possibility of their ever beginning to understand the atonement till they had grasped the truth of the incarnation. To this day the one is intelligible only in the light of the other. Those to whom Jesus of Nazareth is only "one of the prophets" cannot begin to see how He *must* suffer and die. Only those who with the apostles rise to the realisation of His divine glory are prepared to understand anything of the mystery of His Cross and Passion.

As yet, however, the mystery is too deep and the prospect too dark even for them, as becomes painfully evident from the conduct of the bravest of them all, who "took Him, and began to rebuke Him, saying, Be it far from Thee, Lord: this shall not be unto Thee."

We naturally and properly blame the presumption of the apostle, who, when he did not understand, might at least have been silent, or have contented himself with some modest question, instead of this unbecoming remonstrance with One Whose Messiahship and Divine Sonship he had just confessed. But, though we may blame him for what he said, we cannot wonder at what he thought and felt. The lesson of the cross is just beginning. The disciples are just entering a higher form in the Master's school; and it does not follow, because they have undergone so well their examination on the great lesson of the past, that they are prepared all at once to take in what must be the great lesson of the future. They have had time for the first: may they not be allowed time for the second? Why, then, is Peter reproved so very severely?

We may say, indeed, that faithfulness to Peter himself required it. The strong commendation with which his noble confession has been greeted, instead of making him humble, as it ought to have done, inasmuch as it reminded him that it was not of himself but from above he had the power to make it, seems to have made him over-confident, trustful to that very flesh and blood to which he had been assured he was, in regard to that confession, in no wise indebted. It was therefore necessary that the warm commendation accorded to the strength of his faith should be balanced by an equally strong condemnation of his unbelief. But there is more than this to be said. Christ is looking at Peter, and speaking to Peter; but he recognises another, whom He names and whom in the first place He addresses: "Get thee behind Me, Satan." He recognises the same old enemy, with the same old weapon of assault: for it is the same temptation as that which formed the climax of the conflict in the wilderness, a temptation to prosecute His work by methods which would spare Him the awful agony of the cross. The devil had departed from Him then; but only, as we were informed, "for a season"; and there are frequent indications in the subsequent history that at critical times the great adversary took opportunities of renewing the old temptation. This is one of these occasions. Let us by all means bear in mind that our Lord was true man—that He was "compassed with infirmity," that He was "tempted in all points like as we are," though ever without sin; let us not imagine, then, that His human soul was always on so serene a height that the words of one who loved Him and whom He loved so much would have no effect on Him. It was hard enough for Him to face the awful darkness, without having this new stumbling-block set in His path. It is a real temptation, and a most dangerous one; He may not therefore tamper with it for a moment: He may not allow His affection for His true disciple to blind Him to the real source of it; He must realise with whom He has to deal; He must behind the love of the apostle recognise the malice of the evil one, who is using him as his instrument; accordingly, with His face set as a flint, with His whole being braced for resistance, so that not a hair's-breadth shall be yielded, He says: "Get thee behind Me, Satan: thou art a stumbling-block unto Me" (R.V.)—words which clearly indicate that He had recognised the danger, and summoned the resources of His faith and obedience to put the stumbling-block away.

"Resist the devil, and he will flee from you." We may be sure, therefore, that so soon as the energetic words were spoken *he* was gone: the stumbling-block was out of the way. The words which follow may therefore be regarded as spoken to Peter himself, to bring to his own consciousness the difference between the heavenly faith which had come by revelation from above, and the earthly doubt and denial, which was evidently not of God, though so natural to flesh and blood: "Thou mindest not the things of God, but the things of men" (R.V.).

Thus once more the Christ of God takes up the cross of man. In doing so He not only sets aside the protest, uttered or unexpressed, of His disciples' hearts; but He tells them plainly that they too must take the same dark path if they would follow Him: "Then said Jesus unto His disciples, If any man will come after Me, let him deny himself, and take up his cross, and follow Me." So He tests them to the uttermost. He withdraws nothing He has said about the blessedness of those who welcome the kingdom of heaven; but the time has come to put the necessary condition in its strongest light, so that, if they still follow, it will be not blindly, but with eyes fully open to all that it involves. He has given hints before of the stringency of the Divine requirement; He has spoken of the strait gate and the narrow way; now He goes to the very heart of that hard matter, and unfolds the innermost secret of the kingdom of heaven. "Let him deny himself:" here is the pivot of all—the *crux*.

Be it observed that this is not "self-denial" as currently understood, a term applied to the denial to self of something or other which perhaps self cares very little about, but something much more radical. It is the denial of self involving as its correlative the giving of the life to God. It is the death of self-will, and the birth of God-will,[13] as the central force of the life.

"Let him deny himself, *and take up his cross*." Each one has "his" cross, some point in which the will of God and self-will come into direct opposition. To the Captain of our salvation the conflict came in its very darkest and most dreadful form. Its climax was in the Garden, when after the great agony He cried: "Not My will, but Thine be done." Our conflict will not be nearly so severe: it may even be on a point that may seem small,—whether or not we will give up some besetting sin, whether or not we will do some disagreeable duty, whether or not we will surrender something which stands between us and Christ,—but whatever that be in which the will of God and our own will are set in opposition, there is our cross, and it must be taken up, and self must be denied that we may follow Christ. "They that are Christ's have *crucified the flesh*."

Is this, then, the great salvation? Does it resolve itself into a species of suicide? Do we enter the kingdom of life by death? It is even so; and the words which follow resolve the paradox: "For whosoever will save his life shall lose it: and whosoever will lose his life for My sake shall find it." It is a surrender of life, certainly, for the giving up of self means the giving up of all; but these words "for My sake" make all the difference. It is a surrender which, in dethroning self, enthrones Christ in the life. It is dying indeed; but it is dying into life: it is an act of faith which puts an end to the old life of the flesh, and opens the gate for the new life of the spirit.

We have seen that all may hinge on some point that may seem quite small, in which case the sacrifice is plainly not to be compared with the compensation; but even when the very greatest sacrifice is demanded, it is folly not to make it: "For what shall a man be profited, if he shall gain the whole world, and forfeit his life?" (R.V.). And, if life is forfeited, how can it be bought back again: "What shall a man give in exchange for his life" (R.V.)? "In Him was life," and in Him is life still; therefore He is more to us than all the world. It is better to suffer the loss of all things for Christ, than to have all that flesh and blood could desire without Him.

The world is very large; and the Son of man must have seemed very small and weak that day, as He told them of the coming days when He should suffer so many things at His enemies' hands, and die; but this is only while the time of testing lasts: things will be seen in their true proportion by-and-by, when "the Son of man shall come" (what a golden background this to the dark prospect immediately before them! He *must go*; yes; but *He shall come*) "in the glory of His Father with His angels; then He shall reward every man according to his works." Thus, with the searching test the Saviour gives the reassuring prospect; and lest by reason of its indefinite distance they may fail to find in it all the encouragement they need for the present distress, He gives them the further assurance that, before very long, there shall be manifest tokens of the coming glory of their now despised and slighted King: "Verily I say unto you, There be some standing here, which shall not taste of death, till they see the Son of man coming in His kingdom."

III.—The Glory (xvii. 1-8)

"After six days"—the interval is manifestly of importance, for the three Evangelists who record the event all lay stress on it. St. Luke says "about an eight days," which indicates that the six days referred to by the others were days of interval between that on which the conversation at Cæsarea Philippi took place and the morning of the transfiguration. It follows that we may regard this important epoch in the life of our Lord as covering a week; and may we not speak of it as His passion week in the north? The shadow of the cross was on Him all His life through; but it must have been much darker during this week than ever before. At the beginning of it He had been obliged for the first time to let that shadow fall upon His loved disciples, and the days which followed seem to have been given to thought and prayer, and quiet, unrecorded conversation. Beyond all question their thoughts would be fixed on the new subject of contemplation which had just been brought before them, and whatever conversation they had with one another and with the Master would have this for its centre. It cannot but have been a very sad and trying week. The first tidings of the approach of some impending disaster is often harder to bear than is the stroke itself when afterwards it falls. To the disciples the whole horizon of the future would be filled with darkest clouds of mystery; for though they had been told also of the rising again and the glory that should follow, they could as yet get little cheer from what lay so far in the dim distance, and was, moreover, so little understood, that even after the vision on the mount, the favoured three questioned with each other what the rising from the dead might mean (Mark ix. 10). To the Master the awful prospect must have been much more definite and real; yet even to His human soul it could not have been free from that namelessness of mystery that must have made the anticipation in some respects as bad as the reality, rendering the week to Him a passion week indeed.

No wonder that at the end of it He has a great longing heavenward, and that He should ask the three most advanced of His disciples, who had been with Him in the chamber of death and were afterwards to be witnesses of His agony in the Garden, to go with Him to a high mountain apart. The wisdom of His taking only these three was afterwards fully apparent, when it proved that the experience awaiting them on the mountain-top was almost too much for even them to bear. It is of no importance to identify the mountain; probably it was one of the spurs of the Hermon range, at the base of which they had spent the intervening week. We can perfectly understand the sacred instinct which led the Saviour to seek the highest point which could be readily reached, so as to feel Himself for the time as far away from earth and as near to heaven as possible. When we think of this, what pathos is there in the reference to the height of the mountain and the loneliness of the spot: He "bringeth them up into a high mountain apart"!

We are told by St. Luke that they went up "to pray." It seems most natural to accept this statement as not only correct, but as a sufficient statement of the object our Saviour had in view. The thought of transfiguration may not have been in His mind at all. Here, as always, He was guided by the will of His Father in heaven; and it is not necessary to suppose that to His human mind that will was made known earlier than the occasion required. We are not told that He went up to be transfigured: we are told that He went up to pray.

It seems probable that the idea was to spend the night in prayer. We know that this was a not infrequent custom with Him; and if ever there seemed a call for it, it must have been now, when about to begin that sorrowful journey which led to Calvary. With this thought agree all the indications which suggest that it was evening when they ascended, night while they remained on the top, and morning when they came down. This, too, will account in the most natural manner for the drowsiness of the apostles; and the fact that their Lord felt none of it only proved how much more vivid was his realisation of the awfulness of the crisis than theirs was. We are to think of the four, then, as slowly and thoughtfully climbing the hill at eventide, carrying their *abbas*, or rugs, on which they would kneel for prayer, and which, if they needed rest, they would wrap around them, as is the Oriental custom. By the time they reached the top, night would have cast its veil of mystery on the grandeur of the mountains round about them; while snowy Hermon in the gloom would rise like a mighty giant to heaven, its summit "visited all night by troops of stars." Never before nor since has there been such a prayer meeting on this earth of ours.

A careful reading of all the records leads us to think of the following as the order of events. Having gone up to pray, they would doubtless all kneel down together. As the night wore on, the three disciples, being exhausted, would wrap themselves in their cloaks and go to sleep; while the Master, to whom sleep at such a time was unnatural, if not impossible, would continue in prayer. Can we suppose that that time of pleading was free from agony? His soul had been stirred within Him when Peter had tempted Him to turn aside from the path of the Cross; and may we not with reverence suppose that on that lonely hilltop, as later in the Garden, there might be in His heart the cry, "Father, if it be possible"? If only the way upward were open now! Has not the kingdom of God been preached in Judæa, in Samaria, in Galilee, away to the very borderlands? and has not the Church been founded? and has not authority been given to the apostles? Is it, then, absolutely necessary to go back, back to Jerusalem, not to gain a triumph, but to accept the last humiliation and defeat? There cannot but have been a great conflict of feeling; and with all the determination to be obedient even unto death, there must have been a shrinking from the way of the cross, and a great longing for heaven and home and the Father's welcome. The longing cannot be gratified: it is not possible for the cup to pass from Him; but just as later in Gethsemane there came an angel from heaven strengthening him, so now His longing for heaven and home and the smile of His Father is gratified in the gladdening and strengthening experience which followed His prayer—a foretaste of the heavenly glory, so vivid, so satisfying, that He will thenceforth be strong, for the joy that is set before Him, to endure the Cross, despising the shame. For behold, as He prays, His face becomes radiant, the glory within shining through the veil of His mortal flesh. We all know that this flesh of ours is more or less transparent, and that in moments of exaltation the faces of even ordinary men will shine as with a heavenly lustre. We need not wonder, then, that it should have been so with our Lord, only in an immeasurably higher degree: that His face should have shone even "as the sun"; and that, though He could not yet ascend to heaven,

heaven's brightness should have descended on Him and wrapped Him round, so that even "His raiment was white as the light." And not only heavenly light is round, but heavenly company; for "behold, there appeared unto them Moses and Elias talking with Him."

The disciples could not sleep through all this. "When they were fully awake, they saw His glory, and the two men that stood with Him" (Luke ix. 32, R.V.). How they recognised them we are not told. It may have been through their conversation, which in part at least they understood; for the substance of it has been preserved in St. Luke's Gospel, where we read that they "spake of His decease (literally, *exodus*) which He should accomplish at Jerusalem." The human soul of Jesus no doubt longed for an exodus here and now, from this very height of Hermon into the presence of God; but He knows this cannot be: His exodus must be accomplished in a very different way, and at Jerusalem. This Moses and Elijah knew; and their words must have brought Him encouragement and strength, and given steadiness and assurance to the wavering hearts of Peter, James and John.

That the conversation was intended for their benefit as well, seems indicated by the way in which Peter's intervention is recorded: "Then *answered* Peter, and said unto Jesus." What he said is quite characteristic of the impulsive disciple, so ready to speak without thinking. On this occasion he blunders in a very natural and pardonable way. He feels as if he ought to say something; and, as nothing more to the purpose occurs to him, he blurts out his thoughtless proposal to make three tabernacles for their abode. Besides the thoughtlessness of this speech, which is manifest enough, there seems to lurk in it a sign of his falling back into the very error which a week ago he had renounced—the error of putting his Master in the same class as Moses and Elias, reckoning Him thus, as the people of Galilee had done, simply as "one of the prophets." If so, his mistake is at once corrected; for behold a bright luminous cloud—fit symbol of the Divine presence: the cloud suggesting mystery, and the brightness, glory—wraps all from sight, and out of the cloud there comes a voice: "This is My beloved Son, in Whom I am well pleased; hear ye Him."

We now see how appropriate it was that just these two should be the heavenly messengers to wait upon the Son of man on this occasion. The one represented the law, the other the prophets. "The law and the prophets were until John;" but both are now merged in the gospel of Jesus, Who is all and in all. Moses and Elijah have long had audience of the people of God; but behold a greater than Moses or Elijah is here, and they must withdraw; and accordingly, when the Voice is silent and the cloud has cleared away, Jesus is left alone. No one remains to divide His authority, and none to share His sorrow. He must tread the winepress alone. Moses and Elijah return to the world of spirits—Jesus, God's beloved Son, to the world of men. And all His human sympathies were fresh and quick as ever; for, finding His three disciples fallen on their faces for fear, He came and touched them, saying, "Arise, and be not afraid." They no doubt thought their Lord had laid aside His human body, and left them all alone upon the mountain; but with His human hand He touched them, and with His human voice He called them as of old, and with His human heart He welcomed them again. Reassured, they lifted up their eyes, and saw their Lord—the man Christ Jesus as before—and no one else. All is over; and as the world is unprepared for it, the vision is sealed until the Son of man be risen from the dead.

Why were their lips sealed? The more we think of it, the more we shall see the wisdom of this seal of secrecy, even from the other nine; for had they been prepared to receive the revelation, they would have been privileged to witness it. The transfiguration was no mere wonder; it was no sign granted to incredulity: it was one of those sacred experiences for rare spirits in rare hours, which nature itself forbids men to parade, or even so much as mention, unless constrained to it by duty.

It is one of the innumerable notes of truth found, wherever aught that is marvellous is recorded in these Gospels, that the glory on the mount is not appealed to, to confirm the faith of any but the three who witnessed it. Upon them it did produce a deep and abiding impression. One of them, indeed, died a martyr's death so very early that we have nothing from his pen (Acts xii. 2); but both the others have left us words written late in their after life, which show how ineffaceable was the impression produced upon them by what they saw that memorable night. John evidently has it in mind, both in the beginning of his Epistle and of his Gospel, as where he says: "We beheld His glory, the glory as of the only begotten of the Father;" and Peter thus conveys the assurance which the experience of that night left with him to the end: "We have not followed cunningly devised fables, when we made known unto you the power and coming of our Lord Jesus Christ, but were eyewitnesses of His majesty. For He received from God the Father honour and glory, when there came such a voice to Him from the excellent glory, This is My beloved Son, in Whom I am well pleased. And this voice which came from heaven we heard, when we were with Him in the holy mount." But while the impression made upon the three who witnessed it was so deep and abiding, it could not be expected to have any direct evidential value to others; accordingly it remained unused in their dealings with others until their Master's work had been crowned by His resurrection from the dead, which was to be *the* sign, as He had again and again said to those who kept asking Him for a sign from heaven. The transfiguration was indeed a sign from heaven; but it was no sign for a faithless generation: it was only for those who by the strength of their faith and the purity of their devotion were prepared to receive it. Signs fitted to satisfy the doubting heart had been wrought in great abundance (xi. 4, 5); and the crowning sign was to be certified by many infallible proofs, after which it would be time to speak of the experience of that sacred night upon the holy mount.

How fitly the transfiguration closes this memorable week! As we linger with the Lord and His disciples at the sources of the Jordan, we realise that we have reached what we may call the water-shed of doctrine in His training of the Twelve. Slowly have they been rising in their thoughts of Christ, until at last they recognise His true divinity, and make a clear and full confession of it. But no sooner have they reached that height of truth than they are constrained to look down into the dark valley before them, at the bottom of which they dimly see the dreadful cross; and then, to comfort and reassure, there is this vision of the glory that shall follow. Thus we have, in succession, the three great doctrines of the faith: Incarnation, Atonement, Resurrection. There is first the glory of Christ as the Son of God; then His shame as Bearer of our sin; then the vision of the glory that shall follow, the glory given to Him as His reward. For may we not regard that company upon the mount as a miniature of the Church in heaven and on earth? There was the great and glorified Head of the Church, and round Him five representative members: two from the family in heaven, three from the family on earth—those from the Church triumphant, these from the Church still militant—those from among the saints of the old covenant, these the firstfruits of the new. Could there have been a better representation of "the whole family in heaven and on earth"? How appropriate that the passion week of the north, which began with the founding of the Church in the laying of its first stone, should end with a vision of it as completed, which must to some extent have been a fulfilment of the promise, "He shall see of the travail of His soul, and shall be satisfied"!

Observe, too, in quick succession, the great key-words of the new age: The Christ (xvi. 16), The Church (ver. 18), The Cross (ver. 24), The Glory (ver. 27): the latter, as still in the future, made real by the glory on the holy mount. The mediæval interpreters, always on the watch for the symbolism of numbers, especially the number three, regarded Peter as the apostle of faith, James of hope, and John of love. And though we may set this aside as a touch of fancy, we cannot fail to observe that just as the mind, in its grasp of truth, is led from the incarnation to the atonement, and thence to the resurrection and the glory that shall follow; so the cardinal graces of the Christian life are called out in quick succession: first faith with its rock-foundation; then love with its self-sacrificing devotion; and finally hope with its vision of heavenly glory. The whole gospel of Christ, the whole life of the Christian, is found in this brief passage of the first Evangelist, ending with the suggestive words, "Jesus only."

IV.—The Descent (xvii. 9-21)

Who can tell what each step downward cost the Son of man? If it seemed good to the disciples to be on the mountain-top, what must it have been to the Master! and what utter denial of self and conscious taking up of the cross it must have been to leave that hallowed spot! We have already seen a reason, as regards the disciples, why the vision should be sealed till the time of the end; but was there not also a reason which touched the Master Himself? It was well that He had enjoyed such a time of refreshing—it would be something to look back to in darkest hours; but it must be a memory only: it may not therefore be a subject of conversation—not the glory, but the cross, must now, both for Himself and for His disciples, fill all the near horizon.

This view of the case is confirmed by the manner in which He deals with their question respecting Elijah. It was a very natural question. It was no doubt perplexing in many ways to be absolutely forbidden to tell what they had seen; but it seemed especially mysterious in view of Elijah's appearance, which they not unnaturally regarded as a fulfilment of the prophecy for which the scribes were waiting. Hence their question, "Why, then, say the Scribes that Elias must first come?" Our Lord's answer turned their thoughts to the true fulfilment of the prophecy which was no shadowy appearance on a lonely hill, but the real presence among the men of the time of a genuine reformer who had come in the spirit and power of Elijah, and who would certainly have restored all things, had not these very scribes and Pharisees, failing to recognise him, left him to the will of the tyrant who had done away with him. Then most significantly He adds, that as it had been with the Elijah, so would it be with the Messiah of the time: "Likewise shall also the Son of man suffer of them." Thus, in showing them where to look for the true fulfilment of the prophecy, He turns their attention as well as His own away from the glory on the mount, which must now be a thing of the past, to that dark scene in the prison cell, which was so painfully impressed upon their minds, and those still darker scenes in the near future of which it was the presage.

At the foot of the mountain there is presented one of those striking contrasts with which, as we have seen, this Gospel abounds. It is very familiar to us through Raphael's great painting; and we shall certainly not make the mistake of attempting to translate into our feeble words what is there seen, and may now be regarded as "known and read of all men." Leaving, therefore, to the imagination the contrast between the glory on the mount and the misery on the plain, let us briefly look at the scene itself. Briefly; for though it well deserves detailed treatment, the proper place for this would be the full record of it in the second Gospel; while the more general way in which it is presented here suggests the propriety of dealing with it in outline only. Without, then, attempting to enter on the striking and most instructive details to be found in St. Mark's Gospel, and without even dealing with it as we have endeavoured to deal with similar cures under the head of the Signs of the Kingdom, it may be well to glance at it in the light of the words used by our Lord when He was confronted with the sorrowful scene: "O faithless and perverse generation, how long shall I be with you? how long shall I suffer you?"

It seems evident from these words that He is looking at the scene, not so much as presenting a case of individual suffering, appealing to His compassion, as a representation in miniature of the helplessness and perverseness of the race of men He has come to save. Remember how well He knew what was in man, and therefore what it must have been to Him, immediately after such a season of pure and peaceful communion on the holy mount, to have to enter into sympathy with all the variety of helplessness and confusion He saw around Him. There is the poor plague-stricken boy in the centre; beside him his agonised father; there, the feeble and blundering disciples, and the scribes (Mark ix. 14) questioning with them; and all around the excited, sympathetic and utterly perplexed multitude. Yet the kingdom of heaven is so near them, and has been so long proclaimed among them! Alas! alas for the perversity of men, that blinds them to the Sun of Righteousness, already arisen with healing in His wings, and for the unbelief even of the disciples themselves, which renders them, identified though they are with the kingdom, as helpless as all the rest! When we think of all this, need we wonder at the wail which breaks from the Saviour's sorrowful heart, need we wonder that He cries "How long? how long?"

"Bring him hither to Me." Here is the solvent of all. "From that very hour" the boy is cured, the father's heart is calmed and filled with gladness, the cavillers are silenced, the multitudes are satisfied and the worn-out faith of the disciples is renewed. Out of chaos, order, out of tumult, peace, by a word from Christ. It was a wilder sea than Galilee at its stormiest; but at His rebuke the winds and waves were stilled, and there was a great calm.

So would it be still, if this generation were not perverse and faithless in its turn—the world perverse, the Church faithless. Above the stormy sea of human sin and woe and helplessness, there still is heard the lamentation

"How long shall I be with you? how long shall I suffer you?" Here are we groaning and travailing in this late age of the world and of the Church, the worst kind of demons still working their will in their poor victims, the cry of anxious parents going up for lost children, disciples blundering and failing in well-meant efforts to cast the demons out, wise and learned scribes pointing at them the finger of scorn, excited and angry multitudes demanding satisfaction which they fail to get—Oh, if only all could hear the voice of the Son of man as the multitude heard it that day; and if we would only with one consent recognise the majesty of His face and mien as they did (see Mark ix. 15), bring to Him our plague-stricken ones, our devil-possessed, bring to Him our difficulties and perplexities, our vexed questions and our hard problems, would He not as of old bring order out of our chaos, and out of weakness make us strong? Oh, for more faith, faith to take hold of the Christ of God, come down from His holy habitation, and with us even to the end of the world, to bear the infirmities and carry the sorrows and take away the sins of men!—then should we be able to say to this mountain of evil under which our cities groan, "Be thou removed, and be thou cast into the sea," and it would be done. If only the Church of Christ in the world to-day had through all its membership that faith which is the only avenue by which the power of God can reach the need of man, our social problems would not long defy solution—"nothing would be impossible"; for over the millions of London, and the masses everywhere, there broods the same great heart of love and longing which prompted the gracious words, "Come unto Me, *all* ye that labour and are heavy laden, and I will give you rest;" and there is not a wretched one in all the world for whom there is not a blessed ray of hope in this pathetic wail which still proceeds from the loving heart of Him Who is the same yesterday and to-day and for ever. "O faithless and perverse generation, how long shall I be with you? how long shall I suffer you? *bring him hither to Me.*"

"Bring him hither"—this is a work of faith as well as a labour of love. The Church on earth is in the same position now as were the nine when the Master was absent from them on the mountain-top. He has ascended up on high, and the work must be carried on by the members of His body on the earth; and it is only in proportion to their faith that any success can attend them in their work.

Is faith, then, all that is necessary? It is: provided it be genuine living faith. This seems to be the point of the reference to the grain of mustard seed. The little seed, small as it is, is set in true relation to the great life-force of Mother Nature, and therefore out of it by-and-by there comes a mighty tree;

and in the same way even feeble faith, if it be genuine, and therefore set in true relation to the power of the Father of our spirits, becomes receptive of a force which in the end nothing can resist. But genuine living faith it must be: there must be the real opening up of the soul to the Spirit of the living God, so that the man's nature becomes a channel through which unobstructed the grace and power of God shall flow. It need scarcely be remarked that the notion which mistakes faith for mere belief of certain doctrines is utterly misleading. In nothing is the perversity of a faithless generation more conspicuous than in the persistency with which this absurd and unscriptural notion of faith holds its ground, even with those who are supposed to be leaders of thought in certain directions. If only that mountain of folly could be cleared away, there would be a decided brightening of the spiritual outlook; for then men everywhere would see that the faith which Christ expects of them, and without which nothing can be accomplished, is no mere intellectual belief, but the laying open and leaving open of the entire nature to the Spirit of Christ. Thus spurious dead faith would be utterly discredited, and genuine living faith would alone be recognised; and while the first effect would be to disclose the exceeding scantiness of the Church's faith, the result would be that even though what stood the test should be small as a grain of mustard seed, it would have in it such vitality and power that by-and-by it would become mighty and all-pervading, so that before it mountains would disappear (ver. 20).

The last words of the paragraph[14] carry us back to the ultimate necessity for prayer. It is plain that our Lord refers to habitual prayer. We cannot suppose that these nine disciples had utterly neglected this duty; but they had failed to live in an atmosphere of prayer, as was their Master's rule. We may be sure that they had not prayed at the base of the mountain as their Lord had prayed on the summit, or they would certainly not have failed in their attempt to cure the lunatic child. This demand for prayer is not really anything additional to the faith set forth as the one thing needful. There has been a good deal of discussion lately as to whether we can think without words. We shall not presume to decide the question; but it may safely be affirmed that without words we could not think to any purpose. And just as the continuance and development of our thinking is dependent on words, so the continuance and development of our faith is dependent on prayer. Is not the weak spot of our modern Christianity just here? In this age of tear and wear, bustle and excitement, what becomes of prayer? If the amount of true wrestling with God in the daily life of the average Christian could be disclosed, the wonder might be, not that he accomplishes so little, but that God is willing to use him at all.

FOOTNOTES

[12] A touching fulfilment of the Messianic spirit of these prophetic words: "How shall I give thee up, Ephraim? how shall I deliver thee, Israel? how shall I make thee as Admah? how shall I set thee as Zeboim? mine heart is turned within me, my repentings are kindled together." Compare chap. xi. 21-24.

[13] "Our wills are ours, we know not how:
Our wills are ours, *to make them Thine.*"

[14] They are relegated to the margin in R.V.; but the parallel passage in St. Mark's Gospel is acknowledged to be genuine.

XIV
LAST WORDS AT CAPERNAUM

Matt. xvii. 22-xviii. 35.

The Temple Tribute (xvii. 22-27.)

THE way southward lies through Galilee; but the time of Galilee's visitation is now over, so Jesus avoids public attention as much as possible, and gives Himself up to the instruction of His disciples, especially to impressing upon their minds the new lesson of the Cross, which they find it so very hard to realise, or even to understand. A brief stay in Capernaum was to be expected; and there above all places He could not hope to escape notice; but the manner of it is sadly significant—no friendly greeting, no loving welcome, not even any personal recognition, only a more or less entangling question as to the Temple tax, addressed, not to Christ Himself, but to Peter: "Doth not your Master pay the half-shekel?" (R.V.). The impulsive disciple showed his usual readiness by answering at once in the affirmative. He perhaps thought it was becoming his Master's dignity to show not a moment's hesitation in such a matter; but if so, he must have seen his mistake when he heard what his Lord had to say on the subject, reminding him as it did that, as Son of God, He was Lord of the Temple, and not tributary to it.

Some have felt a difficulty in reconciling the position taken on this occasion with His previous attitude towards the law, notably on the occasion of His baptism, when in answer to John's remonstrance, He said, "It becometh us to fulfil all righteousness"; but it must be remembered that He has entered on a new stage of His career. He has been rejected by those who acknowledged allegiance to the Temple, virtually excommunicated, so that He has been constrained to found His Church outside the commonwealth of Israel; He must therefore assert His own rights and theirs in spiritual things (for it must be remembered that the "half-shekel" was not the tribute to Cæsar, but the impost for the maintenance of the Temple worship). But while asserting His right He would not insist on it: He would stand by His disciple's word, and so avoid putting a stumbling-block in the way of those that were without, and who therefore could not be expected to understand the position He took. While consenting to pay the tax, He would provide it in such a way as not to lower His lofty claims in the view of His disciples, but rather to illustrate them, bringing home, as it must have done, to them all, and especially to the "pilot of the Galilean lake," that all things were under His feet, down to the very "fish of the sea, and whatsoever passeth through the paths of the seas" (Psalm viii. 8, l. 10-12). The difficulty which some feel in regard to this miracle, as differing so much in its character from those wrought in presence of the people as signs of the kingdom and credentials of the King, is greatly relieved, if not altogether removed, by remembering what was the special object in view—the instruction of Peter and the other disciples—and observing how manifestly and peculiarly appropriate it was for this particular purpose.

The Little Ones (xviii. 1-14)

The brief stay at Capernaum was signalised by some other lessons of the greatest importance. First, *as to the great and the small in the kingdom of heaven.* We learn from the other Evangelists that by the way the disciples had disputed with one another who should be the greatest. Alas for human frailty, even in the true disciple! It is most humiliating to think that, after that week, with its high and holy lessons, the first thing we hear of the disciples should be their failure in the very particulars which had been special features of the week's instruction. Recall the two points: the first was faith in the Christ, the Son of the living God, and over against it we have from lack of faith the signal failure with the lunatic child; the second was self-denial, and over against it we have this unseemly strife as to who should be greatest in the kingdom.

It is startling and most sad; but is it not true to nature? Is it not after the most solemn impressions that we need to be most watchful? And how natural it is, out of what is taught us, to choose and appropriate what is welcome, and, without expressly rejecting, simply to leave unassimilated and unapplied what is unwelcome. The great burden of the instruction for the last eight or ten days had been the Cross. There had been reference to the rising again, and the coming in the glory of the kingdom; but these had been kept strictly in the background, mentioned chiefly to save the disciples from undue discouragement, and even the three who had the vision of glory on the mount were forbidden to mention the subject in the meantime. Yet they let it fill the whole field of view; and though when the Master is with them He still speaks to them of the Cross, when they are by themselves they dismiss the subject, and fall to disputing as to who shall be the greatest in the kingdom!

How patiently and tenderly their Master deals with them! No doubt the same thought was in His heart again: "O faithless and perverse generation, how long shall I be with you? how long shall I suffer you?" But He does not even express it now. He takes an opportunity, when they are quietly together in the house, of teaching them the lesson they most need in a manner so simple and beautiful, so touching and impressive, as to commend it to all true-hearted ones to the end of time. Jesus called a little child to Him, "and set him in the midst of them." Can we doubt that they felt the force of that striking object-lesson before He said a word? Then, as we learn from St. Mark, to whom we always look for minute details, after having set him in the midst of them for them to look at and think about for a while, He took him in His arms, as if to show them where to look for those who were nearest to the heart of the King of heaven.

Nothing could have been more suggestive. It perfectly suited the purpose He had in view; but the meaning and the value of that simple act were by no means limited to that purpose. It most effectually rebuked their pride and selfish ambition; but it was far more than a rebuke—it was a revelation which taught men to appreciate child-nature as they had never done before. It was a new thought the Lord Jesus so quietly introduced into the minds of men that day, a seed-thought which had in it the promise, not only of all that appreciation of child-life which is characteristic of Christendom to-day, and which has rendered possible such poems as Vaughan's "Retreat," and Wordsworth's grand ode on "Immortality," but also of that appreciation of the broadly human as distinguished from the mere accidents of birth or rank or wealth which lies at the foundation of all Christian civilisation. The enthusiasm of humanity is all in that little act done so unassumingly in heedless Capernaum.

The words spoken are in the highest degree worthy of the act they illustrate. The first lesson is, *None but the lowly are in the kingdom*: "Except ye be converted (from the selfish pride of your hearts), and become (lowly and self-forgetful) as little children, ye shall not enter into the kingdom of heaven." A most heart-searching lesson! What grave doubts and questions it must have suggested to the disciples! They had faith to follow Christ in an external way; but were they really following Him? Had He not said, "If any man will come after Me, let him deny himself"? Were they denying self? On the other hand, however, we need not suppose that this selfish rivalry was habitual with them. It was probably one of those surprises which overtake the best of Christians; so that it was not really a proof that they did not belong to the kingdom, but only that for the time they were acting inconsistently with it; and therefore, before they could think of occupying any place, even the very lowest in the kingdom, they must repent, and become as little children.

The next lesson is, *The lowliest in the kingdom are the greatest*: "Whosoever therefore shall humble himself as this little child, the same is greatest in the kingdom of heaven." Again a most wonderful utterance, now so familiar to us, that we are apt to regard it as a thing of course; but what a startling paradox it must have been to the astonished disciples that day! Yet, as they looked at the bright, innocent, clear-eyed, self-unconscious little child, so simple, so trustful, there must have come a response from that which was deepest and best within them to their Master's words. And though the thought was new to them at the time, it did come home to them: it passed into their nature, and showed itself afterwards in precious fruit, at which the world still wonders. They did not indeed get over their selfishness all at once; but how grandly were they cured of it when their training was finished! If there is one thing more characteristic of the apostles in their after life than any other, it is their self-forgetfulness—their self-effacement, we may say. Where does Matthew ever say a word about the sayings or doings of Matthew? Even John, who was nearest of all to the heart of the Saviour, and with Him in all His most trying hours, can write a whole gospel without ever mentioning his own name; and when he has occasion to speak of John the Baptist does it as if there were no other John in existence. So was it with them all. We must not forget that, so far as this lesson of self-denial is concerned, they were only beginners now (see xvi. 21); but after they had completed their course and received the Pentecostal seal, they did not disgrace their Teacher any more: they did then really and nobly deny self; and thus did they at last attain true greatness in the kingdom of heaven.

So far we have what may be called the Saviour's direct answer to the question as to the greatest; but He cannot leave the subject without also setting before them the claims of the least in the kingdom of heaven. He has shown them how to be great: He now teaches them how to treat the small. The two things lie very close together. The man who makes much of himself is sure to make light of others; and he who is ambitious for worldly greatness will have little regard for those who in his eyes are small. The lesson, then, would have been incomplete had He not vindicated the claims of the little ones.

It is manifest, from the whole strain of the passage which follows, that the reference is not exclusively to children in years, but quite as much to children in spiritual stature, or in position and influence in the Church. The little ones are those who are small in the sense corresponding to that of the word "great" in the disciples' question. They are those, therefore, that are small and weak, and (as it is sometimes expressed) of no account in the Church, whether this be due to tender years or to slender abilities or to scanty means or to little faith.

What our Lord says on this subject comes evidently from the very depths of His heart. He is not content with making sure that the little ones shall receive as good a welcome as the greatest: they must have a special welcome, just because they are small. He identifies Himself with them— with each separate little one: "Whoso shall receive one such little child in My name receiveth Me." What a grand security for the rights and privileges of the small! what a word for parents and teachers, for men of influence and wealth in the Church in their relations to the weak and poor!

Then follow two solemn warnings, wrought out with great fulness and energy. The first is against putting a stumbling-block in the way of even one of these little ones—an offence which may be committed without any thought of the consequences. Perhaps this is the very reason why the Master feels it necessary to use language so terribly strong, that He may, if possible, arouse His disciples to some sense of their responsibility: "Whoso shall offend one of these little ones which believe in Me, it were better for him that a millstone were hanged about his neck, and that he were drowned in the depth of the sea." How jealously He guards the little ones! Verily he that toucheth them "toucheth the apple of His eye."

From the corresponding passage in St. Mark, it would appear that Christ had in view, not only such differences of age and ability and social position as are found in every community of disciples, but also such differences as are found between one company and another of professing Christians (see Mark ix. 38-42). This infuses a new pathos into the sad lament with which He forecasts the future: "Woe unto the world because of offences! for it must needs be that offences come; but woe to that man by whom the offence cometh!" The solemn warnings which follow, not given now for the first time (see chap. v. 29, 30), coming in this connection, convey the important lesson that the only effectual safeguard against causing others to stumble is to take heed to our own ways, and be ready to make any sacrifice in order to maintain our personal purity, simplicity and uprightness (vv. 8, 9). How often alas! in the history of the Church has the cutting off been applied in the wrong direction; when the strong, in the exercise of an authority which the Master would never have sanctioned, have passed sentence of excommunication against some defenceless little one; whereas if they had laid to heart these solemn warnings, they would have cut off, not one of Christ's members, but one of their own—the harsh hand, the hasty foot, the jealous eye, which caused them to stumble!

The other warning is: "Take heed that ye despise not one of these little ones." To treat them so is to do the reverse of what is done in heaven. Be their guardian angels rather, if you would have the approval of Him

Who reigns above; for their angels are those who always have the place of honour there. Is there not something very touching in this home reference, "My Father which is in heaven"?—especially when He is about to refer to the mission of mercy which made Him an exile from His home. And this reference gives Him an additional plea against despising one of these little ones; for not only are the highest angels their honoured guardians, but they are those whom the Son of man has come to seek and to save. The little lamb which you despise is one for whom the heavenly Shepherd has thought it worth His while to leave all the rest of His flock that He may go after it, and seek it on the lonely mountains, whither it has strayed, and over whose recovery He has greater joy than even in the safety of all the rest. The climax is reached when He carries thoughts above the angels, above even the Son of man, to the will of the Father (now it is *your* Father; for He desires to bring to bear upon them the full force of that tender relationship which it is now their privilege to claim): "Even so it is not the will of your Father which is in heaven, that one of these little ones should perish."

Trespasses (xviii. 15-35)

The transition is natural from those solemn words in which our Lord has warned His disciples against offending "one of these little ones," to the instructions which follow as to how they should treat those of their brethren who might trespass against them. These instructions, occupying the rest of this chapter, are of perennial interest and value, so long as it must needs be that offences come.

The trespasses referred to are of course real. Much heartburning and much needless trouble often come of "offences" which exist only in imagination. A "sensitive" disposition (often only another name for one that is uncharitable and suspicious) leads to the imputing of bad motives where none exist, and the finding of sinister meanings in the most innocent acts. Such offences are not worthy of consideration at all. It is further to be observed that our Lord is not dealing with ordinary quarrels, where there are faults on both sides, in which case the first step would be not to tell the brother his fault, but to acknowledge our own. The trespass, then, being real, and the fault all on the other side, how is the disciple of Christ to act? The paragraphs which follow make it clear.

"The wisdom that is from above is first pure, then peaceable;" accordingly we are first shown how to proceed in order to preserve the purity of the Church. Then instructions are given with a view to preserve the peace of the Church. The first paragraph shows how to exercise discipline; the second lays down the Christian rule of forgiveness.

"If thy brother shall trespass against thee,"—what? Pay no heed to it? Since it takes two to make a quarrel, is it best simply to let him alone? That might be the best way to deal with offences on the part of those that are without; but it would be a sad want of true brotherly love to take this easy way with a fellow-disciple. It is certainly better to overlook an injury than to resent it; yet our Lord shows a more excellent way. His is not the way of selfish resentment, nor of haughty indifference; but of thoughtful concern for the welfare of him who has done the injury. That this is the motive in the entire proceeding is evident from the whole tone of the paragraph, in illustration of which reference may be made to the way in which success is regarded: "If he shall hear thee, thou hast gained thy brother." If a man sets out with the object of gaining his cause or getting satisfaction, he had better let it alone; but if he wishes not to gain a barren triumph for himself, but to gain his brother, let him proceed according to the wise instructions of our Lord and Master.

There are four steps: (1) "Go and tell him his fault between thee and him alone." Do not wait till he comes to apologise, as is the rule laid down by the rabbis, but go to him at once. Do not think of your own dignity. Think only of your Master's honour and your brother's welfare. How many troubles, how many scandals might be prevented in the Christian Church, if this simple direction were faithfully and lovingly carried out! In some cases, however, this may fail; and then the next step is: (2) "Take with thee one or two more, that in the mouth of two or three witnesses every word may be established." The process here passes from private dealing; still there must be no undue publicity. If the reference to two or at most three (see R.V.) fail, it becomes a duty to (3) "tell it unto the church," in the hope that he may submit to its decision. If he decline, there is nothing left but (4) excommunication: "Let him be unto thee as an heathen man and a publican."

The mention of church censure naturally leads to a declaration of the power vested in the church in the matter of discipline. Our Lord had already given such a declaration to Peter alone; now it is given to the church as a whole in its collective capacity: "Verily I say unto you, Whatsoever ye shall bind on earth shall be bound in heaven: and whatsoever ye shall loose on earth shall be loosed in heaven." But the question comes: What is the church in its collective capacity? If it is to have this power of discipline, of the admission and rejection of members—a power which, rightly exercised on earth, is ratified in heaven—it is important to know something as to its constitution. This much, indeed, we know: that it is an assembly of believers. But how large must the assembly be? What are the marks of the true church?

These questions are answered in vv. 19 and 20. It is made very plain that it is no question of numbers, but of union with one another and the

Lord. Let it be remembered that the whole discourse has grown out of the strife with one another which should be the greatest. Our Lord has already shown that, instead of ambition to be the greatest, there must be readiness to be the least. He now makes it plain that instead of strife and division there must be agreement, unity in heart and desire. But if only there be this unity, this blending of hearts in prayer, there is found the true idea of the Church. Two disciples in full spiritual agreement, with hearts uplifted to the Father in heaven, and Christ present with them, — there is what may be called the primitive cell of the Church, the body of Christ complete in itself, but in its rudimentary or germinal form. It comes to this, that the presence of Christ with His people and of His spirit in them, uniting them with one another and with Him, is that which constitutes the true and living church; and it is only when thus met in the name of Christ, and acting in the spirit of Christ, that assemblies of believers, whether large or small, have any guarantee that their decrees on earth are registered in heaven, or that the promise shall be fulfilled to them, that what they ask "shall be done for them of My Father which is in heaven."

These words were spoken in the day of small things, when the members of the Church were reckoned by units; therefore it is a mistake to use them as if very small gatherings for prayer were especially pleasing to the great Head of the Church. It does indeed remain true, for the encouragement of the faithful few, that wherever two or three are met in the name of Jesus He is there; but that makes it no less disappointing when the numbers might be reasonably expected to be very much larger. Because our Lord said, "Better two of you agreed than the whole twelve at strife," does it follow that two or three will have the power in their united prayers which two or three hundred would have? The stress is not on the figure, but on the agreement.

The words "There *am I* in the midst of them" are very striking as a manifestation of that strange consciousness of freedom from limitations of time and place, which the Lord Jesus felt and often expressed even in the days of His flesh. It is the same consciousness which appears in the answer to the cavil of the Jews as to the intimacy with Abraham He seemed to them to claim, — "Before Abraham was, I am." As a practical matter also it suggests that we do not need to ask and wait for the presence of the Master, when we are truly met in His name. It is not *He* that needs to be entreated to draw near to us: "There *am I*."

So far the directions given have been with a view to the good of the offending brother and the honour of Christ and His cause. It remains to show how the offended person is to act on his part. Here the rule is very simple: *forgive him*. What satisfaction, then, is the offended party to get? The satisfaction of forgiving. That is all; and it is enough.

It will be observed, indeed, that our Lord, in His discourse up to the point we have reached, has said nothing directly about forgiveness. It is fairly implied, however, in the manner of process, in the very first act of it indeed; for no one will go to an offending brother with the object of gaining him, unless he have first forgiven him in his heart. Peter appears to have been revolving this in his mind, and in doing so he cannot get over a difficulty as to the limit of forgiveness. He was familiar, of course, with the rabbinical limit of the third offence, after which the obligation to forgiveness ceased; and, impressed with the spirit of his Master's teaching, he no doubt thought he was showing great liberality in more than doubling the number of times the offence might be repeated and still be considered pardonable: "Lord, how oft shall my brother sin against me, and I forgive him? till seven times?" It has been thought that some of his brethren had been treating Peter badly, so that his patience was sorely tried. Be that as it may, the question was not at all unnatural. But it was founded on a fallacy, which our Lord cleared away by His answer, and thoroughly exposed by means of the striking parable which follows. The fallacy was this: that we have a right to resent an injury, that in refraining from this we are forbearing to exercise our right, and consequently that there is a limit beyond which we have no call to exercise such forbearance. Our Lord by His answer clears away the limit, and makes the obligation unconditional and universal (ver. 22).

The parable shows the reason why there should be no limit—viz., that all believers, or members of the Church, by accepting from God the unlimited forgiveness He has extended to them, are thereby implicitly pledged to extend a like unlimited forgiveness to others. There is no duty on which our Lord insists more strenuously than this duty of forgiving those who trespass against us, always connecting closely together our forgiving and our being forgiven; and in this parable it is set in the strongest light.

The greatest offence of which our fellow-man can be guilty is as nothing to the sins we have committed against God. The proportion suggested is very startling. The larger sum is more than two millions sterling on the lowest computation; the smaller is not much more than four guineas. This is no exaggeration. Seven times altogether for a brother's offences seems almost unpardonable: do we never offend against God as many times in a single hour? Then think of the days, and the years! This is a startling thought on the one side; but how cheering on the other! For the immensity of the debt does not interfere in the slightest with the freeness and fulness and absoluteness of the forgiveness. Verily there is no more satisfying or reassuring presentation of the gospel than this parable, especially these very words, which rang like a knell of doom in the unmerciful servant's ear: "I forgave thee *all that debt.*" But just in proportion to the grandeur of the gospel here unfolded is the rigour of the requirement, that as we have been forgiven so must we forgive. While we gladly take the abounding comfort, let us not miss the stern lesson, evidently given with the very strongest feeling. Our Lord paints the picture of this man in the most hideous colours, so as to fill our minds and hearts with a proper loathing of the conduct of those he represents. The same intention is apparent in the very severe terms in which the punishment is denounced: "His lord was wroth, and delivered him to the tormentors." After this how awful is the closing sentence: "So likewise shall My heavenly Father do also unto you, if ye from your hearts forgive not every one his brother their trespasses."

Is that tender name of Father out of place? By no means; for is it not the outraged love of God that cries out against the unforgiving soul? And the words "from your hearts,"—are they not too hard on poor frail human nature? It is easy enough to grant forgiveness with the lips,—but from the heart? Yet so it stands written; and it only shows the need we have, not only of unmeasured mercy, but of unmeasured grace. Nothing but the love of Christ can constrain to such forgiveness. The warning was a solemn one, but it need have no terror for those who have truly learned the lesson of the Cross, and welcomed the Spirit of Christ to reign in their hearts. "I can do all things through Christ Who strengtheneth me."

There is an admirable fulness and harmony in Christ's teaching on this subject, as on every other. The duty of unlimited forgiveness is most plainly enjoined; but not that weak forgiveness which consists simply in permitting a man to trespass as he chooses. Forgiveness and faithfulness go hand in hand. The forgiveness of the Christian is in no case to be the offspring of a weak unmanly indifference to wrong. It is to spring from gratitude and love: gratitude to God, Who has forgiven his enormous debt, and love to the enemy who has wronged him. It must be combined with that faithfulness and fortitude which constrains him to go to the offending party and frankly, though kindly, tell him his fault. Christ's doctrine of forgiveness has not an atom of meanness in it, and His doctrine of faithfulness has not a spark of malice. "The wisdom that is from above is first pure, then peaceable, gentle, and easy to be entreated, full of mercy and good fruits, without partiality and without hypocrisy. And the fruit of righteousness is sown in peace of them that make peace."

XV
LAST DAYS IN PERÆA

Matt. xix. 1-xx. 16.

THERE were two main roads from Galilee to Jerusalem. One passed through Samaria, on the west of the Jordan, the other through Peræa, east of it. It was by the former that our Lord went northward from Judæa to begin His work in Galilee; it is by the other that He now goes southward to complete His sacrifice in Jerusalem. As "He must needs go through Samaria" then, so He must needs go through Peræa now. The main thought in His mind is the journey; but He cannot pass through the large and important district beyond the Jordan without bringing the kingdom of heaven near to the people, and accordingly we read that "great multitudes followed Him, and He healed them there." We learn from St. Luke's Gospel that "He went through the cities and villages teaching, and journeying towards Jerusalem"; and from the details there recorded, especially the mission of the seventy which belongs to that period, it is evident that these circuits in Peræa must have occupied several months. Concerning the work of these months our Evangelist is silent, just as he was silent concerning the earlier work in Judæa and Samaria, as recorded by St. John. We are reminded by this of the fragmentariness of these memorials of our Lord; and when we consider how much is omitted in all the narratives (see John xxi. 25) we can understand how difficult it is to form a closely connected history without any gaps between, and with accurately fitted joinings at the intersections of the different accounts.

There is, however, no difficulty here; for by comparison with the third Gospel we find that our Evangelist omits all the circuits in Peræa, and takes up the story again when our Lord is just about to leave that region for Jerusalem. When we take his point of view, we can see how natural this was. It was his special calling to give a full account of the work in Galilee. Hence the haste with which he passes from what it was necessary for him to tell of the early years in the south till the work in Galilee began; and in the same way, now that the work in Galilee is done, he hastens to the great crisis in Jerusalem. In following the journey southward he lingers only in two places, each of them associated with special memories. The one is Capernaum, where Jesus, as we have seen, tarried for a few days before taking final leave of Galilee; the other is the place beyond Jordan, in the region where in baptism He had solemnly entered on His work (cf. John x. 40), where again He remains for a brief period before going up to Jerusalem for the last time.

Marriage and Divorce (vv. 3-12)

There it was, and then, that the Pharisees came to Him with their entangling question concerning divorce. To know how entangling it was it is necessary to remember that there was a dispute at the time between two rival schools of Jewish theology—the school of Hillel and that of Shammai—in regard to the interpretation of Deut. xxiv. 1. The one school held that divorce could be had on the most trivial grounds; the other restricted it to cases of grievous sin. Hence the question: "Is it lawful for a man to put away his wife for every cause?" The answer Jesus gives is remarkable, not only for the wisdom and courage with which He met their attack, but for the manner in which He availed Himself of the opportunity to set the institution of marriage on its true foundation, and give perpetual security to His followers for the sanctity of home, by laying down in the clearest and strongest manner the position that marriage is indissoluble from its very nature and from its divine appointment (vv. 4-6). As we read these clear and strong utterances, let us bear in mind, not only that the laxity which unhappily prevailed in Rome had extended to Palestine, but that the monarch of the country through which our Lord was passing was himself one of the most flagrant offenders. How inspiring it is to think that then and there should have been erected that grand bulwark of a virtuous home: "What God hath joined together, let not man put asunder."

The Pharisees must have felt that He spoke with authority; but they are anxious not to lose their opportunity of getting Him into a difficulty, so they press Him with the disputed passage in Deuteronomy: "Why did Moses, then, command to give a writing of divorcement, and to put her away?" Our Lord's answer exposes the double fallacy lurking in the question. "Why did Moses command?" He did not command; he only suffered it—it was not to further divorce, but to check it, that he made the regulation about the "writing of divorcement." And then, not only was it a mere matter of sufferance,—it was a sufferance granted "because of the hardness of your hearts." Since things were so bad among your fathers in the matter of marriage, it was better that there should be a legal process than that the poor wives should be dismissed without it; but from the beginning it was not so—it was not intended that wives should be dismissed at all. Marriage is in itself indissoluble, except by death or by that which in its very nature is the rupture of marriage (ver. 9).

The wide prevalence of lax views on this subject is made evident by the perplexity of the disciples. They were not at all prepared for such stringency, so they venture to suggest that if that is to be the law, better not marry at all. The answer our Lord gives, while it does admit that there are circumstances in which celibacy is preferable, plainly intimates that it is only in quite exceptional cases. Only one of the three cases he mentions is voluntary; and while it is certainly granted that circumstances might arise in which for the kingdom of heaven's sake celibacy might be chosen (cf. 1 Cor. vii. 26), even then it must be only in cases where there is special grace, and such full preoccupation with the things of the kingdom as to render it natural; for such seems to be the import of the cautionary words with which the paragraph closes: "He that is able to receive it, let him receive it." How completely at variance with this wise caution have been the Romish decrees in regard to the celibacy of the clergy may go without saying.

The Children (vv. 13-15)

"*Then* were there brought unto Him little children"—a happy interruption! The Master has just been laying the solid foundations of the Christian home; and now the group of men by whom He is surrounded is joined by a troop of mothers, some carrying infants in their arms (for the passage in St. Luke expressly mentions infants), and some leading their little ones by the hand, to receive His blessing. The timeousness of this arrival does not seem to have struck the disciples. Their hearts had not yet been opened to the lambs of the fold, notwithstanding the great lesson at Capernaum. With as little regard for the feelings of the mothers as for the rights of the children, they "rebuked those that brought them," (Mark x. 13) and motioned them away. That this wounded the heart of the Saviour appears in His answer, which is stronger, as indicating displeasure, than is shown in our translation; while in the second Gospel it is expressly mentioned that Jesus "was much displeased." How can we thank the Lord enough for that sore displeasure? A distinguished opponent of Christianity has lately been asking whether he is expected to accept the kind and peaceful Jesus, Who smiles in one place, or the stern Judge, Who frowns in another—with the evident implication that it is impossible to accept both. How any person of intelligence can find difficulty in supposing that Christ could without inconsistency be either gentle or stern, as the occasion required, is very marvellous; but here is a case in which the sternness and gentleness are blended together in one act; and who will say that there is the least incompatibility between them? He was much displeased with the disciples; His heart was overflowing with tenderness to the children; and in that moment of conflicting feeling He utters that immortal sentence, these noblest and now most familiar of household words, "Suffer little children, and forbid them not, to come unto Me: for of such is the kingdom of heaven."

The rights of woman had been implicitly taught in the law of marriage carried back to the original creation of male and female; the treatment of woman had been vindicated from the rudeness of the disciples which would have driven the mothers away; and this reception of the children, and these words of welcome into the kingdom for all such little ones, are the charter of the children's rights and privileges. It is very plain that Christ has opened the kingdom of heaven, not only to all believers, but to their children as well. That "the kingdom of heaven" is here used in its ordinary sense throughout this Gospel, as referring to the heavenly kingdom which Christ had come to establish upon earth, cannot be denied; but it is a very fair inference from the Saviour's words that, seeing the children are acknowledged as having their place in the kingdom on earth, those of them who pass away from earth in childhood certainly find as sure and cordial a welcome to the kingdom above.

> "The holy to the holiest leads,
> The kingdoms are but one."

The porch is on earth, the palace is in heaven; and we may be very sure that all whom the King acknowledges in the porch shall be welcome in the palace.

What a rebuke in these words of our Lord to those who deal with children indiscriminately, as if they were all dead in trespasses and sins. How it must grieve the Saviour's heart when lambs of His own fold who may have been His from their earliest infancy are taught that they are utterly lost, and must be lost for ever, unless they pass through some extraordinary change, which is to them only a nameless mystery. It is a mistake to think that children as a rule need to be dragged to the Saviour, or frightened into trusting Him: what they need is to be *suffered* to come. It is so natural for them to come, that all they need is very gentle leading, and above all nothing done to hinder or discourage them: "Suffer little children, and forbid them not, to come unto Me: for of such is the kingdom of heaven."

The Rich Young Man (vv. 16-22)

Another inference from these precious words of Christ is the importance of seeking to win the children for Christ while yet they are children, ere the evil days come, or the years draw nigh, when they will be apt to say they have no pleasure in Him. It is a sad thing to think how soon the susceptibility of the child-nature may harden into the impenetrability which is sometimes found even in youth. Is there not a suggestion of this in the story of the young man which immediately follows?

There was everything that seemed hopeful about him. He was young, so his heart could not be very hard; of good moral character, amiable in disposition, and stirred with noble aspirations; moreover, he did the very best thing in coming to Christ for guidance. Yet nothing came of it, because of one obstacle, which would have been no hindrance in his childhood, but which proved insurmountable now. Young as he was, his affections had had time to get so intertwined with his worldly possessions, that he could not disengage them, so that instead of following Christ "he went away sorrowful."

The manner of our Lord's dealing with this young man is exceedingly instructive. Some have found a difficulty in what seems to them the strange answer to the apparently straightforward and admirable question "What good thing shall I do, that I may have eternal life?" Why did He not give the same answer which St. Paul afterwards gave to the Philippian jailer? Why did He not only fail to bring Himself forward as the way, the truth and the life, but even disclaim the goodness which the young man had imputed to Him? And why did He point him to the law instead of showing him the Gospel? Everything becomes quite clear when we remember that Christ dealt with people not according to the words they spoke, but according to what He saw to be in their hearts. Had this young man been in a state of mind at all like that of the Philippian jailer when he came trembling and fell down before Paul and Silas, he would no doubt have had a similar answer. But he was in the very opposite condition. He was quite satisfied with his own goodness; it was not salvation he was seeking, but some new merit to add to the large stock he already had: "what good thing shall I do" in addition to all the well-known goodness of my character and daily life? what extra claim can I establish upon the favour of God? Manifestly his idea of goodness was only conventional; it was the goodness which passes muster among men, not that which justifies itself before the all-searching eye of God; and having no higher idea of goodness than that, he of course used it in no higher sense, when he addressed Christ as "good Master." There could, then, be no more appropriate or more heart-searching question than this,—"*Why* callest thou Me good?" (it is only in the conventional sense you use the term, and conventional goodness is no goodness at all); "there is none good but One, that is God." Having thus stimulated his easy conscience, He sends him to the law that he may have knowledge of his sin, and so may take the first step towards eternal life. The young man's reply to this reveals the secret of his heart, and shows that Christ had made no mistake in dealing with him as He did. "Which?" he asks, evidently expecting that, the Ten Commandments being taken for granted, there will be something higher and more exacting, the keeping of which will bring him the extra credit he hopes to gain.

The Lord's answer to his question was well fitted to take down his spiritual pride, pointing him as it did to the commonplace Decalogue, and to that part of it which seemed the easiest; for the first table of the law is passed over, and only those commandments mentioned which bear upon duty to man. And is there not special skill shown in the way in which they are marshalled, so as to lead up to the one which covered his weak point? The sixth, the seventh, the eighth, the ninth, the fifth are rapidly passed in review; then the mind is allowed to rest on the tenth, not, however, in its mere negative form, "Thou shalt not covet," but as involved in that positive requirement which sums up the whole of the second table of the Law, "Thou shalt love thy neighbour as thyself." We can imagine how the Saviour would mark the young man's countenance, as one after another the commandments were pressed upon his conscience, ending with that one which should have pierced him as with a two-edged sword. But he is too strongly encased in his mail of self-righteousness; and he only replies, "All these things have I kept from my youth up: what lack I yet?" Clearly it is a surgical case; the medicine of the Commandments will not do; there must be the insertion of the knife: "Go, and sell that thou hast, and give to the poor."

Let us not, however, mistake the tone. "Jesus beholding him loved him" (Mark x. 21); and the love was never warmer than at the moment when He made this stern demand. There was sorrow on His face and in His tone when He told him of the hard necessity; and there was a heart full of love in the gracious invitation which rounded off the sharp saying at the end: "Come, and follow Me." Let us hope that the Saviour's compassionate love was not finally lost on him; that, though he no doubt did lose the great opportunity of taking a high place in the kingdom, he nevertheless, before all was done, bethought him of the Master's faithful and loving words, repented of his covetousness, and so found an open door and a forgiving welcome.

Danger of Riches (vv. 23-26)

So striking an incident must not be allowed to pass without seizing and pressing the great lesson it teaches. No lesson was more needful at the time. Covetousness was in the air; it was already setting its mark on the Hebrew people, who, as they ceased to serve God in spirit and in truth, were giving themselves over more and more to the worship of mammon; and, as the Master well knew, there was one of the twelve in whom the fatal poison was even then at work. We can understand, therefore, the deep feeling which

Christ throws into His warning against this danger, and His special anxiety to guard all His disciples against an over-estimate of this world's riches.

We shall not, however, fully enter into the mind of our Lord, if we fail to notice the tone of compassion and charity which marks His first utterance. He is still thinking kindly of the poor rich young man, and is anxious to make all allowance for him. It is as if He said, "See that you do not judge him too harshly; think how hard it is for such as he to enter the kingdom." This will explain how it is that in repeating the statement He found it desirable, as recorded by St. Mark, to introduce a qualification in order to render it applicable to all cases: "How hard is it for them that trust in riches to enter into the kingdom!" But while softening it in one direction, He puts it still more strongly in another: "Again I say unto you, it is easier for a camel to go through the eye of a needle, than for a rich man to enter into the kingdom of God." We shall not enter into the trivial discussion as to the needle's eye; it is enough to know that it was a proverbial phrase, probably in common use, expressing in the strongest way the insurmountable obstacle which the possession of riches, when these are trusted in and so put in place of God, must prove to their unfortunate owner.

The disciples' alarm expressed in the question "Who, then, can be saved?" does them much credit. It shows that they had penetration enough to see that the danger against which their Master was guarding them did not beset the rich alone; that they had sufficient knowledge of themselves to perceive that even such as they, who had always been poor, and who had given up what little they had for their Master's sake, might nevertheless not be free enough from the well-nigh universal sin to be themselves quite safe. One cannot help thinking that the searching look, which St. Mark tells us their Lord bent on them as He spoke, had something to do with this unusual quickness of conscience. It reminds us of that later scene, when each one asked, "Lord, is it I?" Is there any one of us, who, when that all-seeing Eye is fixed upon us, with its pure and holy gaze into the depths of our being, can fail to ask, with the conscience-stricken disciples, "Who, then, can be saved?"

The answer He gives does not at all lighten the pressure on the conscience. There is no recalling of the strong words which suggest the idea of utter impossibility. He does not say, "You are judging yourselves too strictly"; on the contrary, He confirms their judgment, and tells them that there they are right: "With men this *is* impossible"; but is there not another alternative? "Who art thou, O great mountain? before Zerubbabel thou shalt become a plain;" "With God all things are possible." A most significant utterance this for those to ponder who, instead of following our Lord's dealing with this case to its close, treat it as if the final word had been "If thou wilt enter into life, keep the commandments." This favourite passage of the legalist is the one of all others which most completely overthrows his hopes, and shows that so deep are the roots of sin in the heart of man, even of the most amiable and most exemplary, that none can be saved except by the power of divine grace overcoming that which is to men an impossibility. "Behold, God is my salvation."

It is worthy of note that it is as a hindrance to *entering* the kingdom that riches are here stigmatised, — which suggests the thought that the danger is not nearly so great when riches increase to those who have already entered. Not that there is even for them no serious danger, nor need of watching and of prayer that as they increase, the heart be not set upon them; but where there is true consecration of heart the consecration of wealth follows as a natural and easy consequence. Riches are a responsibility to those that are in the kingdom; they are a misfortune only to those who have not entered it.

As on the question of marriage or celibacy, so on that of property or poverty, the Romanist has pushed our Lord's words to an extreme which is evidently not intended. It was plain even to the disciples that it was not the mere possession of riches, but the setting the heart on them, which He condemned. If our Lord had intended to set forth the absolute renunciation of property as a counsel of perfection to His disciples, this would have been the time to do it; but we look in vain for any such counsel. He saw it to be necessary for that young man; but when He applies the case to disciples in general, He does not say "If any man will come after Me, let him sell all that he has, and give to the poor," but contents Himself with giving a very strong warning against the danger of riches coming between man and the kingdom of God. But while the ascetic interpretation of our Lord's words is manifestly wrong, the other extreme of reducing them to nothing is far worse, which is the danger now.

Rewards (xix. 27-xx. 16[15])

The thought of sacrifice very naturally suggests as its correlative that of compensation; so it is not at all to be wondered at that, before this conversation ended, the impulsive disciple, so much given to think aloud, should blurt out the honest question: "Behold, we have forsaken all and followed Thee; what shall we have therefore?" He could not but remember that while the Master had insisted on His disciples denying self to follow Him, He had spoken no less clearly of their finding life through losing it, and of their being rewarded according to their deeds (see xvi. 24-27). A more cautious man would have hesitated before he spoke; but it was no worse to speak it than to think it: and then, it was an honest and fair question; accordingly our Lord gives it a frank and generous answer, taking care, however, before leaving the subject, to add a supplementary caution, fitted to correct what was doubtful or wrong in the spirit it showed.

Here, again, we see how thoroughly natural is our Saviour's teaching. "Not to destroy, but to fulfil," was His motto. This is as true of His relation to man's nature as of His relation to the law and the prophets. "What shall we have?" is a question not to be set aside as wholly unworthy. The desire for property is an original element in human nature. It was of God at the first; and though it has swelled out into most unseemly proportions, and has usurped a place which does by no means belong to it, that is no reason why it should be dealt with as if it had no right to exist. It is vain to attempt to root it out; what it needs is moderating, regulating, subordinating. The tendency of perverted human nature is to make "What shall we have?" the first question. The way to meet that is not to abolish the question altogether, but to put it last, where it ought to be. To be, to do, to suffer, to enjoy—that is the order our Lord marks out for His disciples. If only they have it as their first anxiety to be what they ought to be, and to do what they are called to do, and are willing, in order to this, to take up the cross, to suffer whatever may be theirs to suffer, then they may allow as large scope as they please to the desire for possession and enjoyment.

Observe the difference between the young man and the disciples. He was coming to Christ for the first time; and if our Lord had set before him what he would gain by following Him, He would have directly encouraged a mercenary spirit. He therefore says not a word to him about prospects of reward either here or hereafter. Those who choose Christ must choose Him for His own sake. Our Saviour dealt in no other way with Peter, James and John. When first He called them to follow Him, He said not a word about thrones or rewards; He spoke of work: "Follow Me, and I will make you fishers of men"; and it was not till they had fully committed themselves to Him that He went so far as to suggest even in the most general way the thought of compensation. It would have spoiled them to have put such motives prominently before them at an earlier stage. But it is different now. They have followed Him for months, even years. They have been tested in innumerable ways. They are not certainly out of danger from the old selfishness; but with the exception of one of them, who is fast developing into a hypocrite, all they need is a solemn word of caution now and then. The time had come when their Master might safely give them some idea of the prospects which lay before them, when their cross-bearing days should be over.

The promise looks forward to an entirely altered state of things spoken of as "the regeneration"—a remarkable term, reminding us of the vast scope of our Saviour's mission as ever present to His consciousness even in these days of smallest things. The word recalls what is said in the book of Genesis as to "the generation of the heaven and of the earth," and suggests by anticipation the words of the Apocalypse concerning the regeneration, "Behold, I make all things new," and "I saw a new heaven and a new earth." That the reference is to that final restitution of all things, and not merely to the new dispensation, seems evident from the words which immediately follow: "When the Son of man shall sit on the throne of His glory." Why, then, was the promise given in words so suggestive of those crude notions of an earthly kingdom, above which it was so difficult and so important for the disciples to rise? The answer is to be found in the limitation of human language: "Eye hath not seen, nor ear heard, neither have entered into the heart of man, the things which God hath prepared for them that love Him"; accordingly, if the promise was to be of any use to them in the way of comfort and encouragement, it must be expressed in terms which were familiar to them then. To their minds the kingdom was as yet bound up with Israel; "the twelve tribes of Israel" was as large a conception of it as their thoughts could then grasp; and it would certainly be no disappointment to them when they afterwards discovered that their relation as apostles of the Lord was to a much larger "Israel," embracing every kindred and nation and people and tribe; and though their idea of the thrones on which they would sit was then and for some time afterwards quite inadequate, it was only by starting with what ideas of regal power they had, that they could rise to those spiritual conceptions which, as they matured in spiritual understanding, took full possession of their minds.

The Lord is speaking, however, not for the apostles alone, but for all His disciples to the end of time; so He must give a word of cheer, in which even the weakest and most obscure shall have a part (ver. 29). Observe that here also the promise is only for those who have left what they had for the sake of Christ. We are not authorised to go with a message after this form: "If you leave, you will get." The reward is of such a nature that it cannot be seen until the sacrifice is made. "Except a man be born again, he cannot see the kingdom of God;" until a man loses his life for Christ's sake, he cannot find it. But when the sacrifice has been made, then appears the compensation, and it is seen that even these strong words are not too strong: "Every one that hath forsaken houses, or brethren, or sisters, or father, or mother, or wife, or children, or lands, for My name's sake, shall receive an hundredfold, and shall inherit everlasting life." The full consideration of this promise belongs rather to St. Mark's Gospel, in which it is presented without abridgment.

The supplementary caution—"But many that are first shall be last; and the last shall be first"—is administered in apparent reference to the spirit of the apostle's question, which exhibits still some trace of mercenary motive, with something also of a disposition to self-congratulation. This general statement is illustrated by the parable immediately following it, a connection which the unfortunate division into chapters here obscures; and not only is an important saying of our Lord deprived in this way of its illustration, but the parable is deprived of its key, the result of which has been that many have been led astray in its interpretation. We cannot attempt to enter fully into the parable, but shall only make such reference to it as is necessary to bring out its appropriateness for the purpose our Lord had in view. Its main purport may be stated thus: many that are first in amount of work shall be last in point of reward; and many that are last in amount of work shall be first in point of reward. The principle on which this is based is plain enough: that in estimating the reward it is not the quantity of work done or the amount of sacrifice made that is the measure of value, but the spirit in which the work is done or the sacrifice made. The labourers who made no bargain at all, but went to work on the faith of their Master's honour and liberality, were the best off in the end. Those who made a bargain received, indeed, all they bargained for; but the others were rewarded on a far more liberal scale, they obtaining much more than they had any reason to expect. Thus we are taught that those will be first who think least of wages as wages, and are the least disposed to put such a question as, "What shall we then have?" This was the main lesson for the apostles, as it is for all who occupy places of prominence in the kingdom. It is thus put in later years by one of those who now for the first time learned it: "Look to yourselves, that we lose not those things which we have wrought, but that we receive a full reward" (2 John 8). "Look to yourselves," see that your spirit be right, that there be nothing selfish, nothing mercenary, nothing vainglorious; else much good labour and real self-denial may miss its compensation.

Besides the lesson of caution to the great ones, there is a lesson of encouragement to the little ones in the kingdom—those who can do little and seem to themselves to sacrifice little for Christ. Let such remember that their labour and self-denial are measured not by quantity but by quality, by the spirit in which the service, however small it be, is rendered, and the sacrifice, trifling as it seems, is made. Not only is it true that many that are first shall be last; but also that many of the last shall be first. "If there be first a willing mind, it is accepted according to that a man hath, and not according to that he hath not."

Neither in the general statement of our Lord, nor in the parable which illustrates it, is there the slightest encouragement to idlers in the vineyard—to those who do nothing and sacrifice nothing for Christ, but who think that, when the eleventh hour comes, they will turn in with the rest, and perhaps come off best after all. When the Master of the vineyard asks of those who are standing in the market-place at the eleventh hour, "Why stand ye here all the day idle?" their answer is ready, "Because no man hath hired us." The invitation came to them, then, for the first time, and they accepted it as soon as it was given them. Suppose the Master of the vineyard had asked them in the morning, and at the first hour and the second and the third, and so on all the day, and only at the eleventh hour did they deign to notice His invitation, how would they have fared?

FOOTNOTE

[15] The latter part of ver. 16—"Many be called, but few chosen"—does not properly belong to this passage (see R.V.); its consideration will therefore be postponed till its proper place is reached (see chap. xxii. 14).

XVI
TO JERUSALEM

Matt xx. 17-xxi. 17.

I.—The Going Up (xx. 17-34)

WE have now reached the last stage of the long and sorrowful journey to Jerusalem. From the corresponding passage in the second Gospel we learn that the disciples were greatly moved by something in their Master's manner: "they were amazed; and as they followed, they were afraid." It would appear, indeed, that they had considerable hesitation in following at all, for it is pointedly mentioned that "Jesus went before them," a hesitation which was no doubt due to the same feeling which prompted Peter, on the first announcement of the journey to Jerusalem and what it would involve, to say "Be it far from Thee, Lord"; and as then, so now, the Saviour felt it as an obstacle in His onward path which He must resolutely put out of the way; and it was doubtless the new and severe effort required of that heroic will to set it aside, and in doing so to face the gathering storm alone, which explained His unwonted agitation as He addressed Himself to the last stage of the fatal journey.

Still, He longs to have His disciples in sympathy with Him. He knows well that not yet have they fully appreciated what He has said to them; accordingly, at some convenient point on the way, He takes them by themselves and tells them once again, more distinctly and definitely than ever, what must be the issue of the step He is now taking (vv. 17-19). St. Luke tells us that even yet "they understood none of these things." Their minds must have been in a state of great bewilderment; and when we think of this, we may well admire that strong personal devotion to their Master which made them willing, however reluctantly and hesitatingly, still to follow Him into the dark unknown. With the one sad exception, they were thoroughly loyal to their King; they trusted Him absolutely; and though they could not understand why He should be mocked and scourged and crucified in His own capital, they were willing to go with Him there, in the full expectation that, in some way they then could not imagine, He should triumph over his enemies and erect those thrones and bring in that glory of the kingdom of which He had spoken.

This failure of theirs to comprehend the real situation, which one Evangelist mentions, is well illustrated by an incident which happened on the road as recorded by the others—one of those evidently undesigned coincidences which continually meet us, and which, in a higher degree than mere circumstantial agreements, confirm our faith in the accuracy of the sacred writers. "Then came to Him the mother of Zebedee's children with her sons, worshipping Him, and desiring a certain thing of Him,"—the "certain thing," as it turned out, being that the two sons should have the chief places of honour in the kingdom. From the form in which the request was presented it would seem as if it had been founded on a misapprehension of one of His own sayings. In St. Mark's Gospel, where the part which the two sons themselves had in it is related, the very words of the application are given thus: "Master, we would that Thou shouldest do for us whatsoever we shall desire," as if to remind Him of His promise to any two of them who should agree as touching anything they should ask (xviii. 19), and to claim the fulfilment of it. It need not be assumed that the request was a purely selfish one. However vague their ideas may have been as to the days of darkness that awaited them in Jerusalem, we cannot suppose that they left them wholly out of view; and if not, they must have been prepared, or have thought themselves prepared, to take foremost places in the battlefield as well as in the triumph that would surely follow. There may well have been, then, a touch of chivalry along with the grosser motive which, it is to be feared, was their main inspiration.

This makes it easier for us to understand the possibility of their coming with such a request at such a time. We all know how easy it is to justify a selfish proceeding when there is something to offset it. We ourselves know how natural it is to think of those scriptures which suit our purpose, while we conveniently forget for the moment those that do not. Was it, then, unnatural that James and John, forgetting for the moment what their Lord had taught them as to the way to true greatness in His kingdom, should satisfy themselves with the thought that they were at all events taking up their cross in the first place, and as to the ulterior object were certainly acting up to the very plain and emphatic word of the Master Himself: "I say unto you, that if two of you shall agree on earth as touching anything that they shall ask, it shall be done for them."

This view of their state of mind is confirmed by our Lord's way of dealing with them. He first asks them what it is they have agreed upon; and, when the mother tells Him, He quietly shows them that, so far from agreeing together, none of them know what they are asking. They are all using the same words, but the words might as well be in an unknown tongue,—better perhaps, inasmuch as to misunderstand is a degree worse than not to understand at all. He then proceeds to show them that the fulfilment of their request would involve issues for which as yet they were by no means prepared: "Jesus answered and said, Ye know not what ye ask. Are ye able to drink of the cup that I shall drink of?" Their answer confirms the view suggested, that they did not leave out altogether the thought of cross-bearing; but we have only to remember what took place in the course of a week to see that in saying "We are able," they knew as little of what they were promising as they had known of what they were asking. He will not, however, break the bruised reed of their devotion, nor quench the feeblest spark of self-denying courage; accordingly He does not slight their offer, but, in accepting it, He reminds them that the honours of the kingdom of heaven are not for favourites, or for those who may first apply, but only for those who approve themselves worthy in the sight of Him Who seeth all, and who rewards every man according to his deeds (ver. 23).

The ten were not much better than the two. It was natural, indeed, that, when they heard it, they should be "moved with indignation"; but, though natural, it was not Christian. Had they remembered the lesson of the little child, or even thought deeply enough of that very recent one about the last and the first, they would have been moved with something else than indignation. But need any one wonder that selfishness should be so very hard to kill? Is it not true to nature? Besides, the Spirit had not yet been given, and therefore we need not wonder that even the plainest teaching of the Lord Himself failed to cast the selfish spirit out of His disciples then. "*Knowledge* comes, but *wisdom* lingers." On the other hand, think of the marvellous patience of the Master. How disappointing it must have been at such a time to see in all of them a spirit so wholly at variance with all that by precept and example He had been labouring to instil into them! Yet without one word of reproach He teaches them the old lesson once again, gives them liberally the wisdom which they lack, and upbraids them not.

The words of Christ not only meet the case most fully, but reach far beyond the immediate occasion of their utterance. Thus He brings good out of evil, and secures that even the strife of His disciples shall make for "peace on earth." He begins by showing how absolutely in contrast to the kingdoms of the world is the kingdom He has come to establish. In them the great ones "lord it over" (R.V.) others; in it the great ones are those who serve. What a revolution of thought is involved in this simple contrast! of how much that is great and noble has it been the seed! The dignity of labour, the royalty of service, the pettiness of selfish ambition, the majesty of self-sacrificing love; the utter condemnation of the miserable maxim "Every man for himself"; the world's first question "What shall we have?" made the last, and its last question "What shall we give?" made the very first,—such are some of the fruits which have grown from the seed our Lord planted in so ungenial soil that day. We are, alas, still very far from realising that great ideal; but ever since that day, as an ideal, it has never been quite out of sight. Early Christianity under the guidance of the apostles strove, though with all too little success, to realise it; the chivalry of the middle ages, with its glorification of knighthood,[16] was an attempt to embody it; and what is the constitutionalism of modern times but the development of the principle in political life, the real power being vested not in the titular monarch, who represents ideally the general weal, but in a *ministry*, so designated to mark the fact that their special function is to minister or serve, the highest position in the realm bearing the humble title of *Prime Minister*, or first servant of the state. It is of value to have the principle before us as an ideal, even though it be buried under the tombstone of a name, the significance of which is forgotten; but when the kingdom of heaven shall be fully established on the earth, the ideal will be realised, not in political life only, but all through society. If only the ambition to serve our generation according to the will of God were to become universal, then would God's kingdom come and His will be done on earth even as it is in heaven.

Of this great principle of the heavenly kingdom the King Himself is the highest illustration: "even as the Son of man came not to be ministered unto, but to minister, and to give His life a ransom for many." There are those who write about "the service of man" as if the thought of it were a development of nineteenth-century enlightenment; but there it is in all its truth and grandeur in the life, and above all in the death, of our Lord and Saviour Jesus Christ! His entire life was devoted to the service of man; and His death was but the giving up in one final act of surrender what had all along been consecrated to the same high and holy ministry.

These closing words of the great lesson are memorable, not only as setting before us the highest exemplification of the law of service, which as "Son of Man" Christ gave to the world; but as presenting the first intimation of the purpose of the great sacrifice He was about to offer at Jerusalem. Again and again He had told the disciples that it was necessary; but now for the first time does He give them an idea why it was necessary. It is too soon, indeed, to give a full explanation; it will be time enough to unfold the doctrine of atonement after the atonement has been actually made. Meantime He makes it plain that, while His whole life was a life of ministering as distinguished from being ministered unto, the supreme service He had come to render was the giving of His life as a ransom, something to be rendered up as a price which must be paid to redeem His people. It is plain from this way of putting it, that He viewed the giving up of His life as the means by which alone He could save the "many" who should, as His redeemed or ransomed ones, constitute His kingdom.

On the way to Jerusalem lay the beautiful city of Jericho. The place now called by that name is such a wretched assemblage of miserable hovels that it is difficult for the traveller to realise that the Jericho of the days of our Lord was not only the most luxurious place of resort in Palestine, but one that might vie with its fashionable rivals throughout the Roman Empire. Since the days of Herod the Great it had been the winter residence of the Court. Jerusalem being on the cold hilltop, it was convenient to have within easy reach a warm and sheltered spot in the deep valley of the Jordan; and with a delightful winter climate and a rich and fertile soil, Jericho needed only the lavish expenditure of money to make it into "a little Paradise," as Josephus calls it. With its gardens of roses and groves of palm, it was, even before the time of Herod, so beautiful a place, that, as a gem of the East, Antony bestowed it on Cleopatra as an expression of his devotion; after it passed into the hands of Herod, a theatre was erected and an amphitheatre, and many other noble and costly buildings; and during the season it was thronged by the rich and the great of the land, among whom would be distinguished visitors from foreign parts. What effect would all this grandeur have on Christ and His disciples as they passed through it on their way to Jerusalem? We are not told. Two things only are noted as worthy of record: the salvation of a rich publican (Luke xix. 1-10), and the healing of two poor blind men. Not the gardens and palaces of the city, but its sins and sorrows, engage the Saviour's thoughts and occupy His time.

As a rule, we regard it as waste of time to deal with the "discrepancies" between the different Evangelists; but as one of the most serious of them all has been found here, it may be well to look at it, to see how much, or how little, it amounts to. First, the other Gospels speak of the cure of a blind man, and tell his name, Bartimæus; this one says that two blind men were cured, and does not mention any name. If the other Evangelists had said that only one was healed, there would have been a real discrepancy; but they do not. Another "discrepancy" which has been noticed is that St. Matthew says Christ "touched their eyes," while the others do not mention the touch, but only tell us what He said; but surely there is no difficulty in supposing that Christ both touched the eyes and spoke the words at the same time. It is true that the words as recorded by St. Mark and St. Luke are not identical, but they are precisely to the same effect; and it is quite possible that every word which both of them report was actually said, and that other words besides were spoken which have not been preserved.

These differences are not discrepancies at all; but there remains one which may fairly enough be so characterised. The first and second Gospels represent the cure as taking place on the way into Jericho; the third puts it on the way out.

Various suppositions, more or less plausible, especially less, have been made to "reconcile" these two representations: such as the fact that there were really two Jerichos, the old and the new, the cure being wrought as the Saviour passed from the one to the other, so that both accounts would be strictly accurate; or again, that cures may have been wrought both in entering and in leaving Jericho. But why should we trouble ourselves to reconcile so small a difference? It is not of the slightest consequence whether the cure took place on the way in or on the way out. If it had been a point on which strict accuracy was essential, care would doubtless have been taken to note the very moment and the very spot where it took place—as, for example, in the case of the cure of the nobleman's son at Capernaum (John iv. 52); but it was not; and therefore we have no more reason to wonder at the variation in so unimportant a detail than at those variations from the accurate text which we continually find in the quotations from the Old Testament Scriptures. The discrepancy does not in the slightest degree affect the credibility of any of the witnesses; it only serves, together with the other variations, to show the independence of the different accounts. How small must be the minds, or how strong the prejudices, of those who find support for their unbelief in discrepancies of which this is acknowledged to be one of the gravest examples!

It so happens, too, that there is no story in all the Gospels which shines more lustrously in its own light. It is full of beauty and pathos in all the versions of it which have come down to us; but most of all in the graphic story of St. Mark, to whose Gospel therefore its illustration may be regarded as belonging by special right.

II.—The Royal Entry (xxi. 1-17)

Travelling from Jericho, it is probable that our Lord reached Bethany on the evening of Friday, a week before His crucifixion. The next day, being the Jewish Sabbath, He would spend in retirement, probably in the house of Lazarus, whom a short time before He had raised from the dead. The following day, the first day of the week, would therefore be the date of His entry into Jerusalem as the Royal Son of David, come to claim His kingdom.

That this entrance into the capital is a most important event in the history of Jesus is evident not only from its nature and consequences, but also from the fact that it is one which all the four Evangelists record. Indeed, it is just at this point that the four narratives converge. The river of the water of life, which "was parted and became four heads" diverging at times in their course, now unites its waters in one channel broad and deep; and all the four Evangelists, though in different accents still, and with variation in the selection of details, combine to tell the same wondrous story of our Saviour's passion, the story of "the decease which He should accomplish at Jerusalem."

This was the first occasion on which our Lord distinctly put forth His claim to royalty. From the beginning of His ministry He had shown Himself to be a "prophet mighty in word and in deed," and to those who followed Him it became manifest that He was the Prophet foretold by Moses, for whose coming they had been taught to look with eager eyes (see Deut. xviii. 15-19). From the beginning of His ministry, too, the Saviour had been proclaiming "the gospel of the kingdom"; but when we examine carefully all He says about it, we find that He never expressly asserts that He Himself is King. Not that He conceals the all-important truth: He speaks of the kingdom in such a way that those who have ears to hear may learn that He is King Himself—as, for instance, when He says, "Suffer the little children to come unto Me, and forbid them not: for of such is the kingdom of heaven." One might quite readily infer from these words that Jesus Himself was King; but the claim is not thereby formally made. Besides, not only is it true that up to this time He did not formally assume the royal title, but He even resisted attempts made to thrust it upon Him (e.g., John vi. 15). For this refusal to be crowned by the multitude there was only too good reason. Their ideas of royalty were entirely different from His. Had He allowed Himself to be borne on the tide of popular favour to royal honours, His kingdom would have been thereby marked as "of this world," it would have been stamped as something very different from the kingdom of "righteousness and peace and joy in the Holy Ghost" He had come to establish. Had He been a mere enthusiast, He would undoubtedly have yielded to such a tidal wave of public excitement; but His unerring wisdom taught Him that He must reach His throne by another path than that of popular favour. Rather must it be through popular rejection—through the dark portals of despite and death; and for that, His hour had not then come.

Now it has come. He has been steadily advancing to Jerusalem for the very purpose of accomplishing that decease which is to be the portal of His royalty. Already fully revealed as Prophet, He is about to be made "perfect through suffering" as our great High Priest. It is time, therefore, that He reveal Himself as King, so that no one may have it afterwards to say that He never really claimed the throne of His father David.

How, then, shall He assert His right? Shall a herald be sent to proclaim with the sound of a trumpet that Jesus of Nazareth is King over Israel in Jerusalem? To take such a course would be to court misunderstanding. It would be to raise the standard of revolt against the Romans. It would stir the city in a very different fashion from that in which the Prince of Peace would have it stirred. It would be the signal for tumult, bloodshed, and disastrous war. The ordinary method is evidently not to be thought of. How, then, shall it be done?

Our Lord is never at a loss for means to accomplish His designs in His own way, which is always the best. He sends to a neighbouring village for a young ass, mounts it, and rides into the city. That is all He does. Not a word said about royalty, no herald, no trumpeter, no proclamation, no royal pomp, nothing whatever to rouse the Roman jealousy or ire—nothing but the very ordinary circumstance of a man riding into the city on an ass's colt, a mode of conveyance not in itself calculated to attract any special notice. What was there, then, in such an act to secure the end? Nothing in itself; but a great deal when taken in connection with a remarkable prophecy in the Book of Zechariah well known to every Jew, and much in the thoughts of all who were looking for the promised Messiah. It is true, indeed, that an ordinary man might have done the same thing and the people have taken no notice of him. But Jesus had become the object of very great interest and attention to large numbers of the people on account of the miracles He had been working—notably that great miracle which still stirred the minds of the whole community, the raising of Lazarus from the dead. The chief priests and scribes, indeed, and the men of influence in Jerusalem, regarded Him with all the greater rancour on account of His miracles of mercy, and they had been specially embittered against Him since the raising of Lazarus; but it was different with the body of the people, especially those who had come or were coming from Galilee and other distant parts of the land to be present at the great Paschal feast. We are told by St. John that a large number of these had gone out the day before to Bethany, both to see Lazarus, who was naturally an object of curiosity, and also to see Jesus Himself; these accordingly were precisely in the state of mind in which they would most readily catch up the idea so naturally suggested by the significant act of our Saviour's riding into the city of David on a colt the foal of an ass. The result, accordingly, was as had been intended, and is thus described by our Evangelist; "The most part of the multitude spread their garments in the way; and others cut branches from the trees and spread them in the way. And the multitudes that went before Him, and that followed, cried, saying, Hosanna to the Son of David; Blessed is He that cometh in the name of the Lord; Hosanna in the highest" (R.V.).

The excellence of the method adopted by our Saviour to set forth His royal claims will still further appear when we consider that it arose quite naturally out of the circumstances in which He was placed. So much was this the case that some have thought He was taken by surprise, that He had no intention of calling forth the testimony of the people to His royal claims, that in fact He was only giving way to a movement He could not well resist; but this shallow view is plainly set aside, not only by what has been already advanced, but also by the answer He gives to the Pharisees who ask him to rebuke and silence His disciples: "I tell you that if these should hold their peace, the stones would immediately cry out" (Luke xix. 39, 40).

Not only did the means adopted by our Lord rise naturally out of the circumstances in which He and His followers were placed, but they were specially suited to suggest important truths concerning the kingdom He claimed as His own. We have already seen that, if He had entered the city in regal pomp and splendour, it would have conveyed an entirely false idea of the kingdom. The method He did adopt was such as to give a true idea of it.

First, it strikingly suggested the kingliness of lowliness, which, as we have seen, was one of its great distinctive principles. As we look back over His recent instructions to His disciples, we see how very much this thought was in His heart and how great was the importance He attached to it. He had just taught them that the Son of man had come, not to be ministered unto, but to minister and to give His life a ransom for many; and His manner of entering into His capital must be in harmony with the lowly, self-renouncing work He has come to do. Thus He shows in the most impressive way that His kingdom is not of this world. There is no suggestion of rivalry with Cæsar; yet to those who look beneath the surface He is manifestly more of a king than any Cæsar. He has knowledge of everything without a spy (ver. 2); He has power over men without a soldier (ver. 3); He has simply to say "The Lord hath need," and immediately His royal will is loyally fulfilled. Evidently He has the mind of a King and the will of a King; has He not also the heart of a King, of a true Shepherd of the people? See how He bears the burden of their future on His heart, a burden which weighs so heavily upon Him that He cannot restrain His tears (Luke xix. 41-44). There is no kingly state; but was not His a kingly soul, Who in such humble guise rode into Jerusalem that day?

Not less than lowliness, is peace suggested as characteristic of His kingdom. First by the manner of His entrance; for while the horse and the chariot were suggestive of war, the ass was the symbol of peace. And then, the prophecy is one of peace. Immediately after the words quoted by the Evangelist there follows this remarkable promise: "I will cut off the chariot from Ephraim, and the horse from Jerusalem, and the battle bow shall be cut off; and He shall speak peace unto the heathen; and His dominion shall be from sea even to sea, and from the river even to the ends of the earth." It would seem, indeed, that some at least in the multitude realised that through the Messiah was to be expected a deeper peace than that between man and man. This deeper peace may have been suggested to their minds by the words following next in the prophecy, which goes on to speak of prisoners of hope rescued from the pit, and turning to the stronghold; or by the Psalm from which their cry "Hosanna in the highest" was taken (Ps. cxviii.); certain it is that their minds did rise to a higher conception of the work of the Messiah than they had given token of before; for the cry of some of them at least was "Peace in heaven, and glory in the highest" (Luke xix. 38). A striking proof this, of the fitness of His manner of entering into His capital to suggest the purest, highest and best thoughts concerning the kingdom which He claimed as His own.

As Jerusalem was the city of the great King, the Temple was His house, His royal palace, and accordingly He enters it and takes possession in His Father's name. We are told by St. Mark that "when He had looked round about upon all things, it being now eventide, He went out unto Bethany with the twelve." But St. Matthew, who is accustomed to pay more attention to the logical than to the exact chronological sequence of events, proceeds at once to relate the purging of the Temple, which really took place the following day, but which was so plainly the natural sequel of His royal entrance that he very properly gives it in close connection therewith. Besides, what the King did on entering the Temple the next day admirably illustrates the prophecy. For what saith the prophet? "Behold thy King cometh unto thee: He is just, and having salvation." "He is *just*," —therefore He will not tolerate the unholy traffic in the Temple, but "cast out all them that sold and bought in the Temple, and overthrew the tables of the money-changers and the seats of them that sold the doves; and He saith unto them, My house shall be called a house of prayer; but ye make it a den of robbers" (R.V.): "*and having salvation*" —accordingly, when He sees the blind and the lame in the Temple He does not turn them out, He does not turn away from them, "He healed them." The casting out of the traders illustrated the *righteousness* of the kingdom, the healing of the blind and lame, its *peace*, and the shouts of the children which followed, its *joy*.

This coming of the King to His capital has been familiarly spoken of as "the triumphal entry." The term seems unfortunate and misleading. The waving of palms, the strewing of branches and leaves, the spreading of garments on the way—all this gave it something of the aspect of a triumph; but that it was no triumph none knew better than the Man of Sorrows, Who was the centre of it all. There was certainly no triumph in His heart that day. If you wish to look into His heart, watch Him as He comes to the turn of the road where first the great city bursts upon His sight. How it glitters in the sun, its palaces and towers gleaming in the splendour of the day, its magnificent Temple, which had taken nearly half a century to build, rearing its stately head high above all, into the glorious heaven—a city and a temple for a king to be proud of, especially when seen through waving palm branches held in the hands of a rejoicing throng who shout "Hosanna to the Son of David, Hosanna in the highest!" Surely His soul must be thrilled with jubilant emotion!

Ah! but look at Him: look at Him closely. Go up to Him, near enough to see His face and hear what He is saying. Is He jubilant? His eyes are wet with tears; and with tears in His voice He is speaking "the saddest words of tongue or pen": O Jerusalem, "if thou hadst known, even thou, at least in this thy day, the things which belong unto thy peace! but now they are hid from thine eyes. For the days shall come upon thee, that thine enemies shall cast a trench about thee, and compass thee round, and keep thee in on every side, and shall lay thee even with the ground, and thy children within thee; and they shall not leave in thee one stone upon another; because thou knewest not the time of thy visitation." Ah! well the Man of Sorrows knew what all that shouting and rejoicing were worth; not even for a moment was He misled by it; no less certainly now, when the plaudits of the multitudes were ringing around Him, than when He had been on the way going up to Jerusalem, did He know that, though He was the rightful King, He should receive no king's welcome, but should suffer many things and die. He knew that it was to no royal palace, but to the bitter cross, He was advancing, as He rode down Olivet, across the Kedron, and up to the city of David. Yet it is not the thought of His own cross that draws the tears from His eyes; it is the thought of the woes impending over those whom He has come to save, but who will have none of Him. O the depth of divine love in these self-forgetful tears!

One thrill of joy the day had for the King of sorrows. It was His welcome from the children. The plaudits of the multitude He seems to have received in silence. Why should He be moved by *hosannas* from the lips of those who, as soon as they shall find out what manner of King He is, will cry "Away with Him"? But the hosannas of the children are genuine music to His soul. The little ones at least are true. There is no guile in their spirits. "Of such is the kingdom of heaven." It is most touching to observe how lovingly the heart of the Saviour goes out to the little ones at this most trying time. The climax of pathos in His lament over Jerusalem is reached when, after speaking of the fate of the city, He adds, "and thy children within thee"; and the same deep sympathy with the little ones is shown in the answer He gives to the mean-spirited priests and scribes who were moved with indignation and tried to silence their sweet voices: "Have ye never read, Out of the mouth of babes and sucklings Thou hast perfected praise?"

"And He left them, and went out of the city into Bethany, and He lodged there,"—not in the house of Lazarus, we may be sure, or He would not have "hungered" when in the morning He returned to the city (ver. 18); no doubt under the open canopy of heaven, or at best under some booth erected as a temporary shelter. What were His thoughts, what His feelings, as He looked back on the day and forward to the week?

FOOTNOTE

[16] The knight was originally a *Knecht* = a servant or slave.

XVII
CONFLICT IN THE TEMPLE

Matt xxi.-xxiii.

IT had been written that the Lord should suddenly come to His Temple (Mal. iii. 1); but He would not too hastily assert His rights. The first day He simply "looked round about upon all things" (Mark xi. 11), and then withdrew to Bethany. The second day—without, however, even yet assailing the authority of those in power—He assumed His prerogative as Lord of the Temple by casting out the traffickers, healing the blind and the lame, and accepting the hosannas of the children. The scribes and Pharisees showed some displeasure at all this, and raised objections; but the answer they received silenced, if it did not satisfy them. Thus two days passed without any serious attempt to dispute His authority; but on the third day the conflict began. It was a dark and terrible day, and of its fateful history we have a full account in this Gospel.

The day opens with the sight on the way to the city of the withered fig tree, a sad symbol of the impending fate of Israel, to be decided ere the day closed by their final rejection of their Saviour-King. This was our Lord's single miracle of judgment; many a stern word of warning did He speak, but there is no severity in His deeds: they are all mercy and love. The single exception, if exception it may be called, makes this great fact stand out only the more impressively. It was necessary for love's sake to show that in that arm, which was always strong to save, there was also strength to smite if the sad necessity should come; but so tender-hearted is He that He cannot bear to strike where the stroke can be felt, so He lets it fall on an unconscious tree. Thus to the end He justifies His name of Jesus, Saviour, and illustrates the blessed truth of which His whole life is the expression, that "God is love." "The Son of man is not come to destroy men's lives but to save them." Judgment is His strange work; from the very thought of it He shrinks, as seems suggested to us here by the fact that, in the use He makes of the circumstance in His conversation with the disciples, He refrains from speaking of its dark significance, but rather takes the opportunity of teaching from it an incidental lesson full of hope and comfort regarding the power of faith and the value of prayer (vv. 21, 22).

As soon as on the third day He enters the Temple the conflict begins. It would seem that the interval our Lord had in mercy allowed for calm reflection had been used for no other purpose than to organise a conspiracy for the purpose of entangling Him in His words and so discrediting His authority. We gather this from the carefully framed questions with which He is plied by one party after another. Four successive attacks are recorded in the passage before us: the first by the chief priests and elders of the people demanding His authority; the next by the Pharisees, assisted by the Herodians, who endeavoured by means of the difficulty of the tribute money to embroil Him with the Roman power; this was again immediately followed by a third, in which the prime movers were the Sadducees, armed with what they considered an unanswerable question regarding the life to come; and when that also broke down there was a renewed attack of the Pharisees who thought to disconcert Him by a perplexing question about the law.

We may not discuss the long sad history of these successive attacks with any fulness, but only glance first at the challenge of our Lord's authority and how He meets it, and next at the ordeal of questions with which it was followed.

I. — The Challenge (xxi. 23-xxii. 14)

"By what authority doest Thou these things? And who gave Thee this authority?" The question was fair enough; and if it had been asked in an earnest spirit, Jesus would have given then, as always to the honest inquirer, a kind and satisfying answer. It is not, however, as inquirers, but as cavillers, they approach Him. Again and again, at times and in ways innumerable, by fulfilment of prophecy, by His mighty deeds and by His wondrous words, He had given proof of His Divine authority and established His claim to be the true Messiah. It was not therefore because they lacked evidence of His authority, but because they hated it, because they would not have this man to reign over them, that now they question Him. It was obvious that their only object was to entangle Him; accordingly our Lord showed how in the net they were spreading for Him their own feet were caught.

He meets their question with a counter question, "The baptism of John, whence was it? from heaven, or of men?" The more we examine this question, the more must we admire the consummate wisdom it displays. We see at once how it turns the tables on His critics; but it is far more important to notice how admirably adapted it was to lead them to the answer of their own question, if only they would follow it out. They dared not repudiate the baptism of John; and had not John baptised Jesus, and solemnly borne repeated testimony to His Messiahship? Had he not most emphatically borne that very testimony to a formal deputation sent by themselves? (John i. 19-27). Finally, were not the ministry and testimony of John closely associated in prophecy with that very coming of the Lord to His Temple which gave them so deep offence: "Behold, I will send My messenger, and he shall prepare the way before Me: and the Lord, whom ye seek, shall suddenly come to His temple: ... behold, He shall come, saith the Lord of hosts." Our Lord's counter question, then, was framed with such exquisite skill as to disappoint their malice, while at the same time it was suited to guide the earnest inquirer to the truth.

The propounders of the question were not true men, but hypocrites. A negative answer they *could* not give. An affirmative they *would* not give. So when they refused to answer, our Lord replied, "Neither tell I you by what authority I do these things."

The Lord of the Temple now assumes the offensive, and directs against His opponents a series of parables which He holds up to them as a triple mirror in which from different points of view they may see themselves in their true character, and as a set of danger signals to warn them of their impending doom. He presents them with such marvellous skill that He makes the Pharisees their own judges, and constrains them to pass sentence on themselves. In the first parable He constrains them to declare their own guilt; in the second, He makes them decree their own punishment; in the third, He warns them of the impending fate of the people they were leading to destruction.

We have said that in these parables Christ assumes the offensive; but this is true only in a very superficial sense. In the deepest sense He spoke them not against the Pharisees, but for them. His object was to carry home to their hearts the conviction of sin, and to impress them with a sense of their danger before it was too late. This was what above all they needed. It was their only hope of salvation. And how admirably suited for His purpose were these three parables! Their application to themselves was plain enough after it was stated, but not beforehand; the effect of which was that they were put in a position to give an impartial verdict on their own conduct. It was the same method so effectively employed by Nathan in bringing conviction to the conscience of David. Had Christ charged the sin of the Pharisees directly home upon them, they would have been at once thrown on the defensive, and it would have been impossible to reach their conscience through the entanglements of prejudice and personal interest. Christ wishes to disentangle them from all that was darkening their moral vision; and He uses the parable as the most effective means. It is a great mistake, then, to suppose that Jesus contented Himself with turning the tables on them, and carrying the war, so to speak, into the enemy's country.

It was with them a war of words, but not with Him. He was seeking to save these poor lost ones. He wished to give them His best for their worst. They had come to entangle Him in His talk. He does His best to disentangle them from the meshes of self-deception. The tone of all three parables is exceptionally severe; but the spirit of them is love.

The Two Sons (vv. 28-32).

The parable of the two sons is exceedingly simple; and the question founded upon it, "Whether of them twain did the will of his father?" admitted of but one answer—an answer which seemed, as it was spoken, to involve only the simplest of all moral judgments; yet how keen the edge of it when once it was disclosed! Observe the emphatic word *did*, suggesting without saying it, that it made comparatively little difference what they *said* (see xxiii. 3). So far as profession went, the Pharisees were all that could be desired. They were the representatives of religion in the land; their whole attitude corresponded to the answer of the second son: "I go, sir." Yet when John—whom they themselves admitted to be a prophet of the Lord—came to them in the way of righteousness, they set his word aside and refused to obey him. On the other hand, many of those whose lives seemed to say "I will not," when they heard the word of John, repented and began to work the works of God. Thus it came to pass that many of these had entered the kingdom, while the self-complacent Pharisee still remained without.

The words with which the parable is pressed home are severe and trenchant; but they are nevertheless full of gospel grace. They set in the strongest light the welcome fact that the salvation of God is for the chief of sinners, for those who have been rudest and most rebellious in their first answers to the divine appeal; and then, while they condemn so very strongly the self-deceiver, it is not for the purpose of covering him with confusion, but in order to open his eyes and save him from the net in which he has set his feet. Even in that terrible sentence which puts him lower down than open and disgraceful sinners, there is a door left still unlatched for him to enter. "The publicans and harlots go into the kingdom of God *before you*"; but you may enter after them. If only you, like them, would "afterward" repent—if you would repent of your hypocrisy and insincerity, as they have repented of their rudeness and rebellion—you would be as gladly welcomed as they into the kingdom of God.

The Husbandmen (vv. 33-46).

The second parable follows hard on the first, and presses the chief priests and Pharisees so closely that they cannot fail to see in the end that it is themselves they have been constrained to judge and condemn (ver. 45). It is indeed difficult to suppose that they had not even from the beginning some glimpse of the intended application of this parable. The vineyard was a familiar symbol, with a definite and well understood meaning, from which our Lord in His use of it does not depart. The vineyard being the nation, the owner is evidently God; the fruit expected, righteousness; the particulars mentioned (the fence, the press, the tower) implying the completeness of the arrangements made by the owner for securing the expected fruit. The husbandmen are the leaders of the people, those who are responsible for their direction and control. The going to a far country represents the removal of God from their sight; so that they are, as it were, put upon their honour, left to act in the matter of the vineyard according to the prompting of their own hearts. All this is contained in the few lines which make up verse 33, and forms the groundwork of this great parable. Thus are set forth in a very striking manner the high privileges and grave responsibilities of the leaders of the Jewish people, represented at the time by the chief priests and Pharisees He was then addressing. How are they meeting this responsibility? Let the parable tell.

It is a terrible indictment, showing in the strongest light the guilt of their fathers, and pointing out to them that they are on the verge of a crime far greater still. Again and again have prophets of righteousness come in the name of the Lord, and demanded the fruits of righteousness which were due. How have they been received? "The husbandmen took his servants, and beat one, and killed another, and stoned another." So have their fathers acted time after time, and still the patience of the owner is not exhausted, nor does He even yet give up all hope of fruit from His favoured vineyard; so, as a last resort, He sends His son, saying, "They will reverence my son."

We can imagine the tone in which the Son of God would speak these words. What a sublime consciousness is implied in His use of them! and how touchingly does He in this incidental way give the best of all answers to the question with which His enemies began! Surely the son, the only and well beloved son,[17] had the best of all authority to act for the father! In the former parable He had appealed to the recognised authority of John; now He indicates that the highest authority of all is in Himself. If only their hearts had not been wholly shut against the light, how it would have flashed upon them now! They would have taken up the cry of the children, and said, "Hosanna! blessed is He that cometh in the name of the Lord"; and the parable would have served its purpose before it had reached its close. But they are deaf and blind to the things of God; so the awful indictment must proceed to the bitter end.

If there was in the heart of Christ an exalted consciousness of His filial relation to God as He spoke of the sending of the Son, what a pang must have shot through it as He proceeded to depict in such vivid colours the crime they are now all ready to commit, referring successively as He does to the arrest, the handing over to Pilate, and the crucifixion without the gate: "They caught him, and cast him out of the vineyard, and slew him." How appalling it must have been to Him to speak these words! how appalling it ought to have been to them to hear them! That they did feel the force of the parable is evident from the answer they gave to the question, "What will he do to those husbandmen?" and, as we have said, they must surely have had some glimpses of its application to themselves; but it did not disturb their self-complacency, until our Lord spoke the plain words with which He followed up the parable, referring to that very psalm from which the children's cry of "Hosanna" was taken. From it He selects the symbol of the stone rejected by the builders, but by God made the head of the corner, applying it to Himself (the rejected stone) and them (the builders). The reference was most appropriate in itself; and it had the further advantage of being followed by the very word which it would be their salvation now to speak. "Hosanna" is the word which immediately follows the quotation He makes, and it introduces a prayer which, if only they will make their own, all will yet be well with them. The prayer is, "Save now, I beseech Thee, O Lord"; followed by the words, "Blessed be He that cometh in the name of the Lord." May we not assume that our Lord paused after making His quotation, to give them the opportunity of adopting it as their own prayer? His whole heart was longing to hear these very words from them. Have we not the proof of it further on, in the sad words with which at last He abandoned the hope: "I say unto you, ye shall not see Me henceforth till ye shall say, Blessed is He that cometh in the name of the Lord" (xxiii. 39)?

Seeing they will not take the warning of the parable, and that they refuse the opportunity given them while yet under its awe-inspiring influence, to repent and return, He must give sentence against them: "Therefore say I unto you, The kingdom of God shall be taken away from you, and given to a nation bringing forth the fruits thereof." This sentence He follows up by setting before them the dark side of the other symbol: "Whosoever shall fall on this stone shall be broken: but on whomsoever it shall fall, it will grind him to powder." They were stumbling on the stone now, and about to be broken upon it; but the danger that lay before them if they persisted in their present unbelief and sin, would be far greater still, when He Whom they now despised and rejected should be at the head of all authority and power.

But all is vain. Steeling their hearts against His faithful words, they are only the more maddened against Him, and fear alone restrains them from beginning now the very crime against which they have just had so terrible a warning: "When they sought to lay hands on Him, they feared the multitudes, because they took Him for a prophet."

The Marriage Feast (xxii. 1-14).

The manner in which this third parable is introduced leaves room for doubt whether it was spoken in immediate connection with the two preceding. The use of the word "answered" (ver. 1) would rather suggest the idea that some conversation not reported had intervened. But though it does not form part of a continuous discourse with the others, it is so closely connected with them in scope and bearing that it may appropriately be dealt with, as concluding the warning called forth by the first attack of the chief priests and elders. The relation between the three parables will be best seen by observing that the first has to do with their treatment of John; the second and third with their treatment of Himself and His apostles. The second and third differ from each other in this: that, while the King's Son, Who is prominent in both, is regarded in the former as the last and greatest of a long series of heavenly messengers sent to demand of the chosen people the fruits of righteousness, in the latter He is presented, not as demanding righteousness, but as bringing joy. Duty is the leading thought of the second parable, privilege of the third; in the one sin is brought home to Israel's leaders by setting before them their treatment of the messengers of righteousness, in the other the sin lies in their rejection of the message of grace. Out of this distinction rises another—viz., that while the second parable runs back into the past, upwards along the line of the Old Testament prophets, the third runs down into the future, into the history of the apostolic times. The two together make up a terrible indictment, which might well have roused these slumbering consciences, and led even scribes and Pharisees to shrink from filling up the measure of their iniquities.

A word may be necessary as to the relation of this parable to the similar one recorded in the fourteenth chapter of St. Luke, known as "The parable of the Great Supper." The two have many features in common, but the differences are so great that it is plainly wrong to suppose them to be different versions of the same. It is astonishing to see what needless difficulties some people make for themselves by the utterly groundless assumption that our Lord would never use the same illustration a second time. Why should He not have spoken of the gospel as a feast, not twice merely, but fifty times? There would, no doubt, be many variations in His manner of unfolding the thought, according to the circumstances, the audience, the particular object in view at the time; but to suppose that because He had used that illustration in Galilee, He must be forbidden from reverting to it in Judæa is a specimen of what we may call the insanity of those who are ever on the watch for their favourite "discrepancies." In this case there is not only much variation in detail, but the scope of the two parables is quite different, the former having more the character of a pressing invitation, with only a suggestion of warning at the close; whereas the one before us, while preserving all the grace of the gospel as suggested by the figure of a feast to which men are freely invited, and even heightening its attractiveness inasmuch as it is a wedding feast—the most joyful of all festivities—and a royal one too, yet has throughout the same sad tone of judgment which has been characteristic of all these three parables, and is at once seen to be specially appropriate to the fateful occasion on which they were spoken.

As essentially a New Testament parable, it begins with the familiar formula "The kingdom of heaven is like." The two previous parables had led up to the new dispensation; but this one begins with it, and is wholly concerned with it. The King's Son appears now, not as a messenger, but as a bridegroom. It was not the first time that Jesus had spoken of Himself as a bridegroom, or rather as *the* Bridegroom.[18] The thought was a familiar one in the prophets of the Old Testament, the Bridegroom, be it remembered, being none other than Jehovah Himself. Consider, then, what it meant that *Jesus* should without hesitation or explanation speak of Himself as the Bridegroom. And let us not imagine that He simply took the figure, and applied it to Himself as fulfilling prophecy; let us not fail to realise that He entered fully into its tender meaning. When we think of the circumstances in which this parable was spoken, we have here a most pathetic glimpse into the sanctuary of our Saviour's loving heart. Let us try with reverent sympathy to enter into the feeling of the King's Son, come from heaven to seek humanity for His bride, to woo and to win her from the cruel bondage of sin and death, to take her into union with Himself, so that she may share with Him the liberty and wealth, the purity and joy, the glory and the hope of the heavenly kingdom! The King "made a marriage for His Son"—where is the bride? what response is she making to the Bridegroom's suit? A marriage for His Son! On Calvary?

It must have been very hard for Him to go on; but He will keep down the rising tide of emotion, that He may set before this people and before all people another attractive picture of the kingdom of heaven. He will give even these despisers of the heavenly grace another opportunity to reconsider their position. So He tells of the invitations sent out first to "them that were bidden"—*i.e.*, to the chosen people who had been especially invited from the earliest times, and to whom, when the fulness of the time had come, the call was first addressed. "And they would not come." There is no reference to the aggravations which had found place in the former parable (xxi. 39). These were connected not so much with the offer of grace, which is the main purport of this parable, as with the demand for fruit, which was the leading thought of the one before. It was enough, then, in describing how they dealt with the invitation, to say, "They would not come"; and, indeed, this refusal hurt Him far more than their buffets and their blows. When He is buffeted, He is silent, sheds no tears, utters no wail; His tears and lamentation are reserved for them: "How often would I have gathered thy children together, even as a hen gathereth her chickens under her wings, and ye would not!" *"They would not come."*

But the love of the King and of His Son is not yet exhausted. A second invitation is sent, with greater urgency than before, and with fuller representations of the great preparations which had been made for the entertainment of the guests: "Again, he sent forth other servants, saying, Tell them which are bidden, Behold, I have prepared my dinner: my oxen and my fatlings are killed, and all things are ready: come unto the marriage." As the first invitation was that which had been already given and which they were now rejecting, the second refers to that fuller proclamation of the gospel which was yet to be made after the work of the Bridegroom-Redeemer should be finished, when it could be said, as not before: "All things are ready."

In the account which follows, therefore, there is a foreshadowing of the treatment the apostles would afterwards receive. Many, indeed, were converted by their word, and took their places at the feast; but the people as a whole "made light of it, and went their ways, one to his farm, another to his merchandise: and the remnant took his servants, and entreated them spitefully, and slew them." What was the consequence? Jerusalem, rejecting the gospel of the kingdom, even when it was "preached with the Holy Ghost sent down from heaven," must be destroyed; and new guests must be sought among the nations that up till now had no especial invitation to the feast. This prophetic warning was conveyed in terms of the parable; yet there is a touch in it which shows how strongly the Saviour's mind was running on the sad future of which the parable was but a picture: "When the king heard thereof, he was wroth: and he sent forth his armies, and destroyed those murderers, and burned up their city." Why "city"? There had been no mention of a city in the parable. True; but Jerusalem was in the Saviour's heart, and all the pathos of His lament over it is in that little word. *"Their* city" too, observe,—reminding us of *"your* house" at the close of this sad day (xxiii. 38). In the same way the calling of the Gentiles is most skilfully brought within the scope of the parable, by the use of the peculiar word translated in the Revised Version—"the partings of the highways," which seems to suggest the thought of the servants leaving the city precincts, and going out in all directions along the main trunk roads to "the partings of the highways," to carry the gospel to all without distinction, wherever could be found an ear of man to listen, or a human heart to welcome the King's grace and the Bridegroom's love. Thus, after all, the wedding was to be furnished with guests.

The parable, as we have seen, is one of grace; but righteousness too must find a place in it. The demand for fruits of righteousness is no less rigid in the new dispensation than it had been in the old. To make this clear and strong the parable of the Feast is followed by the pendant of the Wedding Garment.

There are two ways in which the heavenly marriage feast may be despised: first, by those who will not come at all; next, and no less, by those who try to snatch the wedding joy without the bridal purity. The same leading thought or motive is recognisable here as in the parable of the two sons. The man without the wedding garment corresponds to the son who said "I go, sir," and went not, while those who refuse altogether correspond to the son who answered "I will not." By bearing this in mind we can understand, what to many has been a serious difficulty—how it is that the punishment meted out to the offender in this second parable is so terribly severe. If we simply think of the parable itself, it does seem an extraordinary thing that so slight an offence as coming to a wedding feast without the regulation dress should meet with such an awful doom; but when we consider whom this man represents, we can see the very best of reasons for it. Hypocrisy was his crime, than which there is nothing more utterly hateful in the sight of Him Who desireth truth in the inward parts. It is true that the representation does not at first seem to set the sin in so very strong a light; but when we think of it, we see that there was no other way in which it could be brought within the scope of this parable. It is worthy of notice, moreover, that the distinction between the intruder and the others is not observed till the king himself enters, which indicates that the difference between him and the others was no outward distinction, that the garment referred to is the invisible garment of righteousness. To the common eye he looked like all the rest; but when the all-searching Eye is on the company he is at once detected and exposed. He is really worse than those who would not come at all. They were honest sinners; he was a hypocrite—*at* the feast with mouth and hand and eye, but not *of* it, for his spirit is not robed in white: he is the black sheep in the fold; a despiser within, he is worse than the despisers without.

Even to him, indeed, the king has a kindly feeling. He calls him "Friend," and gives him yet the opportunity to repent and cry for mercy. But he is speechless. False to the core, he has no rallying point within to fall back upon. All is confusion and despair. He cannot even pray. Nothing remains but to pronounce his final doom (ver. 13).

The words with which the parable closes (ver. 14) are sad and solemn. They have occasioned difficulty to some, who have supposed they were meant to teach that the number of the saved will be small. Their difficulty, like so many others, has been due to forgetfulness of the circumstances under which the words were spoken, and the strong emotion of which they were the expression. Jesus is looking back over the time since He began to spread the gospel feast, and thinking how many have been invited, and how few have come! And even among those who have seemed to come there are hypocrites! One He specially would have in mind as He spoke of the man without the wedding garment; for though we take him to be the type of a class, we can scarcely think that our Lord could fail to let His sad thoughts rest on Judas, as He described that man. Taking all this into consideration, we can well understand how at that time He should conclude His parable with the lamentation: "Many are called, but few chosen." It did not follow that it was a truth for all time and for eternity. It was true for the time included in the scope of the parable. It was most sadly true of the Jewish nation then, and in the times which followed on immediately; but the day was coming, before all was done, when the heavenly Bridegroom, according to the sure word of prophecy, should "see of the travail of His soul, and be satisfied." No creed article, therefore, have we here, but a cry from the sore heart of the heavenly Bridegroom, in the day of His sorrow, in the pain of unrequited love.

II.—The Ordeal of Questions (xxii. 15-46)

The open challenge has failed; but more subtle weapons may succeed. The Pharisees have found it of no avail to confront their enemy; but they may still be able to entangle Him. They will at all events try. They will spring upon Him some hard questions, of such a kind that, answering on the spur of the moment, He will be sure to compromise Himself.

1. The first shall be one of those semi-political semi-religious questions on which feeling is running high—the lawfulness or unlawfulness of paying tribute to Cæsar. The old Pharisees who had challenged His authority keep in the background, that the sinister purpose of the question may not appear; but they are represented by some of their disciples who, coming fresh upon the scene and addressing Jesus in terms of respect and appreciation, may readily pass for guileless inquirers. They are accompanied by some Herodians, whose divergence of view on the point made it all the more natural that they should join with Pharisees in asking the question; for it might fairly be considered that they had been disputing with one another in regard to it, and had concluded to submit the question to His decision as to one who would be sure to know the truth and fearless to tell it. So together

they come with the request: "Master, we know that Thou art true, and teachest the way of God in truth, neither carest Thou for any man: for Thou regardest not the person of men. Tell us therefore, What thinkest Thou? Is it lawful to give tribute unto Cæsar, or not?"

But they cannot impose upon Him: "Jesus perceived their wickedness, and said, Why tempt ye Me, ye hypocrites?" Having thus unmasked them, without a moment's hesitation He answers them. They had expected a "yes" or a "no" —a "yes" which would have set the people against Him, or better still a "no" which would have put Him at the mercy of the government. But, avoiding Scylla on the one hand, and Charybdis on the other, He makes straight for His goal by asking for a piece of coin and calling attention to Cæsar's stamp upon it. Those who use Cæsar's coin should not refuse to pay Cæsar's tribute; but, while the relation which with their own acquiescence they sustain to the Roman emperor implied corresponding obligations in the sphere it covered, this did not at all interfere with what is due to the King of kings and Lord of lords, in Whose image we all are made, and Whose superscription every one of us bears: "Render therefore unto Cæsar the things which are Cæsar's; and unto God the things that are God's." Thus He not only avoids the net they had spread for Him, and gives them the very best answer to their question, but, in doing so, He lays down a great principle of far-reaching application and permanent value respecting the difficult and much-to-be-vexed question as to the relations between Church and State. "O answer full of miracle!" as one has said. No wonder that "when they had heard these words, they marvelled, and left Him, and went their way."

2. Next come forward certain Sadducees. That the Pharisees had an understanding with them also seems likely from what is said both in verse 15, which seems a general introduction to the series of questions, and in verse 34, from which it would appear that they were somewhere out of sight waiting to hear the result of this new attack. Though the alliance seems a strange one, it is not the first time that common hostility to the Christ of God has drawn together the two great rival parties (see chap. xvi. 1). If we are right in supposing them to be in combination now, it is a remarkable illustration of the deep hostility of the Pharisees that they should not only combine with the Sadducees against Him, as they had done before, but that they should look with complacency on their using against Him a weapon which threatened one of their own doctrines. For the object of the attack was to cast ridicule on the doctrine of the resurrection, which assuredly the Pharisees did not deny.

The difficulty they raise is of the same kind as those which are painfully familiar in these days, when men of coarse minds and fleshly imaginations show by their crude objections their incapacity even to think on spiritual themes. The case they supposed was one they knew He could not find fault with so far as this world was concerned, for everything was done in accordance with the letter of the law of Moses, the inference being that whatever confusion there was in it must belong to what they would call His figment of the resurrection: "In the resurrection whose wife shall she be of the seven? for they all had her."

It is worthy of note that our Lord's answer is much less stern than in the former case. These men were not hypocrites. They were scornful, perhaps flippant; but they were not intentionally dishonest. The difficulty they felt was due to the coarseness of their minds, but it was a real difficulty to them. Our Lord accordingly gives them a kindly answer, not denouncing them, but calmly showing them where they are wrong: "Ye do err, not knowing the Scriptures, nor the power of God."

Ye know not the power of God, or ye would not suppose that the life to come would be a mere repetition of the life that now is, with all its fleshly conditions the same as now. That there is continuity of life is of course implied in the very idea of resurrection; but true life resides not in the flesh but in the spirit, and therefore the continuity will be a spiritual continuity; and the power of God will effect such changes on the body itself that it will rise out of its fleshly condition into a state of being like that of the angels of God. The thought is the same as that which was afterwards expanded by the apostle Paul in such passages as Rom. viii. 5-11, 1 Cor. xv. 35-54.

Ye know not the Scriptures, or you would find in the writings of Moses from which you quote, and to which you attach supreme importance, evidence enough of the great doctrine you deny. "Have ye not read that which was spoken unto you by God, saying, I am the God of Abraham, and the God of Isaac, and the God of Jacob?" Here, again, Jesus not only answers the Sadducees, but puts the great and all-important doctrine of the life to come and the resurrection of the body on its deepest foundation. There are those who have expressed astonishment that He did not quote from some of the later prophets, where He could have found passages much clearer and more to the point: but not only was it desirable that, as they had based their question on Moses, He should give His answer from the same source; but in doing so He has put the great truth on a permanent and universal basis; for the argument rests not on the authority of Moses, nor, as some have supposed, upon the present tense "I am," but on the relation between God and His people. The thought is that such a relation between mortal man and the eternal God as is implied in the declaration "I am the God of Abraham, and the God of Isaac, and the God of Jacob" is itself a guarantee of immortality. Not for the spirit only, for it is not as spirits merely but as men that we are taken into relation to the living God; and that relation, being of God, must share His immortality: "God is not the God of the dead, but of the living." The thought[19] is put in a very striking way in a well-known passage in the Epistle to the Hebrews: "But now they (the patriarchs) desire a better country, that is, an heavenly: *wherefore God is not ashamed to be called their God*: for He hath prepared for them a city."

Our Lord's answer suggests the best way of assuring ourselves of this glorious hope. Let God be real to us, and life and immortality will be real too. If we would escape the doubts of old Sadducee and new Agnostic, we must be much with God, and strengthen more and more the ties which bind us to Him.

3. The next attempt of the Pharisees is on an entirely new line. They have found that they cannot impose upon Him by sending pretended inquirers to question Him. But they have managed to lay their hands on a real inquirer now — one of themselves, a student of the law, who is exercised on a question much discussed, and to which very different answers are given; they will suggest to him to carry his question to Jesus, and see what He will say to it. That this was the real state of the case appears from the fuller account in St. Mark's Gospel. When, then, St. Matthew speaks of him as asking Jesus a question, "tempting Him," we are not to impute the same sinister motives as actuated those who sent him. He also was in a certain sense tempting Jesus — *i.e.*, putting Him to the test, but with no sinister motive, with a real desire to find out the truth, and probably also to find out if this Jesus was one who could really help an inquirer after truth. In this spirit, then, he asks the question, "Which is the great commandment in the law?"

The answer our Lord immediately gives is now so familiar that it is difficult to realise how great a thing it was to give it for the first time. True, He takes it from the Scriptures; but think what command of the Scriptures is involved in this prompt reply. The passages quoted lie far apart — the one in the sixth chapter of Deuteronomy, the other in the nineteenth of Leviticus, in quite an obscure corner; and nowhere are they spoken of as the first and second commandments, nor indeed were they regarded as commandments in the usually understood sense of the word. When we consider all this, we recognise what from one point of view might be called a miracle of genius, and from another a flash of inspiration, in the instantaneous selection of these two passages, and bringing them together so as to furnish a summary of the law and the prophets beyond all praise, which the veriest unbeliever if only he have a mind to appreciate that which is excellent, must recognise as worthy of being written in letters of light That one short answer to a sudden question—asked indeed by a true man, but really sprung upon Him by His enemies who were watching for His halting—is of more value in morals than all the writings of all the ethical philosophers, from Socrates to Herbert Spencer.

It is now time to question the questioners. The opportunity is most favourable. They are gathered together to hear what He will say to their last attempt to entangle Him. Once more He has not only met the difficulty, but has done so in such a way as to make the truth on the subject in dispute shine with the very light of heaven. There could not, then, be a better opportunity of turning their thoughts in a direction which might lead them, if possible in spite of themselves, into the light of God.

The question Jesus asks (vv. 41-45) is undoubtedly a puzzling one for them; but it is no mere Scripture conundrum. The difficulty in which it lands them is one which, if only they would honestly face it, would be the means of removing the veil from their eyes, and leading them, ere it is too late, to welcome the Son of David come in the name of the Lord to save them. They fully accepted the psalm to which He referred as a psalm of David concerning the Messiah. If, then, they would honestly read that psalm, they would see that the Messiah when He comes must be, not a mere earthly monarch, as David was, but a heavenly monarch, one who should sit on the throne of God and bring into subjection the enemies of the kingdom of heaven. If only they would take their ideas of the Christ from the Scriptures which were their boast, they could not fail to see Him standing now before them. For we must remember that they had not only the words He spoke to guide them. They had before them the Messiah Himself, with the light of heaven in His eye, with the love of God in His face; and had they had any love for the light, they would have recognised Him then—they would have seen in Him, whom they had often heard of as David's son, the Lord of David, and therefore the Lord of the Temple, and the heavenly King of Israel. But they love the darkness rather than the light, because their deeds are evil: therefore their hearts remain unchanged, the eyes of their spirit unopened; they are only abashed and silenced: "No man was able to answer Him a word, neither durst any man from that day forth ask Him any more questions."

III.—The House left Desolate (xxiii.)

The day of grace is over for the leaders of the people; but for the people themselves there may still be hope; so the Lord of the Temple turns to "the multitude," the general throng of worshippers, mingled with whom were several of His own disciples, and solemnly warns them against their spiritual guides. There is every reason to suppose that many of the scribes and Pharisees were within hearing; for when He has finished what He has to say to the people, He turns round and addresses them directly in that series of terrible denunciations which follow (ver. 13, *seq.*).

His warning is couched in such a way as not in the least degree to weaken their respect for Moses, or for the sacred Scriptures, the exposition of which was the duty of their spiritual guides. He separates sharply between the office and the men who hold it. Had they been true to the position they occupied and the high duties they had been called to discharge, they would have been worthy of all honour; but they are false men: "they say, and do not." Not only so, but they do positive evil, making that grievous for the people which ought to be a delight; and when they do or seem to do the right thing, it is some petty observance, which they exaggerate for the sake of vain display, while their hearts are set on personal pre-eminence. Such are the leading thoughts set forth with great vigour of language and force of illustration, and not without a touch of keen and delicate irony in our Lord's remarkable indictment of the scribes and Pharisees recorded by our Evangelist (vv. 2-7).

Then follows one of those passages of profound significance and far-reaching application which, while admirably suiting the immediate occasions on which they were spoken, prove to be a treasury of truth for the ages to come. At first sight it strikes us as simply an exhortation to cultivate a disposition the reverse of that of the scribes and Pharisees. He has been drawing their portrait; now He says, Be ye not like unto them, but unlike in every respect. But in saying this He succeeds in laying down great principles for the future guidance of His Church, the remembrance of which would have averted most of the evils which in the course of its history have weakened its power, hindered its progress, and marred its witness to the truth. With one stroke He abolishes all claims of men to intervene between the soul and God. "One is your Teacher" (R.V.), "One is your Father," "One is your Master." Who is that One? He does not in so many words claim the position for Himself; but it is throughout implied, and at the end almost expressed; for, while in speaking of the Teacher and the Father He says nothing to indicate who the One is, when He comes to the Master, He adds "even the Christ" (R.V.). Standing thus at the end of all, these words suggest that the office of the Christ was to bring God within reach of every soul, so that without any intervention of scribe or Pharisee, priest or pope, each one could go direct to Him for instruction (Teacher), for loving recognition (Father), for authoritative guidance and control (Master).

We must remember, too, that He was speaking to His disciples as well as to the multitude, and to them these words would be full of meaning. When He said, "One is your Teacher," of whom could they possibly think but of Himself? When He said, "One is your Father," they would recall such utterances as "I and My Father are One," and have suggested to them the truth which was so very soon to be plainly stated: "He that hath seen Me, hath seen the Father." It is probable, then, that even before He reached the end, and added the words "even the Christ," the minds of His disciples at least had anticipated Him. Thus we find in these remarkable words an implicit claim on the part of Christ to be the sole Prophet, Priest, and King of His people: their sole Prophet, to teach them by the enlightening and sanctifying grace of the Holy Spirit; their sole Priest, to open up the way of access to a reconciled Father in heaven; their sole King, alone entitled to be the Lord of their conscience and their heart.

If only the Christian Church had been true to all this, how different would her history have been! Then the Word of God would have been, throughout, the only and sufficient rule of faith, and the Holy Spirit dealing directly with the spirits of men its sole authoritative interpreter. Then would there have been no usurping priesthood to stand between the souls of men and their Father in heaven, to bind heavy burdens and grievous to be borne and lay them upon men's shoulders, to multiply forms and observances and complicate what should have been simplest of all—the direct way to the Father in heaven, through Christ the great Priest of humanity. Then would there have been no lordship over men's consciences, no ecclesiastical usurpation, no spiritual tyranny, no inquisition, no persecution for conscience' sake. How inexcusable has it all been! It would seem as if pains had been taken deliberately to violate not only the spirit, but the very letter of the Saviour's words, as *e.g.* in the one fact that, while it is expressly written "Call no man your father upon the earth," the Church of Rome has actually succeeded age after age in getting the millions under its usurped spiritual control, to give a man that very title; for the word "pope" is the very word[20] which our Lord so expressly forbids. But all clerical assumption of priestly power is just as certainly and as clearly in violation of this great charter of our spiritual liberties.

"And all ye are brethren." This is the second commandment of the true canon law, like unto the first, and springing naturally out of it, as naturally as the love of neighbour springs out of love to God. As soon as the time shall come when all Christians shall own allegiance alike, full and undivided, to the one Lord of mind and heart and conscience, then will there be an end to all ecclesiastical exclusiveness, then shall we see realised and manifested to the world the brotherhood in Christ of all believers.

Turning once again to the scribes and Pharisees, the Lord of the Temple denounces them in words perhaps the most terrible in the whole Bible. It is a very thunderstorm of indignation, with flash after flash of scorn, peal after peal of woe. It is "*the* burden of the Lord," "the wrath of the Lamb." Is this at all inconsistent with the meekness and lowliness of His heart, the love and tenderness of His character? Certainly not. Love is no love at all, unless it be capable of indignation against wrong. Besides, it is no personal wrongs which stir the heart of Jesus, "Who when He was reviled, reviled not again, when He suffered, He threatened not"; but the wrong these hypocrites are doing to the poor sheep they are leading all astray. The occasion absolutely demanded a tempest of indignation. There is this further to be considered, that the Lord Jesus, as Revealer of God, must display His justice as well as His mercy, His wrath as well as His love.

This passage, terrible as it is, commends itself to all that is noblest and best in us. Who is there who does not thank God for this scathing denunciation of that most hateful of all abominations—hypocrisy? See how He brands it in every sentence—"Woe unto you, scribes and Pharisees, hypocrites!"—how piece by piece He shows their miserable life to be a lie. *Hypocrites!* because you profess to sit in Moses' seat, to have the key of knowledge, to know the way of life yourselves, and show it to others; and all this profession is a lie (ver. 13). *Hypocrites!* because your pretended charity is a lie, aggravated by the forms of devotion with which it is masked, while the essence of it is most sordid avarice (ver. 14). *Hypocrites!* because your zeal for God is a lie, being really a zeal for the devil, your converts being perverts worse than yourselves (ver. 15). *Hypocrites!* because your morality is a lie, making the law of God of none effect by your miserable casuistry (vv. 16-22). *Hypocrites!* because your devotion is a lie, consisting merely in punctilious attention to the minutest forms, while the weighty matters of the law you set aside, like those who "strain out the gnat and swallow the camel" (vv. 23, 24, R.V.). *Hypocrites!* because your whole demeanour is a lie, all fair without like a whited sepulchre, while within ye are "full of dead men's bones, and of all uncleanness" (vv. 25-28). *Hypocrites!* because your pretended reverence for the prophets is a lie, for had you lived in the days of your fathers you would have done as they did, as is plain from the way in which you are acting now; for you build the tombs of the dead prophets and put to death the living ones (vv. 29-31).

The sin branded, sentence follows: "Fill ye up then the measure of your fathers." Since you will not be saved, there is nothing for it but that you go on in sin to the bitter end: serpents, "for ever hissing at the heels of the holy," a brood of vipers, with no hope now of escaping the judgment of Gehenna!

As in the Sermon on the Mount (see page 102) so here, when He speaks as Judge He cannot conceal His personal majesty. All throughout He has been speaking with authority, but has, as usual, avoided the obtrusion of His personal prerogative. Even in saying "One is your Master, even the Christ," it is not at all the same as if He had said, even Myself. All it necessarily conveyed was, "One is your master, even the Messiah," whoever he may be. But now He speaks as from His judgment throne. He is no longer thinking of Himself as one of the prophets, or even as the King's Son, but as Lord of all; so He says: "Wherefore, behold, I send unto you prophets, and wise men, and scribes: and some of them ye shall kill and crucify; and some of them shall ye scourge in your synagogues, and persecute them from city to city: that upon you may come all the righteous blood shed on the earth," from Abel to Zacharias.[21] And, again, "Verily I say unto you, All these things shall come upon this generation."

But judgment is His strange work. He has been compelled by the fire of His holiness to break forth into this tempest of indignation against the hypocrites, and to pronounce upon them the long-deferred sentence of condemnation and wrath. But there has been a wail in all His woes. His nature and His name is love, and it must have been a terrible strain on Him to keep up the foreign tone so long. "The *wrath* of the *Lamb*" is a necessary but not a natural combination. We may not wonder, then, though well we may adore, when after the tension of these woes, His heart is melted into tenderness as He mourns over the fate which all His love may not avert: "O Jerusalem, Jerusalem, thou that killest the prophets and stonest them which are sent unto thee, how often would I have gathered thy children together, even as a hen gathereth her chickens under her wings, and ye would not!" Again, observe the lofty consciousness shining out in the little pronoun "*I.*" He is a young man of little more than thirty; but His personal consciousness runs back through all the ages of the past, through all the times of the killing of the prophets and stoning of the messengers of God, from Abel on to Zachariah: and not only so, but this Son of Israel speaks in the most natural way as the brooding mother of them all through all their generations—what wonders, not of beauty alone, and of exquisite pathos, but of conscious majesty in that immortal lamentation!

Our Saviour's public ministry is closed. He has yet many things to say to His disciples—a private ministry of love to fulfil ere He leave the world and go to the Father; but His public ministry is ended now. Commenced with beatitudes, it ends with woes, because the blessings offered in the beatitudes have been rudely rejected and trampled underfoot. And now the Lord of the Temple is about to leave it—to leave it to its fate, to leave it as He counselled His disciples to leave any city or house that refused to receive them: shaking the dust off His feet; and in doing so, as He turns from the astonished hierarchs, He utters these solemn words, which close the time of their merciful visitation and leave them to "eat of the fruit of their own way, and be filled with their own devices": "Behold, your house is left unto you desolate." *Your* house. It was Mine. I was its glory, and would have been its defence; but when I came unto My own, Mine own received Me not; and now it is no longer Mine but yours, and therefore desolate. *Desolate*; and therefore defenceless, a ready prey for the Roman eagles when they swoop on the defenceless brood. "For I say unto you, Ye shall not see Me henceforth till"—till when? Is there still a door of hope? There is, even for scribes and Pharisees—hypocrites; the door ever open here on earth: "Him that cometh unto Me, I will in nowise cast out." The door is closed upon them for ever as leaders of the people; as temple authorities they can never be recognised again,—their house is left to them desolate; but for themselves there is still this door of hope; these awful woes therefore are not a final sentence, but a long, loud, last call to enter ere it be too late. And as if to show, after all the wrath of His terrible denunciation, that judgment is "His strange work" and that He "delighteth in mercy," He points in closing to that still open door, and says, "Ye shall not see Me henceforth, *till ye shall say, Blessed is He that cometh in the name of the Lord.*"

Why did they not say it then? Why did they not entreat Him to remain? But they did not. So "Jesus went out, and departed from the Temple" (xxiv. 1); and though eighteen hundred years have rolled away since then, the time has not yet come when as a people they have said, "Blessed is He that cometh in the name of the Lord"; accordingly their house is still desolate, and they are "scattered and peeled"—chickens that will not nestle under the mother's wing.

FOOTNOTES

[17] See the accounts in the second and third Gospels.

[18] Another example of the use of the same illustration more than once. See ix. 15.

[19] Compare the same thought in Ps. xvi. 8-11.

[20] *"Papa,"* pope, is the Latin translation of the Hebrew word for Father.

[21] The reason why these two are named is sufficiently obvious, when we remember that the second Book of Chronicles, in which the martyrdom of Zachariah is recorded, was the last book of the Hebrew Scriptures, just as we might say, *All* the promises from Genesis to Revelation. The difficulty which has been made so much of (Barachias *v.* Jehoiada) is of no importance except to those who will not remember that the letter killeth and the spirit giveth life.

XVIII
THE PROPHECY ON THE MOUNT

Matt xxiv., xxv.

WE have seen that though the Saviour's public ministry is now closed, He still has a private ministry to discharge—a ministry of counsel and comfort to His beloved disciples, whom He soon must leave in a world where tribulation awaits them on every side. Of this private ministry the chief remains are the beautiful words of consolation left on record by St. John (xiii.-xvii.), and the valuable words of prophetic warning recorded by the other Evangelists, occupying in this Gospel two long chapters (xxiv., xxv.).

This remarkable discourse, nearly equal in length to the Sermon on the Mount, may be called the Prophecy on the Mount; for it is prophetic throughout, and it was delivered on the Mount of Olives. From the way in which it is introduced (vv. 1-3) we see that it is closely connected with the abandonment of the Temple, and that it was suggested by the disciples calling His attention to the buildings of the Temple, which were in full view of the little group as they sat on the Mount of Olives that memorable day— buildings which seemed stately and stable enough in their eyes, but which were already tottering to their fall before

"... that Eye which watches guilt
And goodness; and hath power to see
Within the green the mouldered tree,
And towers fallen as soon as built."

Thus everything leads us to expect a discourse about the fate of the Temple. The minds of the whole group are full of the subject; and out of the fulness of their hearts the question comes, "Tell us, when shall these things be? And what shall be the sign of Thy coming, and of the end of the world?" From the latter part of the question it is evident that the coming of Christ and the end of the world were closely connected in the disciples' minds with the judgment that was about to come upon the Temple and the chosen people—a connection which was right in point of fact, though wrong in point of time. We shall not be surprised, therefore, to discover that the burden of the first part of the prophecy is that great event to which the attention of all was at that moment so pointedly directed. But since the near as well as the distant event is viewed as the coming of the Son of man, we may give to what may be called the prophecy proper as distinguished from the pictures of judgment that follow, a title which embodies this unifying thought.

I.—The Coming of the Son of Man (vv. 3-44)

In secular history the destruction of Jerusalem is nothing more than the destruction of any other city of equal size and importance. It is indeed marked out from similar events in history by the peculiarly terrible sufferings to which the inhabitants were subjected before the final overthrow. But apart from this, it is to the general historian an event precisely similar to the destruction of Babylon, of Tyre, of Carthage, or of any other ancient city once the seat of a dominion which now has passed away. In sacred history it stands alone. It was not merely the destruction of a city, but the close of a dispensation—the end of that great age which began with the call of Abraham to come out from Ur of the Chaldees, and be the father of a people chosen of the Lord. It was "the end of the world" (comp. R.V., ver. 3, margin) to the Jews, the end of the world which then was, the passing away of the old to give place to the new. It was the event which bore the same relation to the Jews as the Flood did to the antediluvians, which was emphatically the end of the world to them. If we bear this in mind it will enable us to appreciate the tremendous importance assigned to this event wherever it is referred to in the sacred Scriptures, and especially in this momentous chapter.

But though the destruction of Jerusalem is the primary subject of the prophecy, in its full sweep it takes a far wider range. The Saviour sees before Him with prophetic eye, not only that great event which was to be the end of the world which then was—the close of the dispensation of grace which had lasted two thousand years; but also the end of all things, when the last dispensation of grace—not for Israel alone, but for the whole world—shall have come to a close. Though these two events were to be separated from each other by a long interval of time, yet were they so closely related in their nature and issues that our Lord, having in view the needs of those who were to live in the new dispensation, could not speak of the one without also speaking of the other. What He was then saying was intended for the guidance, not only of the disciples then around Him, and of any other Jews who might from them receive the message, but also for the guidance of the whole Christian Church throughout the world to the end of time,—another marvellous illustration of that sublime consciousness of life and power, infinitely beyond the limits of His mere manhood, which is ever betraying itself throughout this wondrous history. Had He confined Himself to the destruction of Jerusalem, His words would have had no special interest for us, any more, for example, than the burden of Babylon or of Tyre or of Dumah in the Old Testament Scriptures; but when He carries us on to that Last Great Day, of which the day of Jerusalem's destruction (as closing the Old Testament dispensation) was a type, we recognise at once our own personal interest in the prophecy; for we ourselves are individually concerned with that Day — we shall then either be overwhelmed in the ruins of the old, or shall rejoice in the glories of the new; therefore we should feel that this prophecy has an interest for us as personal as it had for those who first heard it on the Mount of Olives.

As might be expected from the nature of its subject, the interpretation of the prophecy in matters of detail is beset with difficulties. The sources of difficulty are sufficiently obvious. One is in the elimination of time. The time of both events is studiously concealed, according to the principle distinctly announced by our Saviour just before His ascension: "It is not for you to know the times or the seasons, which the Father hath put in His own power." There are in each case signs given, by which the approach of the event may be recognised by those who will give heed to them; but anything in the shape of a date is studiously avoided. It is perhaps not too much to say that nine-tenths of the difficulties which have been encountered in the interpretation of this passage have arisen from the unwarrantable attempts to introduce dates into it.

Another difficulty arises from the similarity of the two events referred to, and the consequent applicability of the same language to both of them. This leads to different opinions as to which of the two is referred to in certain places. To show the source of these difficulties is to suggest their solution; for when we consider that one event is the type of the other, that one is as it were the miniature of the other, the same on a much smaller scale, we need not hesitate to apply the same language to both, — it may be literally in the one case and figuratively in the other; or it may be in a subordinate sense in the one case, and in the fullest sense in the other; or it may be in precisely the same sense in both cases. In general, however, it will be observed that the lesser event — the destruction of Jerusalem — stands out in full prominence in the beginning of the prophecy, and the greater event — the Great Day of our Saviour's appearing — in the latter part of it.

Still another source of difficulty is that, while our Saviour's object in giving the prophecy was practical, the object of many who study the prophecy is merely speculative. They come to it to satisfy curiosity, and as a matter of course they are disappointed, for our Lord did not intend when He spoke these words to satisfy so unworthy a desire; and, though

His word never returns to Him void, it accomplishes that which He pleases, and nothing else; it prospers in the thing to which He has sent it, but not in the thing to which He has not sent it. He has sent us this, not to satisfy our curiosity, but to influence our conduct; and if we use it not for speculative but for practical purposes—not to find support for any favourite theory, which parcels out the future, giving days and hours, which neither the angels in heaven nor the Son of man Himself could tell (Mark xiii. 32)—but to find food for our souls, then we shall not be troubled with so many difficulties, and we shall certainly not be disappointed.

Before we pass from the difficulties of this prophecy, observe how strong an argument they furnish for its genuineness. Those who deny the divinity of Christ are greatly troubled with this prophecy, so much so that the only way in which they can get rid of its witness to Him is by suggesting that it was really composed after the destruction of Jerusalem, and therefore never spoken by Christ at all. There are difficulties enough of other kinds in the way of such a disposal of the prophecy; but there is one consideration which absolutely forbids it—viz., that any one writing after the event would have avoided all that vagueness of language which gives trouble to expositors. To those who can judge of internal evidence, its obscurity is clear proof that this discourse could not have been produced in the full light of the subsequent history, but must have been what it professes to be, a foreshadowing of coming events.

We may not, with the limits imposed by the plan of these expositions, attempt a detailed explanation of this difficult prophecy, but must content ourselves with giving only a general view. Our Lord first warns His disciples against expecting the crisis too early (vv. 4-14). In this passage He prepares the minds of His disciples for the times of trouble and trial through which they must pass before the coming of "the great and notable day of the Lord" which was at hand: there shall be false Christs and false prophets—there shall be wars and rumours of wars, and shaking of the nations, and famines, and pestilences, and earthquakes in divers places; yet will all these be only "the beginning of sorrows." He also prepares their minds for the gigantic work which must be done by them and by their brother-disciples before that great day: "This gospel of the kingdom shall be preached in all the world for a witness unto all nations; and then shall the end come." Thus are the disciples taught the very important and thoroughly practical truth, that they must pass through a great trial and do a great work before the Day shall come.

He then gives them a certain sign by which they shall know that the event is imminent, when it does approach. This is not equivalent to fixing a date. He gives them no idea how long the period of trial shall last, no idea how long time they shall have for the great work before them—He simply gives them a sign, by observing which they shall not be taken completely by surprise, but have at least a brief space to make their escape from the condemned city. And so very little time will elapse between the sign and the event to which it points, that He warns them against any delay, and tells them, as soon as it shall appear, to flee at once to the mountains and escape for their lives. It is sufficiently evident, by comparing this passage with the corresponding place in Luke, where our Lord speaks of Jerusalem being compassed with armies, that the "abomination of desolation standing in the holy place" refers to some particular act of sacrilegious impiety committed in the Temple just at the time the Romans were beginning to invest the city. Attempts have been made historically to identify this profanation, but it is doubtful if these have been successful. It is sufficient to know that whether or not the fact has found a place in history, it served its purpose as a sign to the Christians in the city who had treasured up in their hearts their Saviour's warning words.

Having told them what the sign would be, and counselled His disciples to lose no time in making their escape as soon as they should see it, He further warns them, in a few impressive words, of the terrors of those days of tribulation (vv. 19-22), and then concludes this portion of the prophecy by warning them against the supposition—a very natural one in the circumstances—that even then the Son of man should come.

So far we have found the leading ideas to be simple and practical, and all connected with the destruction of Jerusalem. (1) Do not expect that event too early; for you must pass through many trials and do much work before it. (2) As soon as you shall see the sign I give you, expect it immediately, and lose no time in making your escape from the horrors of these awful days. (3) Even then, however, do not expect the personal advent of the Son of man; for though it is a day of judgment, it is only one of those partial judgments which are necessary on the principle that "wheresoever the carcase is, there will the eagles be gathered together." The personal advent of Christ and the day of final judgment are only foreshadowed by, not realised in, the destruction of Jerusalem and the close of the old dispensation.

The three closing verses of this portion of the prophecy refer pre-eminently to the great Day of the coming of the Son of man (vv. 29-31). The word "immediately" has given rise to much difficulty, on account of the hasty conclusion to which some have come that "immediately after the tribulation of those days" must mean immediately after the destruction of Jerusalem; according to which all this must have taken place long ago. It is, indeed, sufficiently obvious that the tribulation of those days began with the destruction, or rather with the besieging, of Jerusalem. But when did it end? As soon as the city was destroyed? Nay. If we wish to get some idea of the duration of those days of tribulation, let us turn to the same place in the same prophecy as given by St. Luke (xxi. 23, 24), where it clearly appears that it embraces the whole period of the Jewish dispersion and of the standing of the Gentile Church. "The tribulation of those days" is going on still, and therefore the events of these verses are still future. We look forward to the Day of the Lord of which that terrible day of judgment, to which their thoughts were first turned, was only a dim foreshadowing—a Day far more august in its nature, far more awful in its accompaniments, far more terrible in its aspect to those who are unprepared for it, yet full of glory and of joy to those who "love His appearing."

Appended to the main prophecy are some additional warnings as to time (vv. 32-44) setting forth in the most impressive manner the certainty, the suddenness, and, to those who are not looking for it, the unexpectedness of the coming of the Day of the Lord. Here again, in the first portion the destruction of Jerusalem, and in the latter portion the Day of the Son of man, is prominent. If we bear this in mind it will remove a difficulty many have found in ver. 34, which seems to say that the events specially referred to in vv. 29-31 would be fulfilled before that generation passed away. But when we remember that the prophecy proper closes with the thirty-first verse, and that the warning as to the imminency of the events referred to commences with ver. 32, the difficulty vanishes; for it is most natural that the practical warning should follow the course of the prophecy itself, referring first to the destruction of Jerusalem, and passing from it to that grand event of which it was the precursor. On this principle vv. 32-35 are quite simple and natural, as well as most impressive, and the statement of ver. 34 is seen to be literally accurate.

The passage from ver. 36 onwards is still quite applicable to the near event, the destruction of Jerusalem; but the language used is evidently such as to carry the mind onward to the more distant event which had been brought prominently forward in the latter part of the prophecy (vv. 36-44). In these verses, again, not only is no date given, but we are expressly told that it is deliberately withheld. What then? Are we to dismiss the subject from our minds? Quite the reverse; for though the time is uncertain, the event itself is most certain, and it will come suddenly and unexpectedly. No time will be given for preparation to those who are not already prepared. True, there will be the sign of the Son of man in heaven, whatever that may be; but, like the other sign which was the precursor of Jerusalem's destruction, it will appear immediately before the event, barely giving time for those who have their lamps trimmed and oil in their vessels with their lamps to arise and meet the Bridegroom; but for those who are not watching, it will be too late—it will be with them as with those who lived at the close of the very first dispensation, who were "eating and drinking, marrying and giving in marriage, until the day that Noah entered into the ark, and knew not until the flood came, and took them all away.... Watch therefore: for ye know not what hour your Lord doth come. But know this, that if the goodman of the house had known in what watch the thief would come, he would have watched, and would not have suffered his house to be broken up. Therefore be ye also ready: for in such an hour as ye think not the Son of man cometh."

II.—Parables and Pictures of Judgment (xxiv. 45-xxv.)

The remainder of this great prophecy is taken up with four pictures of judgment, very striking and impressive, having for their special object the enforcement of the great practical lesson with which the first part has closed: "Watch therefore" (vv. 42, 43); "Be ye also ready" (ver. 44). In the former portion of the prophecy the destruction of Jerusalem was in the foreground, and in the background the coming of the Son of man to judgment in the end of the world. In this portion the Great Day of the Son of man is prominent throughout.

The four pictures, though similar in their scope and object, are different in their subjects. The first represents those who occupy positions of trust in the kingdom; the second and third, all professing Christians,—the one setting forth inward grace, the other outward activity; the fourth is a picture of judgment on the whole world.

1. The Servant set over the Household (xxiv. 45-51).

As in the case of the man without the wedding garment, a single servant is taken as representing a class; and who constitute this class is made quite clear, not only by the fact that the servant is set over the household, but also by the nature of the service: "to give them their food in due season" (R.V.). The application was evidently first to the apostles themselves, and then to all who in the future should be engaged in the same work of providing spiritual nourishment for those under their charge. The very pointed way in which the parable is introduced, together with the fact that only one servant is spoken of, suggests to each one engaged in the work the most careful self-examination. "Who, then, is a faithful and wise servant?" The underlying thought seems to be, that such an one is not very easily to be found; and that therefore there is a special benediction for those who through the trying years are found both "faithful and wise," faithful to their high trust, wise in relation to the momentous issues depending on the manner in which they fulfil it. The benediction on the wise and faithful servant is evidently easy to miss and a great thing to gain.

But there is more to be thought of than the missing of the blessing. There is a fearful doom awaiting the unfaithful servant, of which the picture following gives a terrible presentation. Both offence and punishment are painted in the very darkest colours. As to the former, the servant not only neglects his duty but beats his fellow-servants, and eats and drinks with the drunken. Here a question arises, What was there to suggest such a representation to the Saviour's mind? Surely it could not be intended specially for those who were sitting with Him on the mount that day. If Judas was among the rest, his sin was not of the nature that would have suggested the parable in this particular form, and certainly there is no reason to suppose that any of the rest were in the slightest danger of being guilty of such cruelties and excesses as are here spoken of. Is it not plain then, that the judge of all had in His view the dark days to come, when the clergy of a degenerate Church would be actually guilty of cruelties and excesses such as could not be more fitly set forth in parable than by the disgraceful conduct of "that wicked servant"?

This is still further confirmed by the reason given for such recklessness, — the evil servant saying in his heart, "My Lord delayeth His coming." There is reason to suppose that the early Christians expected the return of the Lord almost immediately. In so far as they made this mistake, it cannot be charged against their Master; for, as we have seen, He warns them against this error throughout the whole of the prophecy. It is plain, however, that those who made this mistake were in no danger of saying in their hearts, "My Lord delayeth His coming." But as time passed on, and the expectation of the Lord's speedy return grew fainter, then there would come in all its force the temptation to those who did not watch against it of counting on the Lord's delay. When we think of this, we see how necessary it was that the danger should be set forth in language which may have seemed unnecessarily strong at the time, but which the future history of the Church only too sadly justified.

The punishment is correspondingly severe. The word used to picture it ("shall cut him asunder") is one to make us shudder; and some have felt surprised that our Lord did not shrink from the horror of the word. Ah! but it was the horror of the thing which He dreaded, and wished to avert. It was the infinite pity of His heart that led Him to use a word which might prove the very strongest deterrent. Besides, how significant it is! Think, again, of whom He is speaking, — servants set over His household to give food in due season, who instead of doing this maltreat their fellow-servants and ruin themselves with excess. Think of the duplicity of such conduct. By office in the church "exalted unto heaven," by practice "brought down to hell"! That unnatural combination cannot last. These monsters with two faces and one black heart cannot be tolerated in the universe of God. They shall be *cut asunder*; and then it will appear which of the two faces really belongs to the man: cut asunder, his place shall be appointed with the hypocrites, where shall be weeping and gnashing of teeth (ver. 51).

2 and 3. *The Virgins; The Talents* (xxv. 1-30).

The second and third pictures, presented in the form of two parables of the kingdom of heaven, set before us the judgment of Christ at His coming on His professed disciples, distinguishing between real and merely nominal Christians, between the pretended and the true members of the kingdom of heaven. In the former parable this distinction is set before us in the contrast between the wise and the foolish virgins; in the latter it appears in the form of the one faithful and the two unfaithful servants. No special significance need be attached to the respective numbers, which are evidently chosen with a view to the consistency of the parables, not to set forth anything in regard to the actual proportion between hypocrites and true disciples in the visible Church.

The relation between the two parables has been already indicated. The first represents the Church as waiting, the second as working, for her Lord; the first shows the necessity of a constant supply of inward grace, the second the need of unremitting outward activity; the teaching of the first is, "Keep thy heart with all diligence, for out of it are the issues of life"; of the second, "Do good as ye have opportunity," "Be faithful unto death, and I will give thee a crown of life." The parable of the Virgins comes appropriately before that of the Talents, inasmuch as a Christian's inner life should be his first care, the outer life being wholly dependent on it. "Keep thy heart with all diligence," is the first command; "Do thy work with all diligence," the second. The first parable calls aloud to every member of the Church, "Be wise"; the second follows it with another call, as urgent as the first, "Be faithful."

The Parable of the Virgins (vv. 1-13), with its marriage feast, recalls the parable of the marriage of the King's Son, so recently spoken in the Temple. The difference between the two is very clearly indicated by the way in which each parable is introduced: there, "the kingdom of heaven *is* likened"; here, "*then shall* the kingdom of heaven *be* likened." The gospel feast which was the subject of the parable spoken in the Temple was already spread; it was a thing of the present; its word was, "All things are ready: come to the marriage"; its preparation had been the object of the heavenly Bridegroom's first coming. The wedding feast of this parable is yet to be prepared; it is "the marriage supper of the Lamb" to which the Lord will call His people at His second coming.

An interval, therefore, of unknown length must pass meantime; and herein, as the sequel will unfold, lies the test which distinguishes the wise from the foolish virgins. This interval is represented by a night, with great appropriateness, seeing that the heavenly Bridegroom is the Sun of the soul. It being night, all alike grow drowsy and fall asleep. To make this a fault, as some do, is to spoil the parable. Had it been wrong to sleep, the wise virgins would certainly have been represented as keeping awake. If, then, we give a meaning to the sleep, it is not that of spiritual torpor, but rather such occupation with the concerns of the present life as is natural and necessary. As the whole of "the life that now is," up till the coming of the Lord, is represented in the parable by the night, and as sleep is the business of night, we may fairly consider that the sleep of the parable represents the business of the life that now is, in which Christians, however anxious to be ready for the coming of the Lord, must engage, and not only so, but must give themselves to it with an engrossment which for the time may amount to as entire abstraction from distinctively spiritual duties as sleep is an abstraction from the duties of the day. In this point of view we see how reasonable is our Lord's requirement. He does not expect us to be always equally wide awake to spiritual and eternal things. The wise as well as the foolish slumber and sleep.

It is not, then, by the temptation to sleep that the interval tests the virgins, but by bringing out a difference which has existed all the while, though at the first it did not appear. All seemed alike at the beginning of the night. Had not every one of them a lamp, with oil in it, and were not the lights of all the ten brightly burning? Yes; and if the Bridegroom had come at that hour, all would have seemed equally ready. But the Bridegroom tarries, and while He tarries the business of the night must go on. In this way time passes, till at an unexpected moment in the very middle of the night as it were, the cry is heard "Behold the Bridegroom cometh; go ye out to meet Him. Then all those virgins arose, and trimmed their lamps." Still no difference: each of the ten lamps is trimmed and lighted. But see, five of them are going out almost as soon as they are kindled! What is the reason? There is no store of oil. Here, then, is the difference between the wise and the foolish, and here lies, therefore, the main point of the parable.

What, then, are we to understand in the spiritual sphere by this distinction? That the wise and the foolish represent the watchful and the unwatchful is plain enough; but is there not something here to let us deeper into the secret of the great difference between the one and the other? In order to get this, it is not at all necessary to ask for the significance of each separate detail—the lamp, the wick, the oil, the oil vessel. The details belong to the drapery of the parable; the essentials are manifestly the light and the source whence it comes. The light is the very familiar symbol of the Christian life; the source whence it comes is divine grace, abiding unseen in the heart. Now, there is a certain superficial goodness which shines for the moment much as the true light of grace shines, but is connected with no perennial supply; there is no oil vessel from which the lamp can be constantly replenished. There may be a flaring up for a moment; but there is no steady enduring light.

All which points to the conclusion that the foolish virgins represent those professing Christians who have religious emotion enough to kindle their lamp of life and make it glow with a flame which looks marvellously like true devotion, but which is little else than the blazing up of natural feeling; while the wise virgins represent those whose constant habit is devotion, whose grace is something they carry with them always, so that at any moment the light of it may shine, the flame glow, pure, bright, steady, inextinguishable. They may be as much engaged in the business of life as the others, so that no flame of devotion may be seen; but deep down, hidden out of sight, like the oil in the vessel, there is abiding grace, which is only waiting the occasion to burst into a flame, of prayer or praise or joyful welcome of the Bridegroom at whatever moment He may come. The distinction, therefore, is between those worldly Christians, whose devotion is a thing of now and then, and those thorough Christians whose devotion is habitual, not always to be recognised on the surface of their life, not always to be seen of men, not so as to hinder their engrossment in business hours with the ordinary duties of life, but so as to be always *there*, the deep abiding habit of their souls. There is the secret of watchfulness; there the secret of readiness for the coming of the Lord.

This explains why the wise virgins cannot help the foolish. It is not that they are selfish, and will not do it; but that it cannot be done. Some commentators, men of the letter, have puzzled themselves as to the advice to go to them that sell and buy. That, again, belongs to the framework of the parable. The thought conveyed is plain enough to those who think not of the letter but of the spirit. It is simply this, that grace is not transferable. A man may belong to the warmest, devoutest, most gracious community of disciples in all Christendom; but if he himself has been foolish, if he has not lived in communion with Christ, if he has not kept himself in communication with the Fountain of grace, not all the saints in whose company he has passed the night of the Lord's personal absence, however willing they may be, will be able to lend him as much as one drop of the sacred oil.

The same principles are applicable to the solemn close of the parable. The question has been asked, Why did not the Bridegroom open the door? Late though the foolish virgins were, they wished to enter, and why should they not be allowed? Again let us look beyond the letter of the parable to the spirit of it—to the great spiritual facts it pictures for us. If it were the mere opening of a door that would remedy the lateness, assuredly it would be done; but the real fact is, that the lateness is now beyond remedy. *The door cannot be opened.* Ponder the solemn words: "I know you not." It is a question of the union of the life with Christ. The wise virgins had lived a life that was always, even in sleep, hid with Christ in God; the foolish virgins had not: they had lived a life which had transient shows of devotion in it, but no reality—a mistake too fatal to be in any wise remedied by the spasms of a few minutes at the close. It is the old familiar lesson, that cannot be taught too often or taken to heart too earnestly: that the only way to die the death of the righteous is to live the life of the righteous.

The Parable of the Talents deals with the same subjects—viz., the professed disciples of Christ; only instead of searching the reality of their inner life, it tests the faithfulness of their service. As in the former parable so in this, stress is laid on the time that must elapse before the Lord's return. The employer of the servants travels "into a far country"; and it is "after a long time" (ver. 19) that "He cometh, and reckoneth with them." Similarly, in the cognate parable of "the pounds," reported by St. Luke, we are told that it was spoken, "because they thought that the kingdom of God should immediately appear" (Luke xix. 11). It would seem, therefore, that both these parables were intended to guard against the temptation to make the anticipation of the Lord's return an excuse for neglect of present duty.

There is evidence that within a short time some Christians in Thessalonica fell into this very temptation,—so much so as to render it necessary that the apostle Paul should write them a letter, his second epistle, for the express purpose of reproving them and setting them right. His first Epistle to the Thessalonians had laid stress on the suddenness of the Lord's coming, as Christ Himself does again and again throughout this discourse; but the result was that some of them, confounding suddenness with imminence, gave themselves up to idle waiting or feverish expectancy, to the neglect even of the most ordinary duties. To meet this he had to call attention to the divine ordinance, that "if any would not work, neither should he eat," and to enforce it with all the authority of Christ Himself: "Now them that are such (viz., those excited "busybodies" "working not at all") we command and exhort by our Lord Jesus Christ, that with quietness they work, and eat their own bread" (2 Thess. iii. 10-12); following it up with a caution, on the other hand, against allowing the Lord's delay to discourage them in their activity in His service: "But ye, brethren, be not weary in well doing."

All this helps us to see how necessary it was that the parable of waiting should be followed by a summons to work, and to admire the marvellous insight of our Lord into human nature in recognising beforehand where hidden dangers would lurk in His people's path. Unhappily, it is not necessary to go back to the case of the Thessalonians to see how needful it is that the parable of work should go along with the parable of waiting; we have painful illustration of it in our own day. Thanks to the clearness and strength of our Lord's teaching, the great majority of those who in our day look for His almost immediate return are not only diligent in work, but an example and a rebuke to many who do not share their expectations; but on the other hand there are not a few who have been so far led astray as to give up positions of great usefulness, and discontinue work in which they had been signally blessed, with the idea that the great event being now so near, the sole duty of the believer is to wait for it.

The parable assumes that all disciples are servants of Christ, and that all of them have work for Christ to do. There is no reason, however, for narrowing the field of service to what is in current phrase distinctively spoken of as "Christian work." All the work of Christian people should be Christian work, and is Christian work, if it be done as it ought to be done, "as to the Lord." There must evidently, however, be the desire and purpose to "serve the Lord Christ," whatever the nature of the service be.

The talents signify ability and opportunity. We must beware of using the word in any limited or conventional sense. In ordinary conversation the word is generally applied to abilities above the average, as, for example, when a man of more than ordinary ability is spoken of as "a man of talent," or "a talented man." The word ability, indeed, is used in the same way. "A man of ability," "an able man," means a man able to do more than most people can; whereas, properly speaking, and in the sense of the parable, a man who is able to do anything—to break stones, to write his name, to speak a sentence of sense—is an able man. He is not generally so called, but he really is a talented man, for God has given him, as He has given to every one, certain ability, and according to that ability is the talent for service with which Christ entrusts him. At first sight this phrase "according to his several ability" seems invidious, as if suggesting that Christ was a respecter of persons, and dealt more liberally with the strong than with the weak. But the talents are not merely gifts,—they are trusts involving responsibility; and therefore it is simple justice to graduate them according to ability. As we shall see, there is no respect of persons in appointing the awards. But as respects the talents, involving as they do a burden of responsibility, it is very evident that it would be no kindness to the man of less ability that he should be made responsible for more than he can easily undertake.

The gradations of five, two, one, appropriately correspond to what we speak of as superior, ordinary and inferior ability. At this point occurs the main distinction between this parable and the similar one of the pounds, spoken at a different time and with a different purpose. Here the servants all differ at first, but the faithful ones are alike in the end, inasmuch as they have done equally well in proportion to their ability. There the servants are all alike at the beginning, but the faithful ones receive different awards, inasmuch as they have differed in the degree of their diligence and faithfulness. The two together bring out with striking clearness and force the great thought that not success but faithfulness is what the Lord insists on. The weakest is at no disadvantage; he may not only do as well as the strongest, but if the measure of his diligence and faithfulness is higher he may even excel him.

It is in keeping with the difference in the scope of the two parables that in the one the sums entrusted should be large (talents), in the other, small (pounds). In the parable which has for its main lesson, "Make the most of the little you have," the amounts entrusted are small; while the large sums are fitly found in the parable which emphasizes what may be called the other side of the great lesson, "To whom much is given, of them much shall be required."

Confining our attention now to the parable before us, we have first the encouraging side in the cases of two of the servants. The number is evidently chosen as the very smallest that would bring out the truth that where abilities differ the reward will be the same, if only the diligence and faithfulness be equal. It is quite probable, indeed, that the number of servants thought of was more than three, perhaps ten,[22] to correspond with the number of the virgins, and that only as many cases are taken as were necessary to bring out the truth to be taught.

These two faithful servants lost no time in setting to work. This appears in the Revised Version, where the word "straightway" is restored to its right place, indicating that immediately on receiving the five talents the servant began diligently to use them (ver. 16, R.V.). The servant with the two talents acted "in like manner" (ver. 17). The result was that each doubled his capital, and each received the same gracious welcome and high promotion when their lord returned (vv. 20-23). They had been unequally successful; but inasmuch as this was not due to any difference in diligence, but only to difference in ability, they were equal in welcome and reward. It is, however, worthy of remark that while the language is precisely the same in the one case as in the other, it is not such as to determine that their position would be precisely equal in the life to come. There will be differences of ability and of range of service there as well as here. In both cases the verdict on the past was "faithful over a few things," though the few things of the one were more than double the few things of the other; and in the same way, though the promise for the future was for the one as well as for the other, "I will set thee over many things," it might well be that the many things of the future might vary as the few things of the past had done. But all will be alike satisfied, a thought which is beautifully put by Dante in the third canto of his "Paradise," where the sainted Piccarda, in answer to the question whether those who, like her, have the lower places have no envy of those above them, gives an explanation of which this is the concluding passage:

> "So that as we, from step to step,
> Are placed throughout this kingdom, pleases all,
> Even as our King, Who in us plants His will;
> And in His will is our tranquillity;
> It is the mighty ocean, whither tends
> Whatever it creates and nature makes."

Whereupon Dante himself says:

> "Then saw I clearly how each spot in heaven
> Is Paradise, though with like gracious dew
> The supreme virtue shower not over all.
> "Canto III. 82-90 (Carey).

It is not suggested, however, in the parable that there is not the same gracious dew showering over all. "The joy of the Lord" would appear to be the same for all; but it is significant that the leading thought of heavenly reward is not joy, but rather promotion, promotion in service, a higher sphere and a wider range of work, the "few things" which have been our glad service here exchanged for "many things," of which we shall be masters there—no more failures, no more bungling, no more mortifications as we look back upon work half done or ill done or much of it undone: "I will *set thee over* many things (R.V.)." That is the great reward; the other follows as of course: "Enter thou into the joy of thy Lord."

As in the parable of the Virgins, so here, the force increases as we pass from encouragement to warning. The closing scene is solemn and fearful. That the man with one talent should be selected as an illustration of unfaithfulness is very significant—not certainly in the way of suggesting that unfaithfulness is more likely to be found among those whose abilities are slender and opportunities small; but so as to make it plain that, though all due allowance is made for this, it can in no case be accepted as an excuse for want of faithfulness. It is just as imperative on the man with one talent, as on him with five, to do what he can. Had the illustration been taken from one with higher endowments, it might have been thought that the greatness of the loss had something to do with the severity of the sentence; but, as the parable is constructed, no such thought is admissible: it is perfectly clear that it is no question of gain or loss, but simply of faithfulness or unfaithfulness: *Hast thou done what thou couldst?*

The offence here is not, as in the first of the four pictures of judgment, painted in dark colours. There was no beating of fellow-servants or drinking with the drunken, no conduct like that of the unjust steward or the unmerciful creditor who took his fellow-servant by the throat—it was simple neglect: "I was afraid, and went and hid thy talent in the earth." The servant had such a modest estimate of his own abilities that he was even afraid he might do mischief in trying to use the talent he had, so he laid it away and let it alone. The excuse he makes (vv. 24, 25) is very true to nature. It is not modesty after all that is at the root of the idleness of those who hide their talent in the earth; it is unbelief. They do not believe in God as revealed in the Son of His love; they think of Him as a hard Master; they shrink from having anything to do with religion, rather wonder at those who have the assurance to think of *their* serving God, or doing anything for the advancement of His kingdom. They know not the grace of the Lord Jesus Christ, and therefore it is that they hold aloof from Him, refusing to confess Him, declining to employ in His service the talents entrusted to their care.

At this point there is an instructive contrast between the parable of the Virgins and the one before us. There the foolish virgins failed because they took their duties too easily; here the servant fails because he thinks his duties too hard. Bearing this in mind, we recognise the appropriateness of the Lord's answer. He might have found fault with his excuse, showing him how easily he might have known that his ideas of his Master were entirely wrong, and how if he had only addressed himself to the work to which he was called, his difficulties would have disappeared and He would have found the service easily within his powers; but the Master waives all this, accepts the hard verdict on Himself, admits the difficulties in the way, and then points out that even at the worst, even though he "was afraid," even though he had not courage enough, like the other servants, to go straightway to the work to which he was first called, he might have found some other and less trying form of service, something that would have avoided the risks he had not courage to face, and yet at the same time have secured some return for his Lord (vv. 26, 27). The Master is ready to make all allowance for the weakness of His servants, so long as it does not amount to absolute unfaithfulness; so long as by any stretch of charity it is possible to call the servant "good and faithful." In this case it was not possible. Not faithful but slothful was the word; therefore good it cannot be, but—the only other alternative—wicked: "thou wicked and slothful servant."

Then follows doom. Instead of promotion, degradation: "take the talent from him." And in this there is no arbitrary punishment, no penalty needing to be *inflicted*—it comes as the result of a great law of the universe, according to which unused powers fall into atrophy, paralysis, and death; while on the other hand faithful and diligent use of power enlarges it more and more: "Take therefore the talent from him, and give it unto him which hath ten talents. For unto every one that hath shall be given, and he shall have abundance: but from him that hath not shall be taken away even that which he hath." As the necessary and natural sequel to promotion in service was the joy of the Lord, so the natural and necessary sequel of degradation is the "outer darkness," where "there shall be weeping and gnashing of teeth."

4. *The Final Separation* (xxv. 31-46).

As in the Sermon on the Mount, and again in the last discourse in the Temple, so here, the language rises into a strain of great majesty and sublimity as the prophecy draws to a close. No one can fail to recognise it. This vision of judgment is the climax of the teaching of the Lord Christ. Alike for magnificence and for pathos it is unsurpassed in literature. There is no departure from His wonted simplicity of style. As little here as everywhere else do we recognise even a trace of effort or of elaboration; yet as we read there is not a word that could be changed, not a clause that could be spared, not a thought that could be added with advantage. It bears the marks of perfection, whether we look at it from the point of view of the Speaker's divinity or from the point of view of His humanity. Divine in its sublimity, it is most human in its tenderness. "Truly this was the Son of God." Truly this was the Son of man.

The grandeur of the passage is all the more impressive by contrast with what immediately follows: "And it came to pass, when Jesus had finished all these sayings, He said unto His disciples, Ye know that after two days is the feast of the passover, and the Son of man is betrayed to be crucified." Into such an abyss was the Son of man looking when in language so calm, so confident, so majestic, so sublime, He spoke of sitting on the throne of His glory as the Judge of all mankind. Did ever man speak like this Man?

It is significant that even when speaking of the coming glory He still retains His favourite designation, "the Son of man." In this we see one of the many minute coincidences which show the inner harmony of the discourses recorded in this Gospel with those of a different style of thought preserved by St. John; for it is in one of these we read that "He (the Father) hath given Him authority to execute judgment, because He is the Son of man." Thus the judgment of humanity proceeds out of humanity itself, and constitutes as it were the final offering up of man to God. This on the God-ward side; and, on the other side, there is for those who stand before the Judge, the certainty that as Son of man He knows by experience all the weaknesses of those He judges and the force of the temptations by which they have been beset.

Nothing could be more impressive than the picture set before us of the throne of glory, on which is seated the Son of man with all the angels around Him and all nations gathered before Him. It is undoubtedly the great assize, the general judgment of mankind. No partial judgment can it be, nothing less than the great event referred to in that passage already quoted from St. John's Gospel, where after speaking of judgment being committed to the Son of man, it is added: "Marvel not at this: for the hour cometh, in which all that are in the graves shall hear His voice, and shall come forth; they that have done good, unto the resurrection of life; and they that have done evil, unto the resurrection of damnation." This view of the passage is supported not only by the universality implied throughout and expressed in the term "all the nations[23]"; but by every reference to the same subject throughout this Gospel, notably the parables of the Tares and the Net (see Matt. xiii. 39-43, 47-50), the general declaration at Cæsarea Philippi, "The Son of man shall come in the glory of His Father, with His angels; and then shall He reward *every man* according to his works" (Matt. xvi. 27); and especially the earlier reference to the same event in this discourse, in that portion of it which we have spoken of as the prophecy proper, where the mourning of all the tribes of earth, and the gathering together of the elect from the one end of heaven to the other, are connected with one another and with the coming of the Son of man (Matt. xxiv. 30, 31).

It seems quite certain, then, that whatever subsequent unfoldings there may be in the later books of the New Testament as to the order in which judgment shall proceed, there is no intention here of anticipating them. It is true that the preceding parables have each given a partial view of the judgment,—the first as affecting those in office in the Church, the second and third as applied to the members of the Church; but just as those specially contemplated in the first parable are included in the wider scope of the second and third, so these contemplated in the second and third are included in the universal scope of the great judgment scene with which the whole discourse is fitly and grandly concluded.

In this great picture of the final judgment the prominent thought is *separation*: "He shall separate them one from another, as a shepherd divideth his sheep from the goats: and He shall set the sheep on His right hand, but the goats on the left." How easily and with what unerring certainty the separation is made—as easily and as surely as the shepherd divideth the sheep from the goats! Nothing eludes the glance of that all-searching Eye. No need of pleading or counter-pleading, of prosecutor or prisoner's counsel, no hope from legal quibble or insufficient proof. All, all is "naked and opened unto the eyes of Him with Whom we have to do." He sees all at a glance; and as He sees, He divides by a single dividing line. There is no middle position: each one is either on the right or on the left.

The dividing line is one entirely new. All nations are there; but not as nations are they divided now. This is strikingly suggested in the original by the change from the neuter (nations, ἔθνη) to the masculine (them, αὐτοὺς), indicating as by a sudden flash of unexpected light that not as nations, but as individuals, must all be judged. The line is one which crosses all other lines that have divided men from one another, so that of all ranks and conditions of men there will be some on the right and some on the left. Even the family line will be crossed, so that husband and wife, parents and children, brothers and sisters, may be found on opposite sides of it. What, then, is this new and final line of separation? The sentence of the King will mark it out for us.

It is the first and only time that Jesus calls Himself the King. He has displayed His royalty in His acts; He has suggested it in His discourses and His parables; He has claimed it by the manner of His entry into His capital and His temple; He will afterwards assent when Pilate shall ask Him the plain question; but this is the only place where He uses the title in speaking of Himself. How significant and impressive is this! It is as if He would once for all before He suffered disclose the fulness of His majesty. His royalty, indeed, was suggested at the very beginning by the reference to the throne of His glory; but inasmuch as judgment was the work which lay immediately before Him, He still spoke of Himself as the Son of man; but now that the separation is made, now that the books have been opened and closed, He rises above the Judge and styles Himself the King.

We must think of Him now as all radiant with His royal glory—that visage which was "so marred more than any man" now shining with celestial light—that Form which was distorted "more than the sons of men," now seen to be the very "form of God," "the chiefest among ten thousand" of the highest angels round Him, "altogether lovely," the personal embodiment of that glorious kingdom He has been preparing through all the centuries from the foundation of the world—disclosed at last as the answer to every longing soul, the satisfaction of every pure desire,—the King.

All this we must realise before we can imagine the awful gulf which lies between these simple words, "Depart" and "Come." That sweet word "Come"—how He has repeated and repeated it through all these ages, in every possible way, with endless variations! Spoken so tenderly with His own human lips, it has been taken up and given forth by those whom He has sent in His name: the Spirit has said "Come"; the Bride has said "Come"; the hearers have said "Come"; whosoever would, has been invited to come. The music of the word has never died away. But now its course is nearly run. Once more it will ring out; but with a difference. No longer now to all. The line of separation has been drawn, and across "the great gulf fixed" the old sweet word of grace can reach no longer. It is to those on the right, and these alone, that now the King says "Come." To those on the left there remains the word, a stranger to His lips before, the awful word, "Depart from Me."

In the contrast between these two words, there already is involved all that follows: all the joy of the welcome—"Come, ye blessed of My Father, inherit the kingdom prepared for you from the foundation of the world"; all the horror of the doom—"Depart from Me, ye cursed, into everlasting fire, prepared for the devil and his angels."

Still the great question remains unanswered, *What is the dividing line?* Inasmuch as this belongs to the hidden man of the heart, to the secrecy of consciousness and conscience, the only way in which it could be made to appear in a picture parable of judgment such as this, is by the introduction of such a conversation as that which follows the sentence in each case. The general distinction between the two classes had been suggested by the simile of the sheep and the goats—the one white, the other black, the one obedient, the other unruly; but it is made much more definite by this dramatic conversation. We call it dramatic, because we regard it as extreme bondage to the letter to suppose this to be a prediction of the words that will actually be used, and therefore look upon it simply as intended to represent, as nothing else could, the new light which both the righteous and the wicked will then see suddenly flashed upon their life on earth, a light so full and clear and self-interpreting that there cannot but be unquestioning acquiescence in the justice of the final award.

There are those who, looking at this conversation in the most superficial way, find in it the doctrine of salvation by works, and imagine that they are warranted on the strength of this passage to set aside all that is written in other parts of Scripture as to the necessity of change of heart, to dismiss from their minds all concern about creed or worship, about doctrine or sacraments or church membership. Be kind to the poor—that will do instead of everything else.

In answer to such a perversion of our Lord's language it should surely be enough to call attention to the fact that all is made to turn upon the treatment of Christ by the one class and by the other. Kindness to the poor comes in, not as in itself the ground of the division, but as furnishing the evidence or manifestation of that devotion to God as revealed in Christ, which forms the real ground of acceptance, and the want of which is the sole ground of condemnation. True it is that Christ identifies Himself with His people, and accepts the kindness done to the poorest of them as done to Himself; but there is obviously implied, what is elsewhere in a similar connection clearly expressed, that the kindness must be done "in the name of a disciple." In other words, love to Christ must be the motive of the deed of charity, else it is worthless as a test of true discipleship. The more carefully the whole passage is read, the more manifest will it be that the great question which determines the separation is this: "How have you treated Christ?" It is only to bring out more clearly the real answer to this question that the other is added: How have you treated Christ's poor? For according to each man's treatment of these will have been his treatment of Christ Himself. It is the same principle applied to the unseen Christ as the apostle applies to the invisible God: "He that loveth not his brother whom he hath seen, how can he love God Whom he hath not seen?"

While there is no encouragement here for those who hope to make up for the rejection of Christ by deeds of kindness to poor people, there is abundant room left for the acceptance at the last of those who had no means of knowing Christ, but who showed by their treatment of their fellow-men in distress that the spirit of Christ was in them. To such the King will be no stranger when they shall see Him on the throne; nor will they be strangers to Him. He will recognise them as His own; and they will recognise Him as the very King of Love for Whom their souls were longing, but Who not till now has been revealed to their delighted gaze. To all such will the gracious words be spoken "Come, ye blessed of My Father"; but they too, as well as all the rest, will be received not on the ground of works as distinguished from faith, but on the ground of a real though implicit faith which worked by love and which was only waiting for the revelation of their King and Lord to make it explicit, to bring it out to light.

Philanthropy can never take the place of faith; and yet no words ever spoken or written on this earth have done so much for philanthropy as these. It were vain to attempt, in so brief a sketch, to bring out even in the way of suggestion the mingled majesty and pathos of the words of the King to the righteous, culminating in that great utterance which touches the very deepest springs of feeling and thrills every fibre of the pure and loving heart: "Inasmuch as ye have done it unto one of the least of these

My brethren, ye have done it unto Me." Besides the pathos of the words, what depth of suggestion is there in the thought, as shedding light upon His claim to be the Son of man! As Son of God He is the King, seated on the throne of His glory; as Son of man He is identified with all His brethren, even with the least of them, and with each one of them all over all the world and through all the ages: "Inasmuch as ye have done it unto one of the least of these My brethren, ye have done it unto Me." How the divinity shines, how the humanity thrills, through these great words of the King!

The scroll of this grand prophecy is finished with the awful words: "These shall go away into eternal punishment; but the righteous into eternal life" (R.V.). Eternal punishment, eternal life—such are the issues which hang upon the coming of the Son of man to judgment; such are the issues which hang upon the treatment of the Son of man in these years of our mortal life that are passing over us now. There are those who flatter themselves with the idea that, because the question has been raised by honest and candid interpreters of Scripture whether absolute endlessness is necessarily involved in the word eternal, therefore these words of doom are shorn of much of their terror; but surely this is a pitiful delusion. There is no possible way of reducing the force of the word "eternal" which will bring the awfulness of the doom within the bounds of any finite imagination; and whatever may be said as to what the word necessarily implies, whatever vague surmise there may be that absolute endlessness is not in it, this much is perfectly certain: that there is not the slightest suggestion of hope in the words; no straining of the eyes can discern even the straitest gate out of that eternal punishment into eternal life. Between the one and the other there is "a great gulf fixed." It is the final judgment; it is the final separation; and scarcely with more distinctness could the awful letters have been traced, "Leave every hope behind, all ye who enter here." "These shall go away into eternal punishment; but the righteous"—none but the righteous—"into eternal life."

FOOTNOTES

[22] In the parable of the pounds the number of servants is ten, and there, too, only three are selected as examples.

[23] It is not forgotten that the word translated "nations" is commonly applied to the Gentiles as distinguished from the Jews; but clearly there is no such limitation here. No commentator, at least of any note, suggests that the Jews as a nation are not among the nations gathered around the throne.

XIX
THE GREAT ATONEMENT DAY

Matt xxvi. 1-xxvii. 56.

WE enter now on the story of the last day of the mortal life of our Lord and Saviour. We have already noticed the large proportionate space given to the Passion Week; but still more remarkable is the concentration of interest on the Passion Day. The record of that single day is very nearly one-ninth of the whole book; and a similar proportion is observed by all the four Evangelists. This proportion of space is very striking even when we bear in mind that properly speaking the Gospels are not the record of thirty-three or thirty-four years, but only of three or four. Of the story of the years of the public ministry one-seventh part is given to the last day; and this, too, without the introduction of any lengthened discourse. If the discourse in the upper room and the intercessory prayer as recorded by St. John were added, it would be, not one-seventh, but almost one-fourth of the whole. Truly this must be the Day of days! Unspeakably sacred and precious as is the entire life of our Lord and Saviour, sacred above all and precious above all is His death of shame and agony. The same pre-eminence was evidently given to the dying of the Lord Jesus in the special revelation granted to St. Paul, as is evident from the fact that, in setting forth the gospel he had been commissioned to preach, he spoke of it as the gospel of "Jesus Christ and Him crucified," and put in the foreground, not the incarnate life, great as he recognised it to be (1 Tim. iii. 16), but the atoning death of Christ: "I delivered unto you *first of all* that which I also received, how that Christ died for our sins according to the Scriptures." Here, then, we have the very gospel of the grace of God. Here we enter the inner shrine of the Word, the Holy of Holies of the new covenant. Let us draw near with holy reverence and deep humility, yet with the eye of faith directed ever upwards in reliance on the grace of Him Who searcheth all things, even the deep things of God, and Whose work and joy it is to take of the things of Christ, even those that are among the deepest things of God, and show them unto us.

"After Two Days" (xxvi. 1-19)

This passage does not strictly belong to the history of the one great day, but it is the approach to it. It opens with the solemn announcement

"After two days is the feast of the Passover, and the Son of man is betrayed to be crucified"; and without any record of the Saviour's doings in the interval,[24] it closes with the preparation for the keeping of the feast with His disciples, the directions for which are introduced by the pathetic words, "My time is at hand."

The incident at Bethany (vv. 6-13) seems to be introduced here in connection with the development of treason in the soul of Judas. This connection would not be so apparent were it not for the information given in St. John's account of the feast, that it was Judas especially who objected to what he called "this waste" of the ointment, and that the reason why he was displeased at it was because "he had the bag, and bare what was put therein." With this in mind we can see how natural it was that, having had no occasion before to tell the story of the feast at Bethany, the Evangelist should be disposed to tell it now, as connected in his mind with the traitor's selling of his Lord for thirty pieces of silver.

The two days of interval would extend from the evening following the abandonment of the Temple to the evening of the Passover feast. It is important always, and especially in studying the days of the Passion week, to bear in mind that, according to the Jewish mode of reckoning, each new day began, not with the morning as with us, but with the evening. In this they followed a very ancient precedent: "The evening and the morning were the first day." The two days, then, would be from Tuesday evening till Thursday evening; so that with Thursday evening began the last day of our Lord's Passion. There is no record at all of how He spent the Wednesday; in all probability it was in seclusion at Bethany. Nor have we any account of the doings of the Thursday save the directions given to prepare the Passover, the keeping of which was to be the first act of the last day.

We may think of these two days, then, as days of rest for our Lord, of holy calm and quietude—a sacred lull before the awful storm. What were His thoughts? what His feelings? What passages of Scripture were His solace? Would not the ninety-fourth psalm be one of them? If so, how fondly would He dwell upon that sentence of it, "In the multitude of my thoughts within me Thy comforts delight my soul." If we only had a record of His prayers, how rich it would be! If we had the spiritual history of these two days it would no doubt be full of pleading as rich and precious as the prayer of intercession His disciples heard and one of them recorded for our sakes, and of yearning as tender and touching as His wail over Jerusalem. But the Spirit, Who takes of the things of Christ and shows them unto us, does not invade the privacy of the Saviour's hours of retirement. No diary is published; and beyond doubt it is better so. It may be that in the lives of the saints there has been too much of this—not too much of spiritual communing, but too much unveiling of it. It may be that there is a danger of leading us to seek after such "exercises" as an end in themselves, instead of as mere means to the end of holy and unselfish living. What the world should see is the life that is the outcome of those secret communings with God—it should see the life which was with the Father manifested in glowing word and self-forgetting deed. Why have we no need to see into that holy, loving heart during these two sacred days in Bethany? Because it is sufficiently revealed in the story of the day that followed it. Ah! the words, the deeds of that day—what revelings of heart, what manifestations of the life within are there!

The very silence of these two days is strikingly suggestive of repose. We are presently to hear of the awful agony in the Garden; but from the very way in which we shall hear of it we shall be strengthened in the impression, which no doubt is the true one, that the two days of interval were not days of agony, but days of soul rest; and in this we recognise a striking contrast to the restlessness of those who spent the time in plotting His destruction. Contrast, for example, the calm of our Lord's announcement in the second verse, with the uneasy plotting in the palace of the high priest. Without agitation He faces the horror of great darkness before Him; without flinching He anticipates the very darkest of it all: "betrayed"—"crucified"; without a tremor on His lips He even specifies the time: "after two days." Now look at that company in the palace of the high priest, as with dark brows and troubled looks they consult how they may take Jesus by subtlety. Observe how in fear they put it off,—as not safe yet, not for nine days at least, till the crowds at the feast, so many of whom had so recently been shouting "Hosanna to the Son of David!" shall have gone home. "Not for nine days," so they resolve. "After two days," so He has said.

> "Oh, but the counsel of the Lord
> Doth stand, for ever sure."

Christ knew far more about it than if there had been a spy in the palace of the high priest, reporting to Him. He was in communication with One Who doeth according to His will in the armies of heaven and among the inhabitants of the earth. Caiaphas and his fellow-conspirators may plot what they please, it shall be done according to the counsel of the Lord; it shall be so done that an apostle shall be able afterwards with confidence to say: "Him, *being delivered by the determinate counsel and foreknowledge of God*, ye have taken."

The means by which their counsels were overruled was the treason of Judas, into whose dark heart the Bethany incident will afford us a glimpse. Its interest turns upon the different values attached to a deed of love, by Judas[25] on the one hand, and by Jesus on the other.

To Judas it meant waste. And such a waste!—three hundred pence thrown away on the foolish luxury of a moment! "This ointment might have been sold for much, and given to the poor." Be it remembered that there was a good deal to be said for this argument. It is very easy for us, who have the limelight of our Lord's words on the whole scene, to see how paltry the objection was; but even yet, with this story now published, as our Lord said it would be, all over Christendom, how many arguments are heard of the very same description! It is not so much to be wondered at that the objection of Judas found a good deal of favour with some of the disciples. They could not see the blackness of the heart out of which the suggestion came, nor could they see the beauty of the love which shed from Mary's heart a perfume far more precious than the odour of the ointment. Probably even Mary was startled; and, if her Lord had not at once taken her part, might not have had a word to say for herself.

"But Jesus, perceiving[26] it, said unto them, Why trouble ye the woman? for she hath wrought a good work on Me." He understood her—understood her perfectly, read at once the whole secret of her loving heart, explained her conduct better even than she understood it herself, as we shall presently see. He deals very tenderly with the disciples; for He understood them too, saw at once that there was no treason in their hearts, that though they took up the suggestion of the traitor it was in no sympathy with his spirit, but simply because of their want of insight and appreciation. He, however, does rebuke them—gently; and then He quietly opens their eyes to the surpassing beauty of the deed they had ventured to condemn. "She hath wrought a good work upon Me." The word translated "good" has prominent in it the thought of beauty. And since our Lord has set that deed of Mary in its true light, there is no one with any sense of beauty who fails to see how beautiful it is. The very impulsiveness of the act, the absence of all calculation, the simplicity and naturalness of it, the womanliness of it—all these add to its beauty as an outburst of love. We can well imagine that these words of Jesus may have furnished much of the inspiration which thrilled the soul of the apostle as he wrote to the Corinthians his noble eulogy of love. Certainly its pricelessness could not have been more notably or memorably taught. Three hundred pence to be weighed against a true woman's love! "If a man would give all the substance of his house for love, it would utterly be contemned."

We are led into still more sacred ground as we observe how highly the Saviour values Mary's affection for Himself. "She hath wrought a good work upon *Me*"—"*Me* ye have not always"—"she did it for My burial." Who can reach the pathos of these sacred words? There is no doubt that amid the hate by which Jesus was surrounded, with His knowledge of the treason in the dark soul of Judas, and His keen sense of the want of sympathy on the part of the other disciples, His human heart was yearning for love, for sympathetic love. Oh, how He loved! and how that love of His was going out to all around Him throughout the Passion week - without return! We may well believe, then, that this outburst of love from the heart of Mary must have greatly cheered Him.

"She hath wrought a good work *upon Me.*" With the ointment on His head, there had come a far sweeter balm to His wounded heart; for He saw that she was not wanting in sympathy—that she had some idea, however vague it might be, of the pathos of the time. She felt, if she did not quite see, the shadow of the grave. And this presentiment (shall we call it?) not as the result of any special thought about it, but in some dim way, had prompted her to choose this touching manner of showing her love: "In that she hath poured this ointment on My body, she did it for My burial." Verily, a true human heart beats here, welcoming, oh! so gladly, this woman's loving sympathy.

But the Divine Spirit is here too, looking far beyond the needs of the moment or the burdens of the day. No one could more tenderly consider the poor; nothing was nearer to His heart than their necessities,—witness that wonderful parable of judgment with which He finished His public ministry; but He knew well that in that personal devotion which was shown in Mary's loving act was to be found the mainspring of all benevolence, and not only so but of all that was good and gracious; therefore to discourage such personal affection would be to seal up the fount of generosity and goodness; and accordingly He not only commends it, but He lifts it up to its proper dignity, He gives a commendation beyond all other words of praise He ever spoke; looking away down the ages, and out to the ends of the earth, and recognising that this love to Himself, this personal devotion to a dying Saviour, was to be the very central force of the gospel, and thus the hope of the world, He adds these memorable words: "Verily I say unto you, Wheresoever this gospel shall be preached in the whole world, there shall also this, that this woman hath done, be told for a memorial of her."

From "this that this woman hath done" the record passes at once to that which was done by the man who had dared to find fault with it. It also is told wherever the gospel is preached as a memorial of him. Behold, then, the two memorials side by side. Has not the Evangelist shown himself the true historian in bringing them together? The contrast intensifies the light that shines from the love of Mary, and deepens the darkness of the traitor's sin. Besides, the story of the three hundred pence is a most fitting prelude to that of the thirty pieces of silver. At the same time, by suggesting the steps which led down to such an abyss of iniquity, it saves us from the error of supposing that the sin of Judas was so peculiar that no one now need be afraid of falling into it; for we are reminded in this way that it was at bottom the very sin which is the commonest of all, the very sin into which Christians of the present day are in greatest danger of falling.

What was it that made so great a gulf between Judas and all the rest? Not natural depravity; in this respect they were no doubt much alike. When the Twelve were chosen there was in all probability as good material, so to speak, in the man of Kerioth as in any of the men of Galilee. What, then, made the difference? Simply this, that his heart was never truly given to his Lord. He tried throughout to serve God and mammon; and if he had been able to combine the two services, if there had been any fair prospect of these thrones on which the Twelve were to sit, and the honours and emoluments of the kingdom with which his fancy had been dazzled, treason would never have entered his mind; but when not a throne but a cross began to loom before him, he found, as every one finds some time, that he must make his choice, and that choice was what it invariably is with those who try to serve the two masters. The god of this world had blinded him. He not only failed to see the beauty of Mary's loving deed, as some of the other disciples did just at the first, but he had become quite incapable of any spiritual insight, quite incapable of seeing his Master's glory, or recognising His claims. In a certain sense, then, even Judas himself was like the other murderers of Christ in not knowing what he did. Only he might have known, would have known, had not that accursed lust of gold been always in the way. And we may say of any ordinary worshipper of mammon of the present day, that if he had been in Judas' place, with the prospects as dark as they were to him, with only the one course left, as it would seem to him, of extricating himself from a losing concern, he would be in the highest degree likely to do the very same thing.

As the two days draw to a close we see Judas seeking opportunity to betray his Master, and Jesus seeking opportunity to keep His last Passover with His disciples. Again what a contrast! The traitor must lurk and lie in wait; the Master does not even remain in Bethany or seek some lonely house on the Mount of Olives, but sends His disciples right over into the city, and with the same readiness with which He had found the ass's colt on which He rode into Jerusalem He finds a house in which to keep the feast.

I.—The Evening (xxvi. 20-30)

The last day of our Lord's Passion begins at eventide on Thursday with the Passover feast,[27] at which "He sat down with the Twelve."

The entire feast would be closely associated in His mind with the dark event with which the day must close; for of all the types of the great sacrifice He was about to offer, the most significant was the paschal lamb. Most fitting, therefore, was it that towards the close of this feast, when its sacred importance was deepest in the disciples' minds, their Master should institute the holy ordinance which was to be a lasting memorial of "Christ our Passover sacrificed for us." Of this feast, then, with its solemn and affecting close, the passage before us is the record.

It falls naturally into two parts, corresponding to the two great burdens on the Saviour's heart as He looked forward to this feast—the Betrayal and the Crucifixion (see ver. 2). The former is the burden of vv. 21-25; the latter of vv. 26-30. There was indeed very much besides to tell—the strife which grieved the Master's heart as they took their places at the table, and His wise and kindly dealing with it (Luke xxii. 24, *seq.*); the washing of the disciples' feet; the farewell words of consolation; the prayer of intercession (John xiii.-xvii.),—but these are all omitted here, that thought may be concentrated on the two outstanding facts: the unmasking and dismissal of the traitor, and the committing to the faithful ones of the sacred charge, "This do in remembrance of Me."

1. It must have been sorrowful enough for the Master as He sat down with the Twelve to mark their unseemly strife, and sadder still to think that, though for the hour so closely gathered round Him, they would soon be scattered every man to his own and would leave Him alone; but He had the comfort of knowing that eleven were true at heart and foreseeing that after all wanderings and falls they would come back again. "He knoweth our frame, and remembereth that we are dust"; and therefore with the eye of divine compassion He could look beyond the temporary desertion, and find satisfaction in the fidelity that would triumph in the end over the weakness of the flesh. But there was one of them, for whom His heart was failing Him, in whose future He could see no gleam of light. All the guiding and counsel with which he had been favoured in common with the rest had been lost on him,—even the early word of special personal warning (John vi. 70), spoken that he might bethink himself ere it were too late, had failed to touch him. There is now only one opportunity left. It is the last night; and the last word must now be spoken. How tenderly and thoughtfully the difficult duty is done! "As they did eat, He said, Verily I say unto you, that one of you shall betray Me." Imagine in what tones these words were spoken, what love and sorrow must have thrilled in them!

The kind intention evidently was to reach the heart of the one without attracting the attention of the rest. For there must have been a studied avoidance of any look or gesture that would have marked the traitor. This is manifest from the way in which the sad announcement is received. It comes, in fact, to all the eleven as a summons to great searchings of heart, a fitting preparation (1 Cor. xi. 28) for the new and sacred service to which they are soon to be invited; and truly there could have been no better sign than the passing from lip to lip, from heart to heart, of the anxious question, "Lord, is it I?" The remembrance of the strife at the beginning of the feast was too recent, the tone of the Master's voice too penetrating, the glance of His eye too searching, to make self-confidence possible to them at that particular moment. Even the heart of the confident Peter seems to have been searched and humbled under that scrutinising look. If only he had retained the same spirit, what humiliation would have been spared him!

There was one who did not take up the question; but the others were all so occupied with self-scrutiny that no one seems to have observed his silence, and Jesus forbears to call attention to it. He will give him another opportunity to confess and repent, for so we understand the pathetic words which follow: "He that dippeth his hand with Me in the dish, the same shall betray Me." This was no mere outward sign for the purpose of denoting the traitor. It was a wail of sorrow, an echo of the old lament of the Psalmist: "Yea, mine own familiar friend, in whom I trusted, which did eat of my bread, hath lifted up his heel against me." How could the heart even of Judas resist so tender an appeal?

We shall understand the situation better if we suppose what is more than probable,[28] that he was sitting very near to Jesus, perhaps next to Him on the one side, as John certainly was on the other. We cannot suppose, from what we know of the customs of the East, that Judas was the only one dipping with Him in the dish; nor would he be the only one to whom "the sop" was given. But if his position was as we have supposed, there was something in the vague words our Saviour used which tended to the singling of him out, and, though not the only one, he would naturally be the first to whom the sop was given, which would be a sufficient sign to John, who alone was taken into confidence at the time (see John xiii. 25, 26), without attracting in any special way the attention of the rest. Both in the words and in the action, then, we recognise the Saviour's yearning over His lost disciple, as He makes a last attempt to melt his obdurate heart.

The same spirit is manifest in the words which follow. The thought of consequences to Himself gives Him no concern; "the Son of man goeth, even as it is written of Him;" it is the awful abyss into which His disciple is plunging that fills His soul with horror: "but woe unto that man by whom the Son of man is betrayed! it had been good for that man if he had not been born." O Judas! Thy treachery is indeed a link in the chain of events by which the divine purpose is fulfilled; but it was not necessary that so it should be. In some other way the counsel of the Lord would have been accomplished, if thou hadst yielded to that last appeal. It was necessary that the Son of man should suffer and die for the world's sin, but there was nothing to compel thee to have thy hand in it.

At last Judas speaks; but in no spirit of repentance. He takes up, it is true, the question of the rest, but not in sincerity—only driven to it as the last refuge of hypocrisy. Moreover, he asks it in so low a tone, that neither it nor the answer to it appears to have been noticed by the general company (see John xiii. 29). And that there is no inclining of the heart to his Lord appears perhaps in the use of the formal title Rabbi, retained in the Revised Version: "Is it I, Rabbi?" Had he repented even at this late hour— had he thrown himself, humbled and contrite, at the Saviour's feet, with the question "Lord, is it I?" struggling to find utterance, or better still, the heart-broken confession "Lord, it is I"—it would not yet have been too late. He Who never turned a penitent away would have received even Judas back again and forgiven all his sin; and in lowliness of heart the repentant disciple might have received at his Master's hands the symbols of that infinite sacrifice which was sufficient even for such as he. But his conscience is seared as with a hot iron, his heart is hard as the nether millstone, and accordingly without a word of confession, actually taking "the sop" without a sign even of shame, he gave himself up finally to the spirit of evil, and went immediately out—"*and it was night*" (see John xiii. 30). There remain now around the Master none but true disciples.

2. The Passover meal is drawing to a close; but ere it is ended the Head of the little family has quite transfigured it. When the traitor left the company we may suppose that the look of unutterable sadness would gradually pass from the Saviour's countenance. Up to this time the darkness had been unrelieved. As he thought of the lost disciple's fate, there was nothing but woe in the prospect; but when from that dark future he turned to His own, He saw, not the horror of the Cross alone, but "the joy set before Him"; and in view of it He was able with a heart full of thanks and praise to appoint for remembrance of the awful day a feast, to be kept like the Paschal feast by an ordinance for ever (see Ex. xii. 14).

The connection of the new feast with the old is closely maintained. It was "as they were eating" that the Saviour took bread, and from the way in which He is said to have taken "a cup" (R.V.) it is plain that it was one of the cups it was customary to take at the Paschal feast. With this in mind we can more readily see the naturalness of the words of institution. They had been feasting on the body of the lamb; it is time that they should look directly at the Lamb of God, which taketh away the sin of the world; so, taking the new symbol and handing it to them, He says, "Take, eat; this is My body."

How strange that into words so simple there should have been imported anything so mysterious and unnatural as some of the doctrines around which controversy in the Church has raged for weary centuries—doctrines sadly at variance with "the simplicity that is in Christ."[29] At the first institution of the Passover the directions for eating it close with these words, "It is the Lord's Passover." Does any one for a single moment suppose that in so putting it Moses meant to assert any mysterious identity of two things so diverse in their nature as the literal flesh of the lamb and the historical event known as the Lord's Passover? Why, then, should any one for a moment suppose that when Jesus says, "This is My body," He had any thought of mysterious transference or confusion of identity? Moses meant that the one was the symbol of the other; and in the same way our Saviour meant that the bread was henceforth to be the symbol of His body. The same appropriateness, naturalness and simplicity, are apparent in the words with which He hands the cup: "This is My blood of the covenant" (R.V. omits *new*, which throws the emphasis more distinctly on *My*) "which is shed"—not, like the blood of the lamb, for a little family group, but—"for many," not as a mere sign (see Heb. x.), but "unto remission of sins."

The new symbols were evidently much more suitable to the ordinance which was to be of world-wide application. Besides, it was no longer necessary that there should be further sacrifice of life. Christ our Passover was sacrificed once for all; and therefore there must be no thought of repetition of the sacrifice; it must be represented only; and this is done both simply and impressively in the breaking of the bread and the pouring of the wine. Nothing could be more natural than the transition from the old to the new Passover feast.

Rising now above all matters of detail and questions of interpretation, let us try humbly and reverently to enter into the mind of Christ as He breaks the bread and pours the wine and institutes the feast of love. As in the earlier part of the evening we had in His dealings with the traitor a touching unveiling of His human heart, so now, while there is the same human tenderness, there is with it a reach of thought and range of vision which manifestly transcend all mortal powers.

Consider first how extraordinary it was that at such a time He should take pains to concentrate the thoughts of His disciples in all time to come upon His death. Even the bravest of those who had been with Him in all His temptations could not look at it now; and to His own human soul it must have seemed in the very last degree repulsive. To the disciples, to the world, it must have seemed defeat; yet He calmly provides for its perpetual celebration as a victory!

Think of the form the celebration takes. It is no mournful solemnity, with dirges and elegies for one about to die; but a *Feast*—a strange way of celebrating a death. It may be said that the Passover feast itself was a precedent; but in this respect there is no parallel. The Passover feast was no memorial of a death. If Moses had died that night, would it ever have occurred to the children of Israel to institute a feast for the purpose of keeping in memory so unutterable a calamity? But a greater than Moses is here, and is soon to die a cruel and shameful death. Is not that a calamity as much more dreadful than the other as Christ was greater than Moses? Why, then, celebrate it by a feast? Because this death is no calamity. It is the means of life to a great multitude that no man can number, out of every kindred and tongue and people and nation. Therefore it is most fitly celebrated by a feast. It is a memorial; but it is far more. It is a feast, provided for the spiritual nourishment of the people of God through all their generations. Think what must have been in the Saviour's mind when He said, "Take, eat"; how His soul must have been enlarged as He uttered the words "shed for many." Simple words, easily spoken; but before they came from these sacred lips there must have risen before His mind the vision of multitudes all through the ages, fed on the strangest food, refreshed by the strangest wine, that mortal man had ever heard of.

How marvellously the horizon widens round Him as the feast proceeds! At first He is wholly engaged with the little circle round the table. When He says, "One of you shall betray Me," when He takes the sop and hands it, when He pours out His last lament over the false disciple, He is the Man of Sorrows in the little upper chamber; but when He takes the bread and again the cup, the horizon widens, beyond the cross He sees the glory that shall follow, sees men of all nations and climes coming to the feast He is preparing for them, and before He closes He has reached the consummation in the heavenly kingdom: "I say unto you, I will not drink henceforth of this fruit of the vine, until that day when I drink it new with you in My Father's kingdom." "Truly this was the Son of God."

Then hear Him singing at the close. How bewildered the disciples, how rapt the Master, must have been! What a scene for the painter, what a study of divine calm and human agitation! The "hymn" they sang was in all probability the latter part of the Great Hallel, which closes with Psalm cxviii. It is most interesting as we read the psalm to think what depths of meaning, into which none of His disciples as yet could enter, there must have been to Him in almost every line.

II.—The Night (xxvi. 31-75)

As the little company have lingered in the upper room evening has passed into night. The city is asleep, as Jesus leads the way along the silent streets, down the steep slope of Moriah, and across the Kedron, to the familiar place of resort on the mount of Olives. As they proceed in silence, a word of ancient prophecy lies heavy on His heart. It was from Zechariah, whose prophecy was often[30] in his thoughts in the Passion week. "Awake, O sword, against My shepherd, and against the man that is My fellow, saith the Lord of hosts: smite the shepherd, and the sheep shall be scattered." It is the last part of it that troubles Him. For the smiting of the Shepherd He is well prepared; it is the scattering of the sheep that makes His heart so sore, and forces Him to break the silence with the sorrowful words, "All ye shall be offended because of Me this night." What pathos in these words *"because of Me"*: how it pained Him to think that what must come to Him should be so terrible to them! And is there not a touch of kind allowance in the words "this night"? "He that walketh in the night stumbleth," and how could they but stumble in such a night? Then the thought of the shepherd and the sheep which fills His mind and suggests the passage He quotes is full of tenderness without even a hint of reproach. Who will blame the sheep for scattering when the Shepherd is smitten? And how trustfully and withal how wistfully does He look forward to the reassembling of the flock in the old home, the sacred region where they gathered first around the Shepherd: "After I am risen again, I will go before you (as the shepherd goes before the flock) into Galilee." Thus after all would be fulfilled His prayer of intercession, so recently offered on their behalf: "Holy Father, keep through Thine own name those whom Thou hast given Me, that they may be one."

The silly sheep were not at all alarmed. This was altogether natural; for the danger was not yet within their sight. Nor was it really at all unnatural that the impulsive Peter should be now at the very opposite pole of feeling from where he stood an hour or two before. Then, sharing the general depression, he joined the rest in the anxious question, "Lord, is it I?" now, having been relieved from the anxiety which for the moment pressed upon him, and having been moreover raised into a glow of feeling and an assurance of faith by his Master's tender and stirring words, and the prayer of intercession which so fitly closed them, he has passed from the depths of self-distrust to the heights of self-confidence, so that he even dares to say, "Though all men shall be offended because of Thee, yet will *I* never be offended."

Ah! Peter, you were safe when you were crying "Lord, is it I?"—you are very far from safe now, when you speak of yourself in so different a tone. Jesus sees it all, and gives him warning in the very plainest words. But Peter persists. He vainly imagines that his Master cannot know how strong he is, how burning his zeal, how warm his love, how steadfast his devotion. Of all this he is himself distinctly conscious. There is no mistake about it. Devotion thrills in every fibre of his being; and he knows, he feels it in his soul, that no torture, not death itself, could move him from his steadfastness: "Though I should die with Thee, yet will I not deny Thee." "Likewise also said all the disciples." Quite natural too. For the moment Peter was the leader of the sheep. They all caught his enthusiasm, and were conscious of the same devotion: why, then, should they not acknowledge it as he had done? They had yet to learn the difference between a transient glow of feeling and abiding inward strength. Only by sad experience can they learn it now; so Jesus lets them have the last word.

And now Gethsemane is reached. The olive trees which in the daytime give a shadow from the heat will now afford seclusion, though the moon is at the full. Here, then, the Son of man will spend some time with God, alone, before He is betrayed into the hands of sinners; and yet, true Son of man as He is, He shrinks from being left alone in that dread hour, and clings to the love and sympathy of those who have been with Him in His temptations hitherto. So He leaves eight of the disciples at the entering in of the olive grove, and takes with Him into the darkness the three most in sympathy with Him—the same three who had been sole witnesses of His power in raising from the dead the daughter of Jairus, and had alone seen His glory on the holy mount. But even these three cannot go with Him all the way. He will have them as near as possible; and yet He must be alone. Did He think of the passage, "I have trodden the winepress[31] alone, and of the people there was none with me"?

That solitude may not be invaded. We can only, like the disciples of old, look reverently at it from afar. There are probably many true disciples who can get no nearer than the edge of the darkness; those who are closest in sympathy may be able to obtain a nearer view, but even those who like John have leant on His breast can know it only in part—in its depth it passeth knowledge. Jesus is alone in Gethsemane yet, and of the people there is none with Him.

> "Ah! never, never can we know
> The depth of that mysterious woe."

While it is not possible for any of us to penetrate the deep recesses of Gethsemane, we have a key to let us in, and open to us something of its meaning. This help is found in that striking passage in the Epistle to the Hebrews, where the experience of the Lord Jesus in the Garden is closely connected with His being "called of God an High Priest after the order of Melchisedec." It is true that at His baptism Jesus entered on His ministry in its largest sense, the Prophet, Priest, and King of men. But there is a sense in which later on, at successive stages, He was "called of God" to each of these offices in succession. At His baptism the voice from heaven was, "This is My Beloved Son, in Whom I am well pleased." On the mount of Transfiguration there was this added, "Hear ye Him," and the withdrawal of Moses and Elias, leaving Jesus alone, indicated that henceforth He was called of God to be the one prophet of humanity. Similarly, though from the beginning He was King, it was not till after He had overcome the sharpness of death that He was "called of God" to be King, to take His seat on the right hand of majesty in the heavens. At what period, then, in His ministry was it that He was called of God to be an high priest? To this natural question the passage in the Epistle to the Hebrews supplies the answer; and when we take the thought with us we see that it is indeed a torch to lighten for us just a little the darkness of the Garden's gloom.

Is there not something in the very arrangement of the group which harmonises with the thought? Three days ago the Temple had been closed for ever to its Lord. Its shrine was empty now for evermore: "Behold, your house is left unto you desolate." But still there is to be a temple, in which shall minister a priest, not of the line of Aaron, rather after the older order of Melchisedec—a temple, not of stone, but of men—of believers, according to the later apostolic word: "Ye are the temple of the living God." Of that new and living temple we have a representation in Gethsemane. The eight disciples are its court; the three are in the holy place; into the holiest of all our great High Priest has gone—alone: for the veil is not yet rent in twain.

But why the agony? The difficulty has always been to account for the sudden change from the calmness of the Paschal feast to the awful struggle of Gethsemane. What had happened meanwhile to bring about so great a change? There was light in the upper chamber—it was dark in the Garden; but surely the darkness and the light were both alike to Him; or if to His human heart there was the difference we all are conscious of, it could not be that the mere withdrawal of the light destroyed His peace. It is altogether probable that both the previous nights had been spent on this same mount of Olives, and there is no hint of agony then. It is true that the prospect before Him was full of unutterable horror; but from the time He had set His face to go up to Jerusalem it had been always in His view, and though at times the thought of it would come over Him as a cold wave that made Him shudder for the moment, there had been up to this hour no agony like this, and not a trace of pleading that the cup might pass.

What, then, was the new element of woe that came upon Him in that hour? What was the cup now put for the first time to His sacred lips, from which He shrank as from nothing in all His sad experience before? Is not the answer to be found in the region of thought into which we are led in that great passage already referred to, which speaks of Him as then for the first time "called of God an High Priest," which represents Him, though He was a Son, learning His obedience (as a Priest) by the things which He suffered?

May we not, then, reverently conceive of Him as in that hour taking on Him the sin of the world, in a more intimate sense than He had ever done before? "He bare our sins in His own body on the tree." In a certain sense He had borne the burden all His life, for He had throughout endured the contradiction of sinners against Himself; but in some special sense manifestly He bore it on the tree. When did He in that special sense take the awful burden on Him? Was it not in the Garden of Gethsemane? If so, can we wonder that the Holy One shrank from it, as He never shrank from simple suffering? To be identified with sin—to be "made sin," as the apostle puts it—how His soul revolted from it! The cup of sorrow He could take without a murmur; but to take on Him the intolerable load of the world's sin—from this He shrank with all the recoil of stainless purity, with all the horror of a heart that could not bear the very thought. It was not the weakness of His flesh, but the purity of His spirit, that made Him shrink, that wrung from Him once and again, and yet again, the cry, "Father, if it be possible, let this cup pass from Me." It was a new temptation, three times repeated, like that old one in the wilderness. That assault, as we found, was in close relation to His assumption at His baptism of His work of ministry; this conflict in the Garden was, we believe, as closely connected with His assuming His priestly work, undertaking to make atonement for sin by the sacrifice of Himself. As that followed His baptism, this followed His institution of the holy supper. In that ordinance He had prepared the minds of His disciples to turn from the Paschal lamb of the old covenant, to behold henceforth the Lamb of God which taketh away the sin of the world. From the feast He goes straightway to this lonely garden, and there begins[32] His dread atoning work.

It must have been a great aggravation of His agony that even the three disciples could not enter into sympathy with Him, even so much as to hold their eyes waking. True, they were very weary, and it was most natural that they should be heavy with sleep; but had they had even a faint conception of what that agony of their Master meant they could not possibly have slept; and we can well fancy that in that hour of anguish the Saviour must have called to mind from the Book of Psalms, with which He was so perfectly familiar, the sad lament: "Reproach hath broken my heart; and I am full of heaviness: and I looked for some to take pity, but there was none; and for comforters, but I found none."

But though He keenly feels His loneliness, His thoughts are far less of Himself than of them. Realising so vividly the horrors now so close at hand, He sees, from the very possibility of their sleeping, how utterly unprepared they are for what awaits them, so He summons them to "watch and pray," to be on the alert against sudden surprise, and to keep in constant touch with God, so that they may not find themselves confronted with temptation which, whatever the devotion of the spirit, may prove too much for the weakness of the flesh. Think of the tender consideration of this second warning, when the first had been so little heeded.

And we cannot but agree with those who see in what He said when He returned for the last time to the three, not irony, no touch of sarcasm, but the same tender consideration He has shown throughout. From the Garden they could easily see the city in the moonlight across the ravine. As yet there was no sign of life about it: all was quiet; there was therefore no reason why they should not for the few moments that might remain to them sleep on now and take their rest. But it can only be for a short time, for "the hour is at hand." We may, then, think of the three lying down to sleep, as the eight had probably been doing throughout, while Jesus, from whose mortal eyes sleep was banished now for ever, would watch until He saw the gleam of lanterns and torches as of men from the city coming down the hill, and then He would wake them and say, "Rise, let us be going: behold, he is at hand that doth betray Me."

The arrest immediately follows the agony; and with it, begins the outward shame and torture of the Passion. The time has now come when all the indignities and cruelties of which Jesus had spoken to His disciples "apart in the way" (see xx. 17-19) shall be heaped upon Him. But none of these things move Him. The inward shame and torture had almost been too much for Him. His soul had been "exceeding sorrowful, even unto death"; so that He was in danger of passing away from the scene of conflict ere yet it would be possible to say "It is finished." Only by "strong crying and tears unto Him that was able to save Him from death" had He obtained the needful strength (Luke xxii. 43) to pass the awful ordeal, and come out of it ready to yield Himself up into the "wicked hands" by which He must be "crucified and slain." But now He is strong. St. Matthew does not tell us that the prayer in the Garden was answered; but we see it as we follow the Son of man along the dolorous way. If He shrank from taking up the load of human sin, He does not flinch in carrying it; and amid all He has to bear at the hands of sinners, He maintains His dignity and self-possession.

When the armed men approach, He goes calmly out to meet them. Even the traitor's kiss He does not resent; but only takes occasion to make one more appeal to that stony heart, "Comrade,"[33] He says, "(do) that for which thou art come" (see R.V.). There is a brokenness in the utterance which makes it difficult to translate, but which is touchingly natural. It would seem as if our Lord, when Judas first appeared, though He knew well for what purpose He had come, and wished to show him that He did, yet shrank from putting it into words. When the traitor had actually done that for which he had come, when he had not only given the traitor's kiss, and that in a shamelessly effusive way, as appears from the strong word used in the account both here and elsewhere, then would come that other appeal which most impressed the eye-witness from whom St. Luke had his information: "Judas, betrayest thou the Son of man *with a kiss?*"

At this point probably occurred an incident of the arrest recorded only in the fourth Gospel, the recoil of the mob when Jesus confronted them and acknowledged Himself to be the man whom they were seeking. Though this is not mentioned here, we recognise the effect of it upon the disciples. It would naturally embolden them when, on the second advance, they saw their Master in the hands of these men, to ask, "Lord, shall we smite with the sword?" And it was most characteristic that "one of them" (whom we should have recognised, even though St. John had not mentioned his name) should not wait for the answer, but should smite at once.

All is excitement and commotion. Jesus alone is calm. In such a sea of trouble, behold the Man! See the heart at leisure from itself to care for and to cure the wounded servant of the high priest (Luke xxii. 51). Think of the mind so free at such a time to look out far into the future, using the occasion to lay down the great principle that force, as a weapon which will recoil on those who use it, must not be employed in the cause of truth and righteousness. Look at that spirit, so serenely confident of power with God at the very moment that the frail body is helpless in the hands of men: "Thinkest thou that I cannot now pray to My Father, and He shall presently give Me more than twelve legions of angels?" How it enlarges our souls even to try to enter into that great mind and heart at such a moment. What an outlook of thought! What an up-look of faith! And again, what mastery! What self-annihilation! We have seen His self-repression in the prayer He offered in the Garden; but think of the prayers He did not offer: think what effort, what sacrifice, what self-abnegation it must have been to Him to suppress that prayer for help from the legions of heaven against these bands of the ungodly. But it was enough for Him to remember, "How then shall the Scriptures be fulfilled, that thus it must be?" It was necessary that He should suffer at the hands of men; therefore He allows them to lead Him away, only reminding them that the force which would have been needful for the arrest of some robber desperado was surely quite unnecessary in dealing with One Whose daily practice it had been to sit quietly teaching in the Temple.

The reference to the Scriptures was probably intended not only to explain His non-resistance, but also to support the faith of His disciples when they saw Him bound and carried off. Had they known the Scriptures as under His teaching they might well have known them, not only would they have seen that "thus it must be," but they would have had before them the sure prospect of His rising from the dead on the third day. But in their case the Scriptures were appealed to in vain; they had not the faith of their Master to venture on the sure Word of God; and so, hope failing, "all the disciples forsook Him and fled." Not all finally, however, even for that dark night; for though faith and hope failed, there remained love enough in the hearts of two to make them presently stop and think, and then turn slowly and follow from afar. Only Peter is mentioned here as doing this, because the sequel concerns him; but that John also went to the palace of the high priest we know from his own account (John xviii. 15).

The night is not yet over, and therefore there can be no formal meeting of the Jewish council, according to an excellent law which enacted that all cases involving the death penalty should be tried in the daytime. This law was, quite characteristically, observed in the letter, transgressed in the spirit; for though the formal sentence was deferred till morning (xxvii. 1), the real trial was begun and ended before the dawn. The reference by St. Matthew to both sessions of the council enables us clearly to understand what would otherwise have appeared a "manifest discrepancy" between his account and that of St. Luke, the former speaking of the trial as having taken place in the night, while the latter tells us it only began "as soon as it was day."

Our Evangelist shows himself to be a true historian in that, while disposing of the formal morning session in half a sentence, he gives a full account of the night conclave which really settled all. They proceed in a thoroughly characteristic manner. Having secured their prisoner, they must first agree upon the charge: what shall it be? It was no easy matter; for not only had his life been stainless, but He had shown consummate skill in avoiding all the entanglements which had been set for Him; and besides, it so happened that nothing they could prove conclusively against Him, such as His breaking the letter of the Sabbath law, or rather of their traditions, would suit their purpose, for they would run the risk on the one hand of calling fresh attention to the works of healing which had made so deep an impression on the popular mind, and on the other of stirring up strife between the opposing factions which had entered into a precarious union based solely on their common desire to do away with Him. Hence the great difficulty of securing testimony against Him, and the necessity of having recourse to that which was false.

We may wonder perhaps that a court so unscrupulous should have made so much of the difficulty of getting witnesses to agree. Could they not, for other "thirty pieces of silver," have purchased two that would have served their purpose? But it must be remembered that men in their position had to pay some respect to decency; and from their point of view to pay a man for helping to arrest a criminal was an entirely different transaction from giving money to procure false witness. Besides, there were men of the council who did not "consent to the counsel and deed of them" (see Luke xxiii. 51, and John vii. 50, 51), and they must be careful. It is not probable of course that Joseph of Arimathæa and Nicodemus would be present at the secret session in the night; but they would of course be present, or have the opportunity of being present, at the regular meeting in the morning.

When, therefore, the attempt to found a charge on the testimony of witnesses against Him failed, the only hope was to force Him, if possible, to incriminate Himself. The high priest accordingly addresses himself to the prisoner, and attempts to induce Him to say something which might tend to clear up the confusion of the witnesses' testimony. It was evident that something had been said about destroying the temple and building it in three days—would He not state exactly what it was? "But Jesus held His peace." He would not plead before such a tribunal, or acknowledge the irregular appeal by so much as a single word.

Caiaphas is baffled; but there is one course left to him, a course which for many reasons he would have preferred not to take, but he sees now no other way of setting up a charge that will bear examination in the morning. He therefore appeals to Jesus in the most solemn manner to assert or deny His Messiahship.

Silence is now impossible. The high priest has given Him the opportunity of proclaiming His gospel in presence of the council, and He will not lose it, though it seal His condemnation. "He cannot deny Himself." In the most emphatic manner He proclaims Himself the Christ, the Son of God, and tells them that the time is coming when their positions shall be reversed— He their Judge, they summoned to His bar: "Henceforth ye shall see the Son of man sitting at the right hand of power, and coming on the clouds of heaven." (R.V.). What light must have been in His eye, what majesty in His mien, as He spoke those thrilling words! And who shall limit their power?

Who of us shall be surprised to find members of that very conclave among the ransomed of the Lord in the New Jerusalem? They might not heed His words that night, but three days after would they not recall them? And fifty days after that again—who can tell?

Meantime the only result is to produce real or affected horror. "The high priest rent his clothes," thereby expressing in a tragic manner how it tore his heart to hear such "blasphemy"; and with one consent, or at least with no voice raised against it, He is condemned to death.

The council have now done with Him for the night, and He is handed over to the custody of the guard and the servants of the high priest. Then follows that awful scene, which cannot be recalled without a shudder. To think that the Holy One of God should suffer these personal indignities—oh, degradation! It is more dreadful to think of than even the nails and the spear. Alas, even the dregs of the bitter cup of sorrow were wrung out to Him! "Is it nothing to you, all ye that pass by? behold and see if there be any sorrow like unto My sorrow!"

Where is Peter now? We left him following afar off. He has summoned up courage enough to follow on into the court of the high priest's palace, and to mingle among the people there. If he had been let alone, he would with John have in some measure retrieved the disgrace of all the disciples forsaking their Master in "that night on which He was betrayed"; but it has been necessary to rally all the remnants of his bravery to come so far, and now he has none of it to spare. Besides, he is very tired, and shivering with cold—in no condition, verily, for anything heroic. Who is there of us will cast the first stone at him? There are those that speak of him in a tone of contempt as "quailing before a servant maid," as if the meanness of the occasion were not the very thing which made it so hard for him. Had he been summoned to the presence of the high priest, with all the eyes of the council fastened on him, his tired-feeling would have left him all at once, his pulse would have beat fast, the excitement would have stirred him so that no fire of coals would have been needed to warm him, and he might then have acquitted himself in a manner worthy of the rock-apostle; but to be suddenly met with a woman's question sprung upon him unawares, with nobody he cared for looking on, with nothing to rouse his soul from the prostration into which it had been cast by the suddenness of what looked like overwhelming defeat—that was more than even Peter could bear; and accordingly he fell—fell terribly. Not to the bottom all at once. He tries first to pass the question off with a show of ignorance or indifference: "I know not what thou sayest." But when the first downward step is taken, all the rest follow with terrible rapidity. As we look down into the abyss into which plunged headlong the foremost of the Twelve, and hear these oaths and curses, what force it lends to the warning in Gethsemane: "Watch and pray, that ye *enter not* into temptation"!

What a lesson of charity is here! Suppose for a moment that one of the Marys had been standing near, and heard Peter denying his Master with oaths and curses, what would her thought of him have been? What else could it have been than a thought of sorrowful despair? She would have felt constrained, however reluctantly, to place him, not with the timid ten, but alongside of "Judas who betrayed Him." Yet she would have been wrong; and many good people are quite wrong when they judge disciples of Christ by what they see of them when at their worst. After all Peter was true at heart; and though from such an abyss he could never have recovered himself, he was so linked to his Master by the true devotion of the days of old that he could not fall utterly away. It was quite otherwise with Judas. His heart had been set on his covetousness throughout, while Peter in his inmost soul was loyal and true. His Master has prayed for him that his faith fail not. His courage has failed; and if that faith which is the only sure foundation for enduring courage had utterly failed too, his case would have been hopeless indeed. But it has not; there is still a link to bind him to the Lord, Whom in word he is denying for the moment; and first the crowing of the cock which reminds him of his Master's warning, and then immediately after, that look which was turned full on Peter as Jesus passed him, led across the court, perhaps with jeerings and buffetings at the very moment— that solemn memory and that sad and loving look recall him to himself again, the old true life wells up from the depths of the genuine and noble heart of him, and overflows in tears. So ends the story of that awful night.

III.—The Morning (xxvii. 1-26)

The formal meeting of the council in the morning would not occupy many minutes. The death sentence had been already agreed upon, and it only remained to take the necessary steps to carry it into effect. Hence the form in which the Evangelist records the morning session: "All the chief priests and elders of the people took counsel against Jesus to put Him to death." This could not have passed as a minute of the meeting; but it was none the less a true account of it. As, however, the law forbade their inflicting the death penalty, "when they had bound Him, they led Him away, and delivered Him to Pontius Pilate the governor."

This delivering up of Jesus is a fact of the Passion on which special stress is laid in the sacred records. It seems, indeed, to have weighed on the mind of Jesus Himself as much as the betrayal, as would appear from the manner in which, as He was nearing Jerusalem, He told His disciples what He should suffer there: "Behold, we go up to Jerusalem; and the Son of man shall be delivered unto the chief priests and scribes, and they shall condemn Him to death, *and shall deliver Him unto the Gentiles* to mock, and to scourge, and to crucify" (Matt xx. 18, 19; see also Mark x. 33, and Luke xviii. 32). Long before this, indeed, "He came unto His own, and His own received Him not." With the sorrow of that rejection He was only too familiar; but it was a new heart-break to be delivered up to the Gentiles. It was a second betrayal on a much larger scale. So Stephen puts it in the impassioned close of his defence, where he charges the council with being "the *betrayers* and murderers" of "the Just One"; and indeed the thought is suggested here, not only by the association with what follows in regard to the traitor's end, but by the use of the very same word as applied to the traitor's act; for the word translated "betrayed" in verse 3 is the very same in the original as that translated "delivered up" in verse 2. Judas is about to drop out of sight into the abyss; but the nation is one Judas now.

It may be, indeed, that it was the seeing of his own sin as mirrored in the conduct of the council which roused at last the traitor's sleeping conscience. As he saw his late Master led away bound, "as a lamb to the slaughter," these very words may have come back to his memory: "They shall deliver the Son of man to the Gentiles to mock, and to scourge, and to crucify." It is quite possible, indeed, that the man of Kerioth was too good a Jew to have been willing to sell his Master to Pilate directly. But now he sees that that is just what he has done. We have no sympathy with those who imagine that Judas only intended to give his Master an opportunity of displaying His power and asserting His rights in a manner that would secure at once the allegiance of the people; but though we see no evidence of any good intentions, we can readily believe that in the act of betrayal his mind did not go beyond the immediate consequences of his action—on the one hand the money; and on the other what was it but the handing of his Master to the chief priests and elders, who were after all His ecclesiastical superiors; and had they not the right to put Him on His trial? But now that he sees Jesus, Whom by long acquaintance he knows to be without spot or stain, bound as a common criminal and led away to execution, his act appears in a new and awful light, he is smitten with a measureless fear, and can no longer bear to think of what he has done.

"He repented himself," so we read in our version; but that it is no true repentance the more expressive Greek makes plain, for the word is quite distinct from that which indicates "repentance after a godly sort." Had there been in his heart any spring of true repentance its waters would have been unsealed long ere this—at the Table, or when in the Garden he heard his Master's last appeal of love. Not love, but fear, not godly sorrow, but very human terror, is what moves him now; and therefore it is not to Jesus that he flies—had he even now gone up to Him, and fallen at His feet and confessed his sin, he would have been forgiven—but to his accomplices in crime. Fain would he undo what he has done; but it is impossible! What he can do, however, he will; so he tries to get the chief priests to take back the silver pieces. But they will have nothing to do with them or with him. To his piteous confession they pay no heed; let him settle his own accounts with his own conscience: "What is that to us? see thou to that."

He is now alone; shut up to himself; alone with his sin. Even the thirty pieces of silver, which had such a friendly sound as he first dropped them in his purse, have turned against him; now he hates the very sight of them, and must be rid of them. As the priests will not take them back, he will cast them "into the sanctuary" (R.V.), and so perhaps find some relief. But oh, Judas! it is one thing to get the silver out of your hands, and quite another to get the stain out of your soul. The only effect of it is to make the solitude complete. He has at last come to himself; and what a self it is to come to! No wonder that he "went and hanged himself."

The chief priests have not yet come to themselves. They will by-and-by, whether after the manner of the prodigal or after the manner of the traitor time will show; but meanwhile they are in the full career of their sin, and can therefore as yet consult to very good purpose. It was not at all a bad way of getting out of their difficulty with the money found in the sanctuary, to buy with it a place to bury strangers in; but little did they dream that when the story of it should be told thereafter to the world they would be discovered to have unconsciously fulfilled a prophecy (Zech. xi. 12, 13), which on the one hand gibbeted their crime as a valuing of the Shepherd of Israel at the magnificent price of thirty pieces of silver, and on the other carried with it the suggestion of those awful woes which Jeremiah had pronounced at the very spot they had purchased with the price of blood (Jer. xix.).

From the end of the traitor Judas we return to the issue of the nation's treason. "Now Jesus stood before the governor." The full study of Jesus before Pilate belongs rather to the fourth Gospel, which supplies many most interesting details not furnished here. We must therefore deal with it quite briefly, confining our attention as much as possible to the points touched in the record before us.[34]

As before the council, so before Pilate, our Lord speaks, or is silent, according as the question affects His mission or Himself. When asked of His Kingship, He answers in the most decided manner ("Thou sayest" was a strong affirmation, as if to say "Certainly I am"); for on this depends the only hope of salvation for Pilate—for His accusers—for all. He will by no means disown or shrink from acknowledging the mission of salvation on which His Father has sent Him, though it may raise against Him the cry of blasphemy in the council, and of treason in the court; but when He is asked what He has to say for Himself, in the way of answer to the charges made against Him, He is silent: even when Pilate himself appeals to Him in the strongest manner to say something in His own defence, "He gave him no answer, not even to one word" (R.V.). "Insomuch that the governor marvelled greatly;" for how could he understand? How can a cautious, cunning, time-serving man of the world understand the selflessness of the Son of God?

Pilate had no personal grudge against Jesus, and had sense enough to recognise at once that the claims of Kinghood advanced by his prisoner did not touch the prerogatives of Cæsar—had penetration also to see through the motives of the chief priests and elders (ver. 18), and therefore was not at all disposed to acquiesce in the demand made on him for a summary condemnation. Besides, he was not without fears, which inclined him to the side of justice. He was evidently impressed with the demeanour of his prisoner. This appears even in the brief narrative of our Evangelist; but it comes out very strikingly in the fuller record of the fourth Gospel. His wife's influence, too, was used in the same direction. She evidently had heard something about Jesus, and had taken some interest in Him, enough to reach the conviction that He was a "righteous man." It was as yet quite early in the morning, and she may not have known till after her husband had gone out that it was for the trial of Jesus he was summoned. Having had uneasy dreams, in which the Man Who had impressed her so much was a leading figure, it was natural that she should send him a hasty message, so as to reach him "while he was sitting on the judgment seat" (R.V.). This message would reinforce his fears, and increase his desire to deal justly with his extraordinary prisoner.

On the other hand, Pilate could not afford to refuse point blank the demand of the Jewish leaders. He was by no means secure in his seat. There had been so many disturbances under his administration, as we learn from contemporary history, that his recall, perhaps something more serious than recall, might be expected from Rome, if he should again get into trouble with these turbulent Jews; so he did not dare to run the risk of simply doing what he knew was right. Accordingly he tried several expedients, as we learn from the other accounts, to avoid the necessity of pronouncing sentence, one of which is here set forth at length (ver. 15, *seq.*), probably because it brings into strong relief the absolute rejection of their Messiah alike by the rulers and by the people.

It was a most ingenious device, and affords a striking example of the astuteness of the procurator. Barabbas may have had some following in his "sedition"; but evidently he was no popular hero, but a vulgar robber or bandit, whose release was not at all likely to be clamoured for by the multitude; and it was moreover reasonably to be expected that the chief priests, much as they hated Jesus, would be ashamed to even hint that He was worse than this wretched criminal. But he did not know how deep the hatred was with which he had to deal. "He knew that for envy they had delivered Him;" but he did not know that at the root of that envy lay the conviction that either Jesus must perish or they must. They felt that He was "of purer eyes than to behold evil, and could not look upon iniquity"; and inasmuch as they had made up their minds to keep their iniquity, they must get rid of Him; they must seal up these eyes which searched them through and through, they must silence these tones which, silvery as they were, were to them as the knell of judgment. They had no liking for Barabbas, and, to do them justice, no sympathy whatever with his crimes; but they had no reason to be afraid of him: they could live, though he was free. It must have been a hard alternative even for them; but there is no hesitation about it. Themselves and their emissaries are busy among the mob, persuading them "that they should ask Barabbas, and destroy Jesus."

The multitudes are only too easily persuaded. Not that they had the dark envy, or anything like the rooted hatred, of their leaders; but what will a careless mob not be prepared to do when excitement prevails and passions are inflamed? It is not at all unlikely that some of the same people who followed the multitude in shouting "Hosanna to the Son of David!" only five days before, would join in the cry which some of the baser sort would be the first to raise, "Crucify Him! crucify Him!" Those who know human nature best—at its basest, as in the hatred of the chief priests and elders; at its shallowest, as in the passions of the fickle crowd—will marvel least at the way in which the alternative of Pilate was received. There is no touchstone of human nature like the cross of Christ; and in the presence of the Holy One of God, sin is forced, as it were, to show itself in all its native blackness and enormity; and what sin is there, however small it seem to be, which if allowed to develop its latent possibility of vileness, would not lead on to this very choice—"Not Jesus, but Barabbas"?

And Pilate, you may wash your hands before the multitude, and say, "I am innocent of the blood of this just Person"; but it is all in vain. There is a Searcher of hearts Who knows you through and through. "See ye to it," you say; and so said to Judas the chief priests and elders, using the very same words. But both they and you must see to that which each fain would put aside for ever. Ay, and it will be less tolerable for you and for them than even for the thoughtless crowd who cry, "His blood be upon us and on our children." It was in vain to ask of people like these, "What shall I do, then, with Jesus which is called Christ?" There was only one thing to do: the thing which was right. Failing to do this, you had no alternative but to share in the sin of all the rest. Even Pilate must take a side, as all must do. Neutrality here is impossible. Those who persist in making the vain attempt will find themselves at last on the same side as Pilate took when he "released unto them Barabbas; but Jesus he scourged and delivered to be crucified."

IV.—From the Third to the Ninth Hour (xxvii. 27-56)

The cool of the morning was passing into the heat of the day, as the soldiers took Jesus and led Him away to be crucified; and the sun was at the same angle in the western sky when He bowed His head and gave up the ghost. In the six hours between lay the crisis of the world (see John xii. 31, Greek): its judgment, its salvation. The great conflict of the ages is concentrated in these hours of agony. In the brief record of them we have the very core and kernel of the gospel of "Jesus Christ *and Him crucified.*"

All we can hope to do is to find some point of view which may afford a general survey of the awful scene; and such point of observation we may perhaps discover in the thought of the marvellous significance of each detail when set in the after light of faith. Most of the incidents are quite simple and natural—what might in every way be expected as concomitants of the deed of blood which darkened the day—and yet the simplest of them is charged with unexpected meaning. The actors in this dark scene are moved by the basest of passions, are destitute of the smallest gleam of insight into what is passing; and yet, in saying what they say and doing what they do, they declare the glory of the Christ of God as signally as if they were saying and doing all by divine direction. In more senses than one "they know not what they do."

From this point of view we might survey all the four records of the Crucifixion, and find striking illustrations of our thought in each of them. As a specimen of this we may refer in passing to the words of Pilate recorded by St. John alone: "Behold the Man!" and again, "Behold your King!" In these remarkable utterances the procurator quite unconsciously furnishes the answer to his own as yet unanswered questions (John xviii. 38; Matt. xxvii. 22), and, Balaam-like, becomes a preacher of the gospel, summoning the whole world to admiration and homage, to faith and obedience. But we may not extend our view over the other Gospels; it will be enough to glance at the particulars found in that which lies before us.

The first is the mockery of the soldiers. A brutal set they must have been; and their treatment of their victim, as they intended it, is too revolting even to think of in detail. Yet, had they been inspired by the loftiest purpose, and been able to look into the meaning of what they did with the most penetrating insight, they could not have in a more striking manner illustrated the true glory of His royalty. Ah! soldiers, you may well plait that crown of thorns, and put it on His head; for He is the Prince of Sufferers, the King of Sorrow! On that head are many crowns—the crown of righteousness, the crown of heroism, the crown of life; but of them all the very best is the crown of thorns, for it is the crown of Love.

The next incident is the impressing of Simon of Cyrene to bear His cross. It was intended as an insult. The service was too degrading even for any of the rabble of Jerusalem, so they imposed it on this poor foreigner, coming out of the country. Little did they think that this same man of Cyrene, who probably had provoked them by showing some sympathy with the Sufferer, and might by no means grudge the toil, unjustly forced upon him though it was, should with his two sons Alexander and Rufus (see Mark xv. 21) be a kind of firstfruits of a great multitude of foreigners coming out of all countries, who should consider it the highest honour of their lives to take up and bear after Jesus the cross which Simon had borne for Him.

The very name Golgotha, though derived in all probability from the natural appearance of the eminence on which the crosses were erected, has a certain dreary appropriateness, not only because of the horror of the deed, but because the thought is suggested that death's Destroyer gained His victory on death's own ground; and the offering of the potion usually given to deaden pain gave the pale sufferer an opportunity of showing by His refusal of it that not only was the death which ended all a voluntary act, but that each pang of the passion was borne in the resoluteness of a love-constrained will:

> "Thou wilt feel all, that Thou may'st pity all;
> And rather wouldst Thou wrestle with strong pain
> Than overcloud Thy soul
> So clear in agony.
>
> O most entire and perfect Sacrifice,
> Renewed in every pulse,
> That on the tedious Cross
> Told the long hours of death."

The dividing of the garments among the soldiers was a most natural and ordinary incident; it would seem, indeed, to have been the common practice at crucifixions; and the fulfilment of prophecy would be the very last thing that would enter the men's minds as they did it: even St. Matthew himself, in recording it, does not view it in this light; for, though he evidently made a point of calling attention to all fulfilments of prophecy that struck him, he seems to have omitted this;[35] yet here again, even in a small but most significant matter of detail, as recorded by St. John (xix. 23, 24), the Scriptures are fulfilled.

The writing on the cross is called "His accusation." So indeed it was; for it was for this he was condemned: no other charge could be made good against Him. But it was not His accusation only,—it was His coronation. In vain the chief priests tried to induce the governor to change it. "What I have written, I have written," was his answer; and there it stood, and a better inscription for the cross the apostles themselves could not have devised. "This is *Jesus*," the Saviour—the name above every name. How it must have cheered the Saviour's heart to know that it was there! "This is Jesus, *the King*" never more truly King than when this writing was His only crown. "This is Jesus, the King *of the Jews*," despised and rejected of them now, but Son of David none the less, and yet to be claimed and crowned, and rejoiced in when at last "all Israel shall be saved." Elsewhere we learn that the inscription was in Hebrew and Greek and Latin,—the first the tongue of the people to whose keeping had been committed the oracles of God, the other two the languages in which God's good tidings of Life through a Crucified Saviour could be best and most quickly carried "to every creature,"—as if to make the proclamation world-wide.

His position between the two thieves is told as simply as all the rest; yet how full of meaning, not only as fulfilling the Scripture which spoke of Him as "numbered with the transgressors," but as furnishing a most impressive picture of the Friend of Sinners, enduring their revilings, and yet as soon as one of them shows the first signs of coming to a better mind, eagerly granting him forgiveness and eternal life, and receiving him into His kingdom as the firstfruits of His redeemed ones.

Again, the mocking cries of the passers-by are exactly what was to be expected from the coarse natures of the men; yet each one of them when seen in the after light of faith becomes a tribute to His praise. As an illustration of this, listen to the cry which comes out of the deepest abyss of hatred. Hear these chief priests mocking Him, with the scribes and elders. With bitter taunt they say, in scorn, "He saved others; Himself He cannot save." With bitter taunt? In scorn? Ah, "fools and blind," you little know that you are making a garland of imperishable beauty to wreathe around His brow! It was indeed most true. It was because He saved others that He could not save Himself. Were He willing to let others perish—were He willing to let you perish—He would this very moment save Himself. But He will bear, not only the cruel nails and spear, but your more cruel mockeries, rather than give up His self-imposed task of saving others by His perfect sacrifice!

It is high noon; but there, at that place of a skull, a deed is being done, from which the sun must hide his face for shame. "From the sixth hour there was darkness over all the land until the ninth hour." The simple-hearted Evangelist has no reflections of his own to offer; he simply records the well-remembered fact, with his usual reticence of feeling, which makes the deep, dread meaning of it only more impressive. For there is not only darkness over all the land; there is darkness in the Sufferer's soul. The agony of the Garden is on Him once again. He sees no longer the faces of the crowd, and the mocking voices are now silent, for the people cannot but feel the solemnising effect of the midday gloom. The presence of man is forgotten, and with it the shame, even the pain: the Redeemer of the world is again alone with God.

Alone with God, and the sin of the world is on Him. "He bare our sins in His own body on the tree," therefore is it that He must enter even into the very deepest darkness of the soul, the feeling of separation from God, the sense of forsakenness, which is so appalling to the awakened sinner, and which even the sinless One must taste, because of the burden laid upon Him. To Him it was a pang beyond all others, forcing from these silent lips the lamentable cry, "My God, My God, why hast Thou forsaken Me?" There is no reason indeed to suppose that the Sufferer was really forsaken by God, even for a moment. Never was the love of the Father deeper and stronger than when His Son was offering up the all-atoning sacrifice. Never was the repeated testimony more sure than now—"This is My beloved Son, in Whom I am well pleased." But none the less was there the *sense* of forsakenness.

This sense of forsakenness seems to have had some mysterious connection with the pains of death. In the Garden, where the experience was similar, He said, "My soul is exceeding sorrowful, *even unto death*," and now that death is on Him, now that His human spirit is about to sink into the unknown abyss, now that darkness is closing over Him on every side, He feels as if He were forsaken utterly: yet His faith fails not; perhaps He thinks of the words, "Yea the darkness hideth not from Thee; but the night shineth as the day: the darkness and the light are both alike to Thee," and though He cannot now say "Father" even, He can at least cry as from the depths, His spirit overwhelmed within Him, "My God, My God." That 22nd Psalm which was certainly in His mind must have suggested thoughts of hope and strength, and ere His spirit leaves the tortured body He has reached the triumphant close of it; for as its opening utterance became His cry of agony, its closing word suggests His shout of victory. The shout is mentioned by St. Matthew; the words we learn from St. John: "It is finished."

From the sixth hour to the ninth the darkness lasted, and at the ninth hour Jesus yielded up the ghost. The agony is over. The feeling of separation, of utter loneliness, is gone, for the last word has been, "Father, into Thy hands I commend My Spirit"; and as the spirit of the Son of man returns to the Father's bosom, the gloom is gone, and the sun shines out again upon the earth.

How appropriate the rending of the veil,[36] the quaking of the earth, the shuddering of the graves, and the visitants from the realm of the unseen greeting the eyes of those for whom heaven was opened now, is all so plain in the light of faith on the Son of God that it needs no pointing out. It was no wonder that even the Roman centurion, unaccustomed as he was to think of such things, could not refrain from exclaiming, "Truly this was the Son of God." Much more may we echo his exclamation when in the light of the glory that has followed we look back on "the things that were done." Recall them, — the crown of thorns, the cross-bearing of Simon, the place of a skull, the parting of the garments, the writing on the cross, the company of the thieves, the mockeries of the people, the darkness of the heavens, the shaking of the earth, the rending of the veil, — is there not profound meaning in it all?

The portents at the close, as was natural, impressed the centurion most; but these are just what make the least impression now, because we do not see them, and those for whom no veil has been rent by the Saviour's sacrifice cannot be expected to recognise them. But think of the other incidents — incidents to which not even the most sceptical can attach a shadow of doubt: observe how utterly unconscious the actors were — the soldiers in plaiting the crown of thorns, Pilate in writing His title, the chief priests in shouting "He saved others; Himself He cannot save" — and yet how these all, viewed in a light that did not shine for them, are seen to have vied with each other in setting forth His glory as the Saviour-King; and then say whether it could all have been the merest chance, whether there be not in it manifestly "the determinate counsel and foreknowledge of God," whether it is possible to escape the conviction of the Roman centurion, "Truly this is the Son of God!"

The reference to the "many women," "beholding afar off," forms a pathetic close to the story of the Great Atonement Day.

FOOTNOTES

[24] The feast in Bethany did not take place during this interval, but some days before (see John xii. 1); in all probability the very day before Christ's entry into Jerusalem.

[25] That the name of Judas is not specially mentioned is probably to be accounted for by the consciousness on the part of St. Matthew that Judas was not alone in the feeling he expressed, that he and others of the disciples present sympathised with him in what he said, so that in fairness he must lay the blame of the objection not alone on the man who expressly made it, but on the disciples generally (in St. Mark's Gospel it is "*some* had indignation"). We may well suppose that John, the beloved disciple, would be the least likely of all to sympathise with the objection, and in this we may see the reason why he should feel no scruple in singling out the traitor as the man who was audacious enough to express the feeling of dissatisfaction.

[26] So R.V. The Authorised Version is peculiarly unhappy at this point. "When Jesus understood it" seems to suggest that it took Him some time to make out what they were grumbling about. It is altogether likely that the murmuring was among themselves, and the speech of Judas was probably spoken not loud enough for Jesus to hear, but in a low tone to the knot of sympathisers around Him. But there is no hint in the original of any time elapsing before Jesus understood the situation. As always, He "knew their thoughts" at once.

[27] We may not enter fully into the vexed question whether our Lord kept the Passover on the day appointed by law, or anticipated it by twenty-four hours, as some suppose to be the necessary inference from the narrative of St. John. It is a long and intricate subject; but much unnecessary difficulty has been imported into it by those who fail to realise two important facts: (1) The word "Passover" is frequently used for the entire Feast of Unleavened Bread (see Luke xxii. 1). This is the regular usage of St. John throughout his Gospel; yet many assume that in his story of the Passion "Passover" must mean Passover Day. (2) "The preparation of the Passover" (see John xix. 14) does not mean, as many suppose, the preparation for the paschal feast, but the preparation for the Sabbath. This is in fact proved, not only by Mark xv. 42, but by a subsequent reference in the same Gospel (John xix. 31). Suppose the paschal feast to have been eaten on Thursday night, Friday would still be the preparation day of the Passover, inasmuch as the next day

(Saturday) was the Sabbath of the Passover. If these facts be borne in mind, little difficulty will remain in accepting as the order of events that our Lord kept the Passover at the proper time, on the evening of the 14th Nisan (Thursday), died on the afternoon of the 15th (Friday), lay in the grave over the Sabbath (Saturday, 16th Nisan), and rose on the morning of the 17th, the first day of the week.

[28] See the interesting discussion on the arrangement of the table in Edersheim, "Life and Times of Jesus the Messiah," vol. ii., p. 494.

[29] The high Sacramentarian view of the Lord's Supper is not only at variance with the simple and obvious meaning of the central words of institution, but seems to disregard in the most wanton manner the plainest statements of the very authority on which the ordinance is based. According to the Gospel it was "as they were eating" that Jesus took the bread and gave it to the disciples; according to the Ritualist it ought to be before anything else has touched the lips. For their mystical act of consecration on the part of the priest, all they can find either in gospel or epistle is the simple giving of thanks (that "blessed" of ver. 26 is the same act precisely is obvious by comparing the corresponding passages in the other Gospels and in the first Epistle to the Corinthians—xi. 24); while in opposition to the emphatic *"Drink ye all of it"* the cup has been refused by the Church of Rome to the great majority of her communicants!

[30] See Zech. ix. 9, xi. 12, xiii. 7.

[31] Gethsemane means *oil-press.*

[32] Observe the emphatic word, *"began* to be sorrowful" (ver. 37).

[33] The word "friend" is too strong. It is not the same word our Lord uses when He says: "I have not called you servants, I have called you friends"; it is a word which indicates not heart-friendship, but that familiar intercourse which is supposed to take place only between friends. The selection of the word is a striking illustration of our Lord's carefulness of the claims of sincerity and truth, while He is anxious if possible to use a word that will touch the traitor's heart.

[34] It is most instructive at this point to note the extreme condensation of this report of the trial before Pilate. This

is especially noticeable at the first stage of the trial. In the fuller reports by St. John (xviii. 29-38) we find indeed the question, "Art thou king of the Jews?" (v. 33), and the answer, "Thou sayest" (v. 37); but how much more besides! So is it beyond question in many other places where there is not the same opportunity of supplying what has been omitted. If this were always borne in mind in reading the Gospels, we should avoid many difficulties, which have often needlessly perplexed the best of people. There is often much to read between the lines, and not only so, but much between the lines we cannot read, the knowledge of which would make crooked things straight and rough places plain. The difficulty of accurately realising a complex scene from a report of it which, however accurate, is highly condensed, ought to be always present to the minds of readers of the Gospels, and ought to be a check on those who attribute to the "mistakes" of the writers what in all probability is due to the ignorance of the readers—ignorance, it may be, of some little matter of detail, or some comparatively unimportant saying, the knowledge of which would at once clear up a difficulty which to the unaided imagination may appear insoluble.

[35] The reference is inserted in our Authorised Version, but without sufficient authority. The Revised Version properly omits it.

[36] "From the top to the bottom,"—rent, therefore, by no human hand.

XX
THE THIRD DAY

Matt. xxvii. 57-xxviii. 15.

NOW that the atoning work of Christ is finished, the story proceeds with rapidity to its close. It was the work of the Evangelist to give the history of the incarnate Son of God; and now that the flesh is laid aside, it is necessary only to give such notes of subsequent events as shall preserve the continuity between the prophetic and priestly work of Christ on earth which it had been His vocation to describe, and the royal work which, as exalted Prince and Saviour, it still remained for Him to do. We need not wonder, then, that the record of the three days should be quite brief, and of the forty days briefer still.

This brevity is a note of truthfulness. The old idea of deliberate falsehood having been quite given up, reliance is placed, by those who wish to discredit the gospel witnesses, on the suggestion that the records of the resurrection are the result of fancy crystallising into so-called fact. But not only was there no time, between the death of Christ and the latest date which can be assigned for the writing of the first Gospel, for the process of crystallisation, but had there been such a process, the result would have been very different. Had fancy, and not observation, been the source, how comes it that nothing is told but what came within the range of actual vision? Why is there not a word about Christ's entry into Paradise, or descent into Hades? What a fruitful field for fancy here!—yet there is not even a hint; for it is not from anything in the Gospels, but solely from a passage in one of the Epistles, that the doctrine of the descent into Hades has been derived. There is not a word or a hint of anything that passed in the unseen; a plain statement of what was done with the body of Jesus is absolutely all. Clearly it is not myth, but history, with which here we have to do.

The Evening of the First Day (vv. 57-61)

Day was passing into evening when Jesus "yielded up His spirit"; for the early evening according to the Jewish reckoning began at the ninth hour. It was probably some time after this—perhaps towards the later evening, which began about the twelfth hour (six o'clock)—that Joseph of Arimathæa thought of claiming the body to give it honourable burial. Why should such a duty have fallen to a stranger? Where were the eleven? Had none of them so far recovered from their fear? Where was Peter? might not his penitence for the past have impelled him to come forward now? Where was John? He had taken the mother of Jesus to his own home; but why did he not come back to see what he could do for the sacred body? How can they all leave this tender office to a stranger?

It may be thought by some sufficient answer simply to say, So the Lord willed it, and so the Scripture was fulfilled which intimated that He Who had died with the wicked should be "with the rich in His death"; but is there not more than this to be said? Is not the disappearance of the eleven and the coming forward of the two secret disciples (for as we learn from the fourth Gospel, Nicodemus—another secret disciple—appears a little later on the scene) true to human nature? Let us remember that the faith of the eleven, while much superior to that of the two, was from the nature of the case exposed to a counter-current of feeling, of which neither Joseph nor Nicodemus could know anything. They had committed themselves and their all to Jesus, as Joseph and Nicodemus had never done. The consequence was that when the terrible tempest broke on Him, it came with all its force on them too. But Joseph and Nicodemus had not as yet ventured their all— had not, it would appear, as yet ventured anything for Christ. They were looking on at the storm, as it were, from the shore; so they could stand it, as those who were in the very midst of it could not. They could stand beholding. Not having made themselves known, they were not exposed to personal danger, hence were in a position calmly and thoughtfully to watch the progress of events. We can imagine them first looking towards Calvary from afar, and then, as the darkness favoured a timid approach, drawing nearer and nearer, and at last coming within the spell of the Divine Sufferer. As they witnessed His patient endurance, they would become more and more ashamed of their half-hearted sympathy, ashamed to think that though they had not consented to the counsel and deed of the rest (Luke xxiii. 51; John vii. 50, 51), they had not had courage to offer any serious opposition. They would feel, as they thought of this, as if they shared the responsibility of what must now appear to them an awful crime; and so, looking to Him whom they had pierced, they would mourn; and, brought at last to decision by His death (John xii. 32), first Joseph, and after him Nicodemus, came out boldly, the one asking for the body of Jesus, the other joining him in those tender and reverent ministrations which all that was best in them now constrained them to render.

The sad duty hastily but tenderly and fitly done, a great stone is rolled to the door of the sepulchre, and they depart. But the sepulchre is not deserted yet. What are these figures in the dusk, these women that advance as the others retire? While the two men were busy they have been keeping at a discreet and respectful distance; but now that all is silent at the tomb, they draw nearer, and though night is coming on apace, they cannot leave it, and the story of the long day ends with this pathetic touch: "And Mary Magdalene was there, and the other Mary, sitting over against the sepulchre."

The Second Day (vv. 62-66)

It was the Jewish Sabbath. The Evangelist for some reason avoids the common designation, preferring to speak of it as "the day after the preparation" — whether it was that he shrank from mentioning the Sabbath in such a connection, or whether it was that the great event of the preparation day had such complete possession of his mind that he must date from it, we shall not attempt to decide.

This is the only record we have of that Sabbath day except that St. Luke tells us that on it the women "rested according to the commandment." But the enemies of Jesus could not rest. They were uneasy and troubled now that the deed was done. They could not but have been impressed with the bearing of their Victim, and with all the portents which accompanied His end. It was natural, therefore, that words of His, which when reported to them before had not seemed worth noticing, should come back to them now with fateful force. "After three days I will rise again" was what He had often said. "What if He should rise? we must see that He does not." It would never do, however, to confess to such a fear; but they may get all needful precautions taken by suggesting that there was danger of the disciples stealing the body, and then saying that He had risen. On this pretext they get a guard from Pilate, and authority to seal the sepulchre. Having thus made all secure, they can sleep in peace.

The Morning of the Third Day (xxviii. 1-15)

The women, having rested on the Sabbath according to the commandment, knew nothing of what had been done at the tomb that day, so, as they set out before daybreak on the third morning, they only thought of the great stone, and wondered how it could be rolled away; but when they came, the sun just rising as they reached the spot, they found the stone already rolled away, and an angel of the Lord at the tomb, so lustrous in the livery of heaven that the keepers had quailed in his presence and were powerless to interfere. The awe with which the sight would naturally inspire the women also was mingled with joy as they heard his kindly greeting and sympathetic words. Altogether worthy of an angel from heaven are the words he is reported to have spoken. There is first the tender response to their looks of dread—"Fear not ye," as if to say, These others well may fear, for there is nothing in common between them and me; but with you it is different: "I know that ye seek Jesus, Which was crucified." Then there is the joyful news: "He is not here; for He is risen, as He said:" and as he observes their look of half-incredulous wonder he kindly adds, to let their sight be helper to their faith, "Come, see the place where the Lord lay." Then he gives them the honour of carrying the glad tidings to the other disciples, and assuring them that the Divine Shepherd will meet them all in Galilee according to His word.

At this point we encounter one of the chief difficulties to be found in St. Matthew's record of the resurrection. There are indeed several particulars in this Gospel, as well as in the others, which it is difficult to fit into a connected account embracing all the facts; but as every person of even moderate intelligence knows that the same difficulty is met in comparing various truthful accounts of any great event in which details are many and complex, it is only the most unreasoning prejudice that can find in this an excuse for doubting the credibility of the writers. Rather is this feature of the records a distinct note of truthfulness; for, had it been easy to fit each fact into its exact place in all the other accounts, we should have heard from the very same doubters, and with far better reason, that there was every sign of its being a made-up story. All the four accounts are brief and fragmentary; there is evidently no attempt whatever to relate all that took place, and we should need to know all in order to form a complete picture of the entire series of events which glorified the first Easter Day. We must therefore be content with the four vivid pictures given us, without insisting on what with our imperfect knowledge is perhaps the impossible task of so combining them as to have one great canvas embracing all the details in each of the four.

The account before us is the briefest of all, and therefore it would be especially out of place in dealing with this Gospel to attempt to fill up the blanks and construct a consecutive history of all that took place on that eventful day. But there is one point with which it is especially necessary to deal in considering St. Matthew's account of the resurrection—viz., the prominence given to the appearance of the Lord to His disciples in Galilee—

whereas in the fuller records of the third and fourth Gospels, not Galilee, but Jerusalem and its vicinity, is the region where He makes Himself known.

Those who are anxious to make the most of this difficulty are much disappointed to find the ninth verse in their way. Wishing to prove a sharp contradiction, as if the one said the Lord appeared only in Galilee, and the other that He appeared only in Jerusalem and its neighbourhood, they are naturally vexed to find one of the Jerusalem appearances actually mentioned here. The attempt has accordingly been made to discredit it; but in vain. It stands there an unquestionable part of the original text. So we must bear in mind that St. Matthew not only does not assert that it was only in Galilee that our Lord appeared, but he expressly mentions one appearance in Jerusalem. On the other hand, while St. Mark mentions no appearance in Galilee, he does mention the Lord's promise to meet His disciples there, and leaves it distinctly to be inferred that it was fulfilled. St. Luke, indeed, makes no mention of Galilee at all; but there is abundance of room for it: for while he occupies almost all his space with the record of one day, he tells us in the beginning of his second volume (Acts i. 3) that Christ "showed Himself alive after His passion by many infallible proofs, *being seen of them forty days,* and speaking of the things pertaining to the kingdom of God." St. John also confines himself to what took place at Jerusalem; but in the interesting appendix to that Gospel there is a striking account of a meeting with the eleven in Galilee—evidently not the same one which is recorded here, but another of the same, affording one more specimen of meetings which were no doubt frequently repeated during the forty days. It is abundantly evident, therefore, that there is no contradiction whatever.

Still the question remains, Why does St. Matthew make so little of what the others make so much of, and so much of what the others make so little of? In answer we might first ask whether this was not in every way to be expected and desired. If, as evidently was the case, there were manifestations of the risen Lord both in the south and in the north, and if we were to have several accounts, was it not desirable that one at least should make it his specialty to bring into prominence the appearances in the north? And if so, who could do it more appropriately than Matthew the publican of Galilee? The favour shown his own northern land had most deeply impressed his mind. It will be remembered that he passed over entirely the early Judæan ministry recorded by St. John, and rejoiced in the Galilean ministry as the dawning of the new Day according to the words of ancient prophecy (Matt. iv. 14-16).

Furthermore, there is every reason to suppose that it was not till they met in Galilee that the scattered flock of the disciples was gathered all together. The appearances in Jerusalem were to individuals and to little companies; whereas in Galilee it would seem that He appeared to as many as five hundred at once (1 Cor. xv. 6); and though the Lord appeared to the ten (Thomas being absent), and again to the eleven, before they left Jerusalem, it is not to these occasions, but rather to the meeting on the shore of the lake, that we look for their fresh commission to address themselves again to their work as fishers of men. This will appear more clearly if we bear in mind our Lord's sad reference, as the crisis approached, to the scattering of the flock, and His promise that after He had risen again He would go before them into Galilee (Matt. xxvi. 31, 32). We have here, then (ver. 7), a repetition of the same promise, "He goeth before you" (as the shepherd goes before his flock) "into Galilee," where all the scattered ones shall be gathered round the Shepherd once again, and thence sent out as under-shepherds (see John xxi. 15-17), to gather in the rest of the flock that are scattered abroad.

The conduct of the chief priests and scribes (vv. 11-15) is the natural sequel of their futile attempt to seal the sepulchre. It is in vain to raise the objection, as some do, that it was too clumsy a device for men so astute; for what else could they do? It was indeed a poor evasion; but, baffled as they were, no better was possible for them. Let the critic say what better expedient they could have thought of, before he assigns its poverty as a reason for discrediting the story. That St. Matthew, and he alone, records it, is sufficiently accounted for by the fact that, his being the first written Gospel, and moreover the Gospel for the Jew, it behoved him to deal with a saying "commonly reported among the Jews until this day"; while its being recorded by him was a sufficient reason why no further notice should be taken of it, when there was so much of greater importance to tell.

Looking back on this very brief record of the great events of Easter Day, nothing is more striking than the prominence of the women throughout. It is a note of the new dispensation. It must have been very strange to all the disciples, and not least to the author of this Gospel, that woman, who had been kept so far in the background, treated almost as if her presence would pollute the sacred places, should, now that the veil was rent in twain from the top to the bottom, not only enter into the sacred presence of the risen Lord as the equal of her brother man, but should be there before him,—that a woman's eyes should be the first to see Him, a group of women the first to receive His loving welcome and to fall in adoration at His sacred feet. Yet so it was. Not that there was any partiality. "In Christ Jesus there is neither male nor female." It is not a question of sex; it is a question of love and faith; and it was because the love of these women was deeper, and their fidelity greater, than that of any of the men, that they had this honour. Had the love of John been as all-engrossing as that of Mary of Magdala, he would not have had to wait for the Easter tidings till she had come to tell him. It is not a question of faith alone, but of faith and love. The women's faith had failed them too. It was with no hope of seeing a risen Lord that they had gone to the tomb—it was with spices to finish the embalming of His dead body; but their love, love stronger than death, even in the wreck of faith, kept them near, and so it was that, when light first broke from out the darkness, they were there to see.

XXI

THE GOSPEL FOR ALL THE NATIONS
THROUGH "ALL THE DAYS"

Matt xxviii. 16-20.

THIS brief concluding passage is all St. Matthew gives us of the thirty-nine days which followed the Resurrection and preceded the Ascension. It would seem as if he fully realised that the manifestations of these days belonged rather to the heavenly than to the earthly work of Jesus, and that therefore, properly speaking, they did not fall within his province. It was necessary that he should bear witness to the fact of the Resurrection, and that he should clearly set forth the authority under which the first preachers of the gospel acted. Having accomplished both, he rests from his long labour of love.

That the commission of the eleven was not restricted to this particular time and place is evident from notices in the other Gospels (Mark xvi. 15; Luke xxiv. 48; John xx. 21-23, xxi. 15-17); but we can see many reasons why this occasion was preferred to all others. We have already seen how natural it was that St. Matthew should call the attention of his readers to the appearances of the risen Lord in Galilee rather than to those in Jerusalem and its vicinity; and the more we think of it, the more do we see the appropriateness of his singling out this one in particular. It was the only formally appointed meeting of the Lord with His disciples. In every other case He came unannounced and unexpected; but for this meeting there had been a distinct and definite appointment.

This consideration is one of many which render it probable that this was the occasion referred to by St. Paul when our Lord was seen by above five hundred brethren at once; for on the one hand there was nothing but a definite appointment that would bring so large a company together at any one point, and on the other hand, when such an appointment was made, it is altogether natural to suppose that the news of it would spread far and wide, and bring together, not the eleven only, but disciples from all parts of the land, and especially from Galilee, where the greater number of them would no doubt reside. That St. Matthew mentions only the eleven may be accounted for by the object he has in view—viz., to exhibit their apostolic credentials; but even in his brief narrative there is one statement which is most easily understood on the supposition that a considerable number were present. "Some doubted," he says. This would seem altogether natural on the part of those to whom this was the only appearance; whereas it is difficult to suppose that any of the eleven could doubt after what they had seen and heard at Jerusalem.

In any case, the doubts were only temporary, and were in all probability connected with the mode of His manifestation. As on other occasions, of which particulars are given in other Gospels, the Lord would suddenly appear to the assembled company; and we can well understand how, when first His form was seen, He should not be recognised by all; so that, while all would be solemnised, and bow in adoration, some might not be altogether free from doubt. But the doubts would disappear as soon as "He opened His mouth and taught them," as of old. To make these doubts, as some do, a reason for discrediting the testimony of all is surely the very height of perversity. All the disciples were doubters at the first. But they were all convinced in the end. And the very fact that it was so hard to convince them, when they were first confronted with so unexpected an event as the Lord's appearing to them after His death, gives largely increased value to their unfaltering certainty ever afterwards, through all the persecution and sufferings, even unto death, to which their preaching the fact of the Resurrection exposed them.

As Galilee was the most convenient place[37] for a large public gathering of disciples, so a mountain was the most convenient spot, not only because of its seclusion, but because it would give the best opportunity for all to see and hear. What mountain it was we can only conjecture. Perhaps it was the mount on which the great Sermon was delivered which gave the first outline sketch of the kingdom now to be formally established; perhaps it was the mount which had already been honoured as the scene of the Transfiguration; but wherever it was, the associations with the former mountain scenes in Galilee would be fresh and strong in the disciples' minds.

The choice of a mountain in the north was moreover suitable as signalising the setting aside of Mount Zion and Jerusalem as the seat of empire. From this point of view we can see still another reason why St. Matthew, the Evangelist for the Jew, should mention the formal inauguration of the new kingdom in the north. The rejection of the Messiah by His own people had gone very deeply to the heart of the author of this Gospel. He certainly never obtrudes his feelings, even when they are strongest, as is most strikingly apparent in his calm record of the Passion itself; but there are many things which show how keenly he felt on this point. Recall how he tells us on the one hand that "Herod the king was troubled, and all

Jerusalem with him," when the report was spread abroad that the Christ was born in Bethlehem, and on the other that the wise men from the East "rejoiced with exceeding great joy." Remember how he speaks of "Galilee of the Gentiles" as rejoicing in the great light which had been unnoticed or unwelcome in Jerusalem, and how he calls special attention to "the coasts of Cæsarea Philippi," the utmost corner of the land, as the place where the Church was founded. And now, having recorded the Lord's final and formal entry into the ancient capital to claim the throne of David, only to be despised and rejected, mocked and scourged and crucified, it is natural that, as the Evangelist for the Jew, he should pass away from what he often fondly calls "the holy City,"[38] but which is now to him an accursed place, to those calm regions of the north which were associated in his mind with the first shining of the light, with so many words of wisdom spoken by the Lord, with the doing of most of His mighty deeds, with the founding of the Church, and with the glory of the Transfiguration.

The words of the Lord on this last occasion are worthy of all that has gone before. Let all doubters ponder well the significance of this. Suppose for a moment that the story of the Resurrection had been only "the passion of a hallucinated woman," as Renan puts it, and then consider the position. No one of course denies that up to the moment of death there was a veritable Jesus, whose sayings and doings supplied the material for the history; but now that the hero is dead and gone, where are the materials? The fishermen and publicans are on their own resources now. They have to make everything out of nothing. Surely, therefore, there must be now a swift descent; no more of those noble utterances to which we have been accustomed hitherto—only inventions of the poor publican now. No more breadth of view—only Jewish narrowness now. It was about this very time that the disciples asked, "Lord, wilt Thou at this time restore the kingdom to Israel?" Suppose, then, these men obliged themselves to invent a Great Commission, how narrow and provincial will it be!

Is there, then, such a swift descent? Are not the reported words of the risen Lord—not in this Gospel merely, but in all the Gospels—as noble, as impressive, as divine as any that have been preserved to us, from the years of His life in the flesh? Search through this Gospel, and say if there can be found anywhere an utterance that has more of the King in it, that is more absolutely free from all Jewish narrowness and from all human feebleness, than this Great Commission which forms its magnificent close. It is very plain that these simple artists have their subject still before them. Manifestly they are not drawing from imagination, but telling what they heard and saw.

There is an unapproachable majesty in the words which makes one shrink from touching them. They seem to rise before us like a great mountain which it would be presumption to attempt to scale. What a mighty range they take, up to heaven, out to all the earth, down to the end of time!—and all so calm, so simple, so strong, so sure. If, as He finished the Sermon on the Mount, the multitude were astonished, much more must these have been astonished who first listened to this amazing proclamation.

"All authority hath been given unto Me in heaven and on earth" (R.V.). What words are these to come from One Who has just been put to death for claiming to be the king of the Jews! King of kings and Lord of lords is the title now He claims. And yet it is as Son of man He speaks. He does not speak as God, and say, "All authority is Mine": He speaks as the man Christ Jesus, saying, "All authority has been given unto Me"—given as the purchase of His pain: authority in heaven, as Priest with God—authority on earth, as King of men.

Having thus laid broad and deep and strong the foundations of the new kingdom, He sends the heralds forth: "Go ye therefore, and make disciples of all the nations, baptising them into the name of the Father and of the Son and of the Holy Ghost: teaching them to observe all things whatsoever I commanded you" (R.V.). These are simple words and very familiar now, and a distinct effort is needed to realise how extraordinary they are, as spoken then and there to that little company. "All nations" are to be discipled and brought under His sway,—such is the commission; and to whom is it given? Not to Imperial Cæsar, with his legions at command and the civilised world at his feet; not to a company of intellectual giants, who by the sheer force of genius might turn the world upside down; but to these obscure Galileans of whom Cæsar has never heard, not one of whose names has ever been pronounced in the Roman Senate, who have excited no wonder either for intellect or learning even in the villages and country-sides from which they come,—it is to these that the great commission is given to bring the world to the feet of the crucified Nazarene. Imagine a nineteenth-century critic there, and listening. He would not have said a word. It would have been beneath his notice. A curl of the lip would have been all the recognition he would have deigned to give. Yes, how ludicrous it seems in the light of reason! But in the light of history is it not sublime?

The hidden power lay in the conjunction: "Go ye *therefore*." It would have been the height of folly to have gone on such an errand in their own strength; but why should they hesitate to go in the name and at the bidding of One to Whom all authority had been given in heaven and on earth? Yet the power is not delegated to them. It remains, and must remain with Him.

It is not, "All authority is given *unto you*." They must keep in closest touch with Him, wherever they go on this extraordinary mission. How this may be will presently appear.

The two branches into which the commission divides—"Baptising them into the name of the Father and of the Son and of the Holy Ghost," "Teaching them to observe all things whatsoever I commanded you"—correspond to the twofold authority on which it is based. By virtue of His authority in heaven, He authorises His ambassadors to baptise people of all nations who shall become His disciples "into the name of the Father and of the Son and of the Holy Ghost." Thus would they be acknowledged as children of the great family of God, accepted by the Father as washed from sin through the blood of Jesus Christ His Son, and sanctified by the grace of His Holy Spirit—the sum of saving truth suggested in a single line. In the same way, by virtue of His authority on earth, He authorises His disciples to publish His commands so as to secure the obedience of all the nations, and yet not of constraint, but willingly, "teaching them to observe all things whatsoever I have commanded you."

Easily said; but how shall it be done? We can imagine the feeling of bewilderment and helplessness with which the disciples would listen to their marching orders, until all was changed by the simple and sublime assurance at the close: "And lo, I am with you alway, even unto the end of the world." This assurance is perhaps the strangest part of all, as given to a company, however small, who were to be scattered abroad in different directions, and who were commissioned to go to the very ends of the earth. How could it be fulfilled? There is nothing in St. Matthew's narrative to explain the difficulty. We know, indeed, from other sources what explains it. It is the Ascension—the return of the King to the heaven whence He came, to resume His omnipresent glory, by virtue of which alone He can fulfil the promise He has made.

This brings us to a question of considerable importance: Why is it that St. Matthew gives no record of the Ascension, and does not even hint what became of the risen Christ after this last recorded interview with His disciples? It seems to us that a sufficient reason is found in the object which St. Matthew had in view, which was to set forth the establishment of the kingdom of Christ upon earth as foretold by the prophets and expected by the saints of old; and inasmuch as it is Christ's kingdom on earth which he has mainly in view, he does not call special attention to His return to heaven, but rather to that earthly fact which was the glorious result of it—viz., His abiding presence with His people on the earth. Had he finished his Gospel with the Ascension, the last impression left on the reader's mind would have been of Christ in heaven at the right hand of God—a glorious thought indeed, but not the one it was his special aim and object to convey. But, concluding as he does, the last impression on the reader's mind is of Christ abiding on the earth, and with all His people even to the end of the world—a most cheering, comforting, and stimulating thought. To the devout reader of this Gospel it is as if his Lord had never left the earth at all, but had suddenly clothed Himself with omnipresence, so that, however far apart His disciples might be scattered in His service, each one of them might at any moment see His face, and hear His voice of cheer, and feel His touch of sympathy, and draw on His reserve of power. Thus was it made quite plain, how they could keep in closest touch with Him to Whom was given all authority in heaven and on earth.

After all, is it quite correct to say that St. Matthew omits the Ascension? What was the Ascension? We think of it as a going up; but that is to speak of it after the manner of men. In the kingdom of heaven there is no geographical "up" or "down." The Ascension really meant the laying aside of earthly limitations and the resumption of divine glory with its omnipresence and eternity; and is not this included in these closing words? May we not fancy one of these doubting ones (ver. 17), who trembled in the presence of that Form in which the Lord appeared to them upon the mount, recalling afterwards the supreme moment when the words "Lo, I am with you," entered into his soul, in language such as this:

"Then did the Form expand, expand—
I knew Him through the dread disguise,
As the whole God within His eyes
Embraced me"—

an embrace in which he remained, when the Form had vanished.

The Ascension is all in that wonderful "I am." It is not the first time we have heard it. Among His last words in Capernaum, when the Saviour was thinking of His Church in the ages to come, gathered together in companies in all the lands where disciples should meet in His name, the great thought takes Him for the moment out of the limitations of His earthly life; it carries Him back, or rather lifts Him up, to the eternal sphere from which He has come to earth, so that He uses not the future of time, but the present of eternity: "*There am I* in the midst of them" (xviii. 20). A still more striking example has been preserved by St. John. When on one occasion He spoke of Abraham as seeing His day, the Jews interrupted Him with the question, "Thou art not yet fifty years old, and hast Thou seen Abraham?" Recognising in this a challenge of His relation to that timeless, dateless sphere from which He has come, He promptly replies, "Before Abraham was,[39] *I am.*" It is as if a foreigner, speaking perfectly the language of the country of his adoption, were suddenly betrayed into a form of expression which marked his origin.

That was a momentary relapse, as it were, into the language of eternity; but this last "I am" marks a change in His relations to His disciples: it is the note of the new dispensation of the Spirit. These forty days were a transition time marked by special manifestations—not wholly material as in the days of the Incarnation, nor wholly spiritual as in the days after Pentecost; but on the borderland between the two, so as to prepare the minds and hearts of the disciples for the purely spiritual relation which was thenceforward to be the rule. Whichever appearance was the last to any disciple would be the Ascension to him. To very many in that large gathering this would be the Saviour's last appearance. It was in all probability the time when the great majority of the disciples bade farewell to the Form of their risen Lord. May we not, then, call this the Ascension in Galilee? And just as the parting on the Mount of Olives left as its deepest impression the withdrawal of the man Christ Jesus, with the promise of His return in like manner, so the parting on the mount in Galilee left as its deepest impression not the withdrawal of the human form, but the permanent abiding of the Divine Spirit—a portion of the truth of the Ascension quite as important as the other, and even more inspiring. No wonder that the great announcement which is to be the Christian's title-deed, for all ages to come, of God's unspeakable gift, should be introduced with a summons to adoring wonder: "*Lo,* I am with you alway, even unto the end of the world."

The Gospel ends by removing from itself all limitations of time and space extending the day of the Incarnation to "all the days," enlarging the Holy Land to embrace all lands. The times of the Son of man are widened so as to embrace all times. The great name Immanuel (i. 23) is now fulfilled for all the nations and for all the ages. For what is this finished Gospel but the interpretation, full and clear at last, of that great Name of the old covenant, the name Jehovah: "I am," "I am that I am" (Exod. iii. 14)? All of the Old Testament revelation is gathered up in this final utterance, "I am—with you"; and it has in it by anticipation all that will be included in that last word of the risen Saviour: "I am Alpha and Omega, the Beginning and the End, the First and the Last" (Rev. xxii. 13).

This last sentence of the Gospel distinguishes the life of Jesus from all other histories, biographies, or "remains." It is the one "Life" in all literature. These years were not spent "as a tale that is told." The Lord Jesus lives in His gospel, so that all who receive His final promise may catch the light of His eye, feel the touch of His hand, hear the tones of His voice, see for themselves, and become acquainted with Him Whom to know is Life Eternal. Fresh and new, and rich and strong, for "all the days," this Gospel is not the record of a past, but the revelation of a present Saviour, of One Whose voice sounds deep and clear across all storms of life: "Fear not: I am the First and the Last: I am He that liveth *and was dead*; and behold I am alive for evermore."

FOOTNOTES

[37] The number at Jerusalem at the time of the Ascension was only a hundred and twenty (Acts i. 15).

[38] St. Matthew alone of the Evangelists uses this designation.

[39] The full significance of the original can scarcely be given in English. The Greek language, rich in the vocabulary of philosophy, has two verbs corresponding to our "to be," one indicating phenomenal, the other absolute being. It is the former which is used of Abraham; the latter is used by our Lord in speaking of Himself. There is, therefore, more than a difference of tense.